Succus Moruli
Succus ex floribus tinctor
Beergelb
Schittgelb
Lacca Brabantia
Rubrum Parisiense
Brabendischer Lac
Paris Rott
2 Presilium
Lacca Venetiana
Presilgen
Venedischer Lacc

1000   1100   1200   1300   1400   1500

THE MEDIEVAL WORLD

400   500   600   700   800   900

1000   1100   1200   1300   1400   1500

THE MEDIEVAL WORLD

CIVILIZATION FROM 1000 TO 1500 AD

DR DAVID NICOLLE

BARNES
&NOBLE
BOOKS
NEW YORK

This edition published by
Barnes & Noble, Inc.,
by arrangement with Hamlyn.

1997 Barnes & Noble Books

M 10 9 8 7 6 5 4 3 2 1

ISBN 0-7607-0730-8

Copyright © 1997
Reed International Books Limited

Printed in China

Publishing Director
Laura Bamford
Executive Editor
Julian Brown
Editor
Conor Kilgallon
Art Director
Keith Martin
Art Editor
Mark Winwood
Design
Birgit Eggers
Production
Dawn Mitchell
Picture Research
Charlotte Deane

CONTENTS

INTRODUCTION

Western Europe

In the Middle Ages the term Western Europe meant Latin or Catholic Christendom as distinct from Orthodox Christendom to the east. It also excluded large areas of what we now know as Western Europe. In the south, much of Spain and Portugal were Muslim in religion and Arabic in culture. Until the late 11th century, Sicily and several other Mediterranean islands were also dominated by Muslim civilization while much of southern Italy still fell within the Byzantine Orthodox Christian orbit. By the end of the 15th century, western Christendom had lost its toe-hold in Greenland but was well on its way to conquering the last Muslim state in Spain and siezing Atlantic islands off the African coast. It would soon also reach India and the Americas.

Eastern Europe

Eastern or Orthodox Christian Europe changed in geographical scope even more than western Catholic Europe during the Middle Ages. The main states were the Byzantine Empire, which shrank in size until finally disappearing in the mid-15th century, and Russia which fragmented and then fell under Mongol domination in the mid-13th century but also expanded eastwards into the territory of Finnish and Ugrian tribes. Other eastern Christian states would also fall under Muslim Turkish domination, from Armenia and Georgia in the east to the Slav, Albanian and Romanian principalities of the Balkans.

The Muslim World

By the 11th century the Muslim world seemed to be on the defensive, losing territory to Christian aggression in the Iberian peninsula and at the hands of the Byzantine Empire. The 11th century then saw a dramatic reversal of fortunes in the Middle East with the arrival of the Seljuq Turks who conquered half of the Byzantine Empire. As a result the Muslim world of the late 15th century was substantially different from that of the early 11th century in geography, language and many aspects of secular culture. Islamic civilization also continued to differ from its Christian rivals. Within Christendom there was only one recognized religion; in the Muslim world, however, Jews and Christians were accepted, although Muslims still considered themselves to be at the top of the religious pecking order.

East and Central Asia

China has often been portrayed as a conservative civilization, resistant to outside influences. But China did change under the influence of Central Asian invaders and foreign religious ideas. The Chinese state also fragmented and reunited several times while its frontiers altered ever more drastically. In the 11th century Sung period, for example, the Chinese Empire was not only smaller than it had been under the T'ang but its centre of gravity had shifted southwards. Then for much of the 13th and 14th centuries China formed the most important part of a vast though fragmented, Mongol World Empire stretching from Korea to the Balkans. As a result Chinese civilization had an astonishingly widespread influence during this period.

India and South-East Asia

Early medieval India was a more outward-looking civilization than in later centuries, spreading Hinduism and Buddhism to a great deal of south-east Asia, Tibet, Central Asia and China, and having a cultural and material influence upon both the Middle East and East Africa. Only in the later Middle Ages, under the growing challenge of Islam, did traditional Hindu Indian civilization largely turn its back on the outside world. By then its cultural colonies in Indonesia and Malaysia were also beginning to look to Islam for inspiration while those in Indo-China and Burma were developing a distinctive civilization of their own.

1 DOMESTIC LIFE

THE MIDDLE AGES WERE ONE OF THE MOST VIGOROUS AND INVENTIVE PERIODS IN HUMAN HISTORY. THIS WAS TRUE OF MOST PARTS OF THE WORLD, SOME OF WHICH SAW THE GREATEST FLOWERINGS OF CIVILIZATION DURING THIS PERIOD. MEANWHILE, ORDINARY PEOPLE GOT ON WITH THEIR LIVES. THEY WERE NOT ISOLATED FROM THE GREAT POLITICAL AND CULTURAL EVENTS OF THE TIME, BUT WERE INFLUENCED BY THEM IN WAYS THAT RANGED FROM FASHIONS IN DRESS TO NEW FORMS OF FOOD AND METHODS OF BUILDING HOUSES. IN FACT THE MIDDLE AGES SAW MORE FUNDAMENTAL CHANGES IN DOMESTIC LIFE THAN ANY OTHER PERIOD UNTIL MODERN TIMES.

WESTERN EUROPE – THE NEW HEARTLAND

Medieval Christendom was not a stagnant civilization awaiting the Renaissance to give Europe new life. It was rapidly changing, varied and open to new ideas in politics, art, trade, science, even religion and above all everyday fashions. Nevertheless, the basic unit remained the family, although in most areas various forms of feudal loyalty could cut across family ties, as almost everyone was 'somebody's man'; the masterless man was an object of pity and fear. Such a pattern of social obligation and support was flexible and varied.

In the urbanized south, this so-called Feudal System was more of an ideal than a reality, while in the far north and north-west, extended family structures were almost tribal and remained more important than superficial feudal relationships imposed by distant governments. Yet the myth remained and led to extraordinary forms of exaggeration as once dominant aristocracies tried to reaffirm a lost social and political superiority.

One way that individuals and family groups identified their status and allegiances was by costume and, for the aristocratic elite, by heraldry. Most clothing was of wool or linen and was at first similar for all classes. By the 13th century, however, the aristocracy distinguished itself by wearing increasingly elaborate clothing, often reinforced by sumptuary laws which made it illegal for non-aristocrats to wear certain things. The degree of similarity between costumes within Europe's feudal elite was, however, remarkable, as new fashions spread rapidly from France, the fountainhead of chivalric culture, to the fringes of western Christendom.

Everyday life in medieval Europe was rarely as primitive as is popularly believed today. It remained the feudal elite's duty to maintain 'grandeur' by entertaining guests and employing a large number of people. The early feudal 'household' could be a huge organization which defended local territory, gathered food, collected tithes and arranged hunting expeditions. The senior ladies organized the servants and helped make and mend the knights' and lord's clothes.

As the centuries passed the household organization became more complex, more formal and often larger. The number of rooms and outbuildings similarly increased as castles became bigger and more concerned with conspicuous display and comfort. Most of the lower ranking aristocracies of England

Opposite: A virtuous lady beats off unwanted sexual advances from a priest. The event was commemorated in the use of a lady's loom in the coat-of-arms of the little town of Sarnen and appears in a book of German Heraldry made in Zürich in the early 14th century.

At a dance at the palace of St. Pol in 1393, King Charles VI of France and five knights dressed as 'wodehouses', or savages, chained themselves together. One of the costumes caught fire and set the rest alight. Four men were killed but the King escaped because the Duchess de Berry smothered the flames with her robe.

Sir Geoffrey Luttrell's wife and daughter in law give him weapons and shield. Sir Geoffrey is wearing his coat-of-arms while the ladies have their own variations on this heraldry on their dresses.

and France moved out of their uncomfortable castles into largely unfortified manor houses, while in Italy they moved into towns during the 13th and 14th centuries. Even so each manor-house or urban palazzo had its household of relatives, dependants and servants.

Another widespread myth is that medieval people were dirty and ill-mannered. In reality, the aristocracy and prosperous middle classes took cleanliness, courtesy and good manners very seriously. For example there are said to have been hundreds of public baths in 13th century Paris; only two remained by the possibly smellier early 18th century.

Education in the hands of the Church

Education was controlled by, and largely confined to, the Church. Schools remained rare and linked to a cathedral, hospital or guild, though some village priests taught a few local boys in church porches. Those lucky enough to get a university education aimed at a system of examinations called the Trivium, which consisted of Latin, rhetoric and logic, or the Quadrivium, which also included mathematics, geometry, astronomy and music. Latin was, of course, used by western European scholars from widely differing linguistic backgrounds. Books were

extremely expensive, being copied by hand on vellum or parchment, while students took their notes on wax tablets.

Some senior members of the aristocracy received a private education, but by the 13th century there was spreading literacy and learning amongst the middle ranking 'country squires' and wealthier urban merchants. Boys from prosperous families attended an increasing number of schools where scholarships were maintained by charities or financial bequests. Some girls were also given a practical education at home by nuns while some literacy, numeracy and grammar was taught by merchant or master-tradesmen to their apprentices. The 14th century saw a similar growth in university education with three 'colleges' founded in Oxford between 1260 and 1275. University students gained a reputation for becoming a large and unruly group in several cities.

Another aspect of medieval life which is often misrepresented is that of relations between the sexes. Sexual attitudes amongst the aristocratic leaders of society changed in the 12th century as the new and initially shocking concept of Courtly Love spread from southern France where it had developed, probably as a result of influence from the Arab-Islamic world. It was based on the idea that men and women could love each other as equals, an idea almost alien to ancient Greeks, Romans and early Christians. The ideal of Courtly Love urged young squires and knights to admire a beautiful woman and do heroic deeds in her name, while she in turn should praise their courage. The ancient sport of falconry was further stimulated by contact with Byzantine and Islamic civilizations and became associated with illicit love affairs in the minds of minstrels and artists.

In a civilization where hospitality on a lavish scale was central to the aristocratic way of life, the preparation of food played an important role, while the diet of ordinary people appears to have been healthy, if monotonous. Bread was the staple diet of all except the rich, and the poorest may have had little else except cheese. In England, pork, chicken, beans, eggs, dairy produce and occasionally honey were the basic foods. The better-off used bread mainly as trenchers, which were large slices with a dip in the middle used as platters to sop up the juices of food placed on top and then gathered in baskets at the end of a meal to be given to the poor.

The main vegetables were peas, cabbage, lettuce, leeks, onions, turnips, carrots and rape, with parsley as the most common herb. Garlic and sage were added by the later Middle Ages, a herb garden being considered almost essential. Mustard and saffron were grown where possible, but pepper had to be imported in huge quantities, whereas salt was obtained by mining or sea evaporation. Salads often included flowers like borage, violets and primroses, while uncooked fruit was viewed with suspicion as it could cause stomach upsets. The poor also supplemented their diet with wild hazel and cob nuts from the forest.

Across most of Europe the most important animal was the pig, which could feed itself in winter by rooting, and even poor peasants had access to salt pork. Sheep were important as they, like the goat, also provided milk, while a cow was another vital possession, not for meat, but for the milk which made butter and cheese. Most farm animals were slaughtered in autumn, a few being kept alive for next year's breeding stock.

Strict laws limited who could take deer from the forest, while fish were essential as the eating of meat was forbidden on Saturdays, Wednesdays, Fridays and the many other holy days throughout the year. The staple fish were salted or pickled herring and dried cod, though people living near coasts might find oysters and whelks while people inland supplemented their diet with river fish and eels.

Strictly speaking the clergy were only permitted to eat birds and fish, while some monastic orders remained strictly vegetarian and fish-eating. Nevertheless monks remained amongst the best-fed people in western Christendom and perhaps had the best

table manners, with various monastic rules instructing brother monks not to wipe their mouths or noses on the tablecloths. At the same time monasteries provided hospitality to travellers, pilgrims and itinerant scholars.

Peas pottage to roast pheasant

Medieval cooking ranged from pottage or thick soup of meat, vegetables and cereal grains, to the extraordinary creations produced for an aristocratic feast. The poor cooked over an open fire, usually in earthenware pots, although small animals were sometimes wrapped in clay and baked in the embers. The better-off might have possessed iron firedogs supporting an iron spit used for roasting meat or hanging a cauldron. Kitchen facilities in a castle or manor house had to cater for a larger number of people and included a large fireplace for roasting, with the ovens for baking bread usually being in a separate bakehouse because of the risk of fire. Boiling would be done in cauldrons while long-handled pans were used for sauces or frying. Grilling was done on a special device over rather than under the fire.

Two meals a day were normal, the main one late in the morning and a second at what would now be called teatime. Breakfast was only for children and invalids. Ale was much more common than wine in northern Europe, wine being more widely drunk in the south.

Roasting chickens and a suckling pig by an open fire in a Psalter made for Sir Geoffrey Luttrell in the early 14th century. Though people enjoyed feasting in the open air, most meals were cooked indoors.

An old man warming his feet by the fire in the *Book of Hours* made for John, Duke of Bedford, in the 1420s when he was Regent of France. The manuscript was painted in Paris and shows how the houses of the elite now had leaded glass windows. There is even something to eat being heated in a pot over the fire.

Other beverages included milk and cider. Noble households would have their own bird-catcher and dovecote, as well as domestic poultry. Hens were raised in great numbers with forced-feeding common, particularly leading up to the Christmas celebrations.

Dairy produce was as important for the aristocracy as for ordinary people, with a variety of creams and soft cheeses being made. Cream was drunk alone or poured on fruit; cooked milk making assorted 'possets and caudles', as well as cream soups, custards and cheesecakes. Seals were classed as fish, as were barnacle geese and puffins, but in England whalemeat, sturgeon and porpoise were reserved for the king. Pickled salmon was an even greater luxury since it had to be imported from Scotland or Ireland.

In rich households, the main meals became increasingly ceremonial and the greatest people in the land might 'feast' almost every day. Most tables remained simple boards laid on trestles, with cups, trenchers and perhaps wooden plates for the majority, while those at the top table ate off pewter, silver or gold. Seating was according to rank with servants and dependants placed 'below the salt', in other words furthest from the lord and lady who occupied the top table. Grace was also said before and after eating.

In the early years, servants carried around joints of meat so that each person could cut off what they wanted, but later on a senior servant, called the carver, entered the hall while most of the guests were washing their hands using the ewers and cloths brought by other servants. The carver then ceremonially cut a small portion of bread before the pantler tasted each dish as a precaution against poison. The lord then washed his own hands and the guests sat down. People also disliked eating after dark for fear of flies and other 'filth' in the food, particularly after the Black Death plague in 1348.

There were normally many different dishes and diners tried to sample them all before finishing the meal with nuts, fruits and sweetmeats. People ate with their own small knives though the host usually provided spoons, forks being a later idea in most areas. Waterproofed leather, wood, pewter or ceramic cups were used for drinking, with the rich using silver goblets or, by the late medieval period, even imported glasses. In a great household, the head butler was in charge of drinks; wine was only considered suitable for the 'old and wise', not the 'young and silly', but there was also ale, cider, perry and mead available.

Citrus fruits were imported into England by the late 13th century, though the most expensive foreign foods were currants, raisins, figs, dates, prunes and almonds. Eastern spices were much in demand. The most common oriental spices were ginger, cinnamon, nutmeg, mace, cardamoms and cloves, and included others which have since disappeared. They were so valuable that they were kept under lock and key in special cupboards, along with imported cones of cane sugar from the eastern Mediterranean.

Courtly dances and singing birds

Music and dancing were popular forms of entertainment for all classes, not merely for guests at aristocratic feasts where the formal dances seemed to mime the heroic ideals of Courtly Love. Ordinary town and country people were more lively with their displays of dexterity and agility, such as in a version of the Scottish sword dance using eggs rather than sharpened blades, or in the originally pagan maypole fertility dance. Children's games included the universal catching game and the knucklestones from ancient times. In Hoodman Blind one player had his or her hood reversed and was then being buffeted by the rolled-up hoods of the other players until the Hoodman caught one.

Newer games also came from the east, including kites and soap bubbles blown through straws. A rough form of football with teams of any size was enjoyed by urban apprentices, along with horse racing, ice-skating, mock battles, archery and wrestling. Crowds flocked to see bull and bear-baiting, cock-fighting, performing animals and acrobats while tournaments, such as the Great Tournament held at Windsor Castle in 1278, gradually became a favourite spectator sport – colourful, exciting and with a chance for viewers to see proud aristocrats getting hurt.

Theatre died out with the collapse of Roman civilization and for centuries the Church remained firmly set against theatrical performances until religious plays evolved as a way of teaching people about Christianity, the famous Mystery Plays of medieval western Christendom. Some Mystery Plays became humorous burlesques where 'wicked' characters could do almost anything to amuse the

audience before, of course, receiving their just punishment in Hell while saints were 'martyred' with excruciating realism. By the late 15th century, at the end of the Middle Ages the plots of such plays remained primitive but their costumes and theatrical effects were not.

Board-games were widely played in the long winter evenings, chess having reached Western Europe by the 11th century from India via Muslim civilization. Playing cards also came from the Islamic world of Egypt, where they had reached something like their modern form.

Hunting was a sport as well as a necessity, with hawks and hounds sometimes being hugely valuable – the sleek ancestors of today's greyhounds had been brought to Europe by the Arabs. Singing birds were similarly prized. Canaries were imported from the Canary Islands and could literally be worth their weight in gold if they were good singers, although the native Guanches had eaten canaries as food.

Playing Blind Man's Buff from a French love poem of the 15th century. Like the earlier game of Hoodman Blind, the man has pulled his hat over his eyes and tries to catch the girls who in turn hit him and run away.

EASTERN EUROPE – A DIFFERENT WORLD

The cultural differences between Catholic societies in western Europe and Orthodox societies in the east grew wider following the great religious Schism of 1054. As in the west, individuals identified themselves firstly by religious faith, then by membership of an extended family network. For ordinary people, life revolved around religious celebrations and festivities, including those associated with family life. Within the Byzantine Empire itself, these patterns were largely rooted in the Roman past. On the other hand costume changed over the centuries under largely Persian and Turkish influence, for example in the widespread wearing of beards. Women's costumes changed less and retained a strong Romano-Greek element. Paradoxically, the wearing of veils by women was a Byzantine fashion, perhaps of Persian origin, subsequently adopted by most Muslims. Both

sexes wore jewellery, while wealthier women also used makeup, virtually unknown in most of western Europe. It included rouged lips and poisonous belladonna (deadly night-shade) to dilate the pupils of their eyes. To-wards the end of the Middle Ages Byzantine and Balkan costume became virtually identi-cal to that of the Ottoman Turks, even to the extent of adopting turbans and other forms of Turkish headgear. Meanwhile in Russia, the ruling elite mirrored the steppe peoples after the Mongol conquest in 1239.

As in western Europe, the Byzantine house-hold was really run by the women. Richer houses normally had more than one sitting room where the men could relax and receive guests; the women and children generally remained in the private sections of the house, and servants tended to live at the top. Many Byzantine houses had flat roofs which were used as terraces in the heat of summer, while the walls were often decorated with religious texts or motifs, although secular paintings became popular in the later Middle Ages.

Byzantines, like the Muslims, took per-sonal cleanliness far more seriously than westerners did. Public baths were abundant, some being large and impressive structures, which included private cubicles, clean lava-tories, and hot and cold pools big enough to swim in. Such baths were used by men dur-ing the day, women in the evenings.

The Greek influence in education

Education was equally important to the Byzantines; in a wealthy household, a child would start to learn reading, writing and clear speech in the women's quarters. Three forms of the Greek language were used: the vernacular or Romaic of uneducated people, classical Attic used when writing, and a more elaborate version used for formal speech. Basic education was built upon the Greek classics, particularly Homer which even the middle classes quoted widely, while Latin was used only by lawyers. The emperors themselves also continued a long-established

tradition of founding schools for orphans, while bishops and many monasteries ran their own schools. Even for middle-class children, primary educa-tion was more widely available than it was in western Europe. Those who stayed at school beyond 12 attended a different institution to study Greek, while a minority went on from 16 to 20 to university, studying rhetoric, law and philosophy.

University education was based upon disciplines inher-ited from the Roman past, though it remained essentially religious. Philosophy formed part of the curriculum in all universities, the study of Plato being added to Aristotle in later centuries. Ancient secu-lar scholarship and scientific works were not confined to libraries as in western Europe, but were generally read everywhere with interest. At the same time Byzantine scholars learned from neighbour-ing Muslim civilization and, following the Mongol conquests, even had access to some Chinese thought. Emperors, senior church-men, the political, social and merchant elites of Byzantium all patronized scholars, collect-ing men of learning as ornaments to their households. In other eastern Christian coun-tries, for example Georgia, the church and monasteries took over responsibility for most forms of education, but Georgian rulers con-tinued to endow schools and libraries.

Christianity improved the status of women since pagan Roman times. Most marriages were still arranged by parents or guardians, girls from 12, boys from 14. On her wedding day, a bride was veiled and richly dressed, this being a chance for the bride's family to display their status. The marriage procession walked to church accompanied by friends and musi-cians. Rings were exchanged and from the 11th century onwards a marriage contract was

This carved relief of a huntsman shooting a deer on the west portal of the Cathedral at Trogir was made by Master Radovan in 1240. Although Dalmatian art was in rather old-fashioned Italian style it included several distinctly Balkan details, including this archer's bow and quiver.

Opposite: Women of the Tribe of David in Byzantine costume on a mosaic donated by Theodoros Metochites to the church in around 1310. Ladies fashions did not change as quickly as men's.

Portraits of the men who
helped build the Cathedral at
Sibenik, carved on the outside
of the building in the mid-15th
century. The culture and
costume of Dalmatia, on
the Adriatic coast of the
Balkans, were almost entirely
westernized and had very
little in common with that
of people who lived inland.

signed. Back at the bride's family's house
there would be a banquet where men and
women sat at separate tables and next morning the guests awoke the newlyweds with
singing. The bride's dowry would be kept
separate from her husband's wealth as a form
of insurance, divorce being legal and increasingly easy from the 11th century onwards.

Unexpected luxuries

Byzantine tastes in food were similar to those
of modern Europe in that anyone who could
afford it ate three meals a day. They liked
roasted meat, pork, ham imported from the
Crimea (a semi-independent Byzantine outpost survived at Theodoros in the Crimea
until 1475, twenty-two years after the fall of
Constantinople) and assorted sweets. In some
areas like Trebizond on the Black Sea, fish
was abundant, with a species of anchovy
appearing in such huge and unpredictable
shoals that they were used to manure the
fields. All Orthodox peoples, except the

Russians whose agricultural situation was
very different, ate a great deal of vegetables,
cheese, fresh or stewed fruits, and nuts, while
methods of cooking were essentially the same
as those still used in Greece and Turkey. The
diners, however, mostly ate with their hands.
The Greek island of Chios was the most famous
centre of wine-making, producing something
similar to today's sweet Mavrodaphne.

Some forms of entertainment had continued uninterrupted since Roman times, including chariot races which were held in
Constantinople's famous Hippodrome, the
last one being recorded in 1204. Between
each race, bawdy comedies were put on
instead of the serious drama supposedly typical of ancient Greece. Tsykanion, or polo, was
introduced from the Turco-Muslim world,
and played by the military elite. A few west-
ern-style tournaments were recorded in the
12th to 14th centuries, but never caught on.
Instead Byzantine soldiers preferred cavalry
games copied from their Muslim neighbours.

In both town and country, however, religious, semi-religious or semi-official gatherings or celebrations provided an excuse for
ordinary people to take a day off work. They
ranged from a parade of icons of a local church
to festivals where masked men lit bonfires in
the streets and young people jumped through
the flames. There were also the fairs and markets linked to agricultural events such as har-
vesting the fields or picking grapes.

Not much is known about the secular
music of the Byzantine Empire. Organs and
flutes were played, while some performances
had features in common with opera. Most,
however, were more like cabaret shows and
the Byzantines had a reputation, at least
amongst some of their neighbours, for dis-
gracefully erotic dancing. The Church tried
to ban all such dubious performances, but
failed – except on Saturdays and Sundays.

Children's toys would have included
model carts and animals made of clay,
knucklebones, bouncing balls, hoops and
tops as well as musical instruments and dolls
made of wax, clay or plaster.

THE WORLD OF ISLAM

In the Muslim world shared lineage, the extended family and real or fictitious tribal affiliations, were the foundations of society, second only to an individual's religious identity. They provided support in business and in resisting government interference. Within the family, relationships were based upon custom, which differed from place to place, and the Sharia or Islamic Law, which was essentially the same everywhere. Women exerted enormous influence from behind the scenes, this 'power of the harem' being the normal way of conducting family or even political affairs.

During the early years of Islam there was no attempt to distinguish Muslims from Christians or Jews in dress, but such distinctions soon appeared. Amongst Muslims themselves there were also clear differences between the clothing of different classes, occupations and ethnic groups. From the 10th century, Arab fashions gave way to Persian or Turkish styles amongst the political and military elites of most Muslim states, while an Arab form of dress became the 'uniform' of high civilian or religious officials. Islamic society was, however, fundamentally egalitarian, with the middle classes consistently imitating those who felt themselves superior, while the latter constantly redefined itself by wearing new fashions.

Despite variations in climate and architectural heritage, private houses had certain features in common stemming from the distinctive organization of Islamic family life. As a result houses tended to have little furniture and rooms were decorated with rugs, while walls might have wooden panelling, stucco, stone inlay or painted patterns. Another feature which set Islamic civilization apart from that of western Europe was its deep-seated love of gardens. These gardens used running water and scent rather than coloured flowers, a characteristic rooted in the Persian and Arab past where a cool and well-watered garden was regarded as a foretaste of Paradise. Gardens and the imagery of flowers were so central to medieval Islamic culture that the Persian poet Sa'di entitled his two greatest works the *Bustan* (Garden) and the *Gulistan* (Rose-garden).

The 'hamam' or 'Turkish bath' featured largely in the life of cities, towns and even villages. It was particularly popular with women who would spent a great deal of time meeting their friends, exchanging news, eating sweets, having their hair cleaned and their body hair carefully removed with tweezers.

Like so many aspects of Islamic life, child rearing was strictly governed by religion, the circumcision of boys being celebrated with the biggest festivities a family could afford. Religious education started as soon as an infant could speak, but physical discipline was not normally imposed before the age of six. Unlike European children, a Muslim child had the same legal rights as an adult; a smack which caused a persistent red mark theoretically made the parent liable to pay compensation just as if the parent had struck an adult.

Reading and writing were taught in the local mosque, free or in return for such gifts as a family could afford. Mathematics, law, grammar and other subjects would be taught in another school attached to a larger mosque in the nearest

A ruler and his advisers in a palace garden, from a dictionary of rare Persian words made in western India in the 15th century.

17

town. Literacy remained the most important aspect of education, not merely for business or scholarship, but as an essential social skill. Girls, meanwhile, were taught music at home by their mothers or servants. University education was based upon the 'madrasah', a special form of 'collegiate mosque' which provided access to higher education in almost all Muslim states by the later medieval period. These madrasahs were maintained by the distinctive Islamic system of religious endowments, money, land or other forms of property known as the 'waqf'.

The myth of the harem

The medieval Islamic attitude towards sex differed considerably from that of medieval Christendom and, in many ways, had more in common with modern ideas. Marriage was regarded as the cement which bound society together and as a way of stopping sexual desires from becoming a public nuisance, but it was a civil contract rather than a religious bond. A man could have up to four wives – if the first agreed, and if he was capable of maintaining them and carrying out his sexual obligations on a basis of strict fairness. A first marriage was normally arranged by the parents, but subsequent partners were more freely chosen and divorce was common.

In contrast to the Christian Church's attitude towards sex, which was tolerated within marriage as a biological necessity, Islamic culture regarded it as an important part of human fulfilment, so much so that respected scholars wrote books on the subject, such as *The Perfumed Garden* written by Shaykh Nefwazi in North Africa late in the late 15th century. Certainly no sin was attached to sex itself, but only to relationships outside the accepted boundaries of marriage or concubinage.

Meanwhile medieval Arab literature paints a clear picture of what was considered female beauty, a woman's main sexual attribute being her long, dark hair. In contrast to the veil which was worn in public, elaborate and often revealing clothes were worn within the privacy of the harem or private 'women's rooms' where none but the closest family were allowed to enter – and from which even the husband could be excluded. When it came to illicit love-affairs, a highly developed language of flowers, fruit and other emblems evolved, whereby messages could be sent without either party having to write anything down. Meanwhile homosexuality, though remaining totally illegal, flourished in a situation where the sexes were strictly segregated.

Islamic culture dietary laws were similar to those of Judaism. Yet the climate of the Muslim heartlands lay behind the different emphasis which was placed on various meals. Breakfast, for example, was very important, whereas light lunch would be eaten in the heat of the day, the main meal being in the evening. Food was only taken with the right hand, as the left was used for washing private parts of the body.

Abu Zaid confuses a schoolmaster while his pupils take notes in an illustration by al-Wasiti, made in Baghdad in 1237. This book of comic stories tells how a clever rogue tricks the rich, powerful and pompous. The picture also shows a servant operating a form of ceiling fan to cool the schoolroom.

A maid dresses her mistress' hair, in a 15th century dictionary of rare Persian words. The difference between the princess's embroidered tunic and her servant's plain dress and headcloth is clear, even in this little picture.

A remarkable number of Arabic cookbooks from the 9th to 13th centuries survive which clearly show that the Muslim elite were very interested in food. They are similar in content and concept to what is now called 'nouvelle cuisine', with an emphasis on small quantities of the best and healthiest ingredients. The recipes were quite simple, with little use of spices and a great concern to bring out the basic flavour. The ingredients, however, could be very varied because of the medieval Middle East's 'green revolution' in agricultural techniques and the introduction of an astonishing array of new food crops from Asia.

Good cooks formed a highly paid elite, even if they were slaves, and in a large house the kitchen was a complex place with its own separate toilet and bathroom for kitchen staff. The main oven was a charcoal-fired 'tannur' for baking bread, pies, rice dishes and casseroles. There was also an open fireplace for pots and pans, while separate knives cut meat and vegetables in another example of the Islamic concern for hygiene. Poor people who lacked full kitchens could use communal neighbourhood ovens, especially when making larger quantities for a family celebration. Kid was considered the finest meat, though mutton was eaten in greater quantities, followed by chicken and fish, with beef considered suitable only for the poor.

Picnicking was an important form of family entertainment while the social elite could also visit Christian monasteries, where they would enjoy the wine which Christians alone were supposed to drink. Despite the widespread consumption of 'sherbets' made from fruit cordials, many people brewed beer and

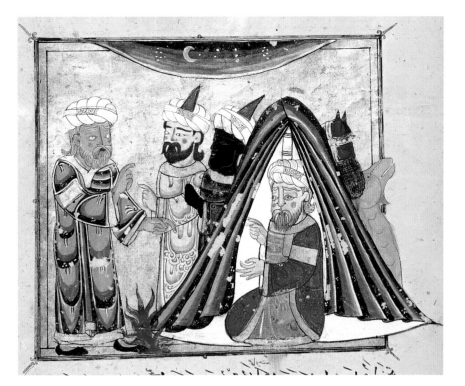

Ibn Hammani meets some
bedouin in the desert, in a
version of the Maqamat made
in Egypt in 1334. Although the
tent has been stylized beyond
recognition, the men's costume
and the horse's nosebag are
very realistic.

an ancient history in the Middle East, with
the long-haired Persian breed spreading to
Turkey in the west and China in the east.
Several Middle Eastern rulers maintained
menageries of exotic animals as a source of
diplomatic gifts to other rulers. In addition,
cheetahs were used as hunting animals, while
in eastern Islamic countries, elephants were
kept for parades or war. Ordinary people
made do with singing birds, and were also
encouraged by their Muslim religion to look
after wild creatures – the pigeons which
swirled around the minarets of Cairo's
mosques were fed from large boat-shaped
copper seed trays on top of some domes while
the children of the Syrian city of Aleppo kept
hamsters long before these were 'discovered'
by a visiting American.

The art of dancing was almost as highly
developed in the medieval Muslim world as
it was in India. Dancing by women was supposedly confined to the harem, yet the traditional dancing which evolved into today's
belly dancing was not necessarily erotic. It
was also performed by women for women as a
celebration of fertility and as exercise during
pregnancy, though it would be naïve to
believe that such dancing was not used to
encourage a jaded husband or lover.

Strictly speaking Islamic culture had a brutally matter-of-fact attitude towards death.
Corpses, for example, had to be buried within
a very brief period after death for reasons of
public health. Nor were graves supposed to be
ostentatious, except in the case of the Prophet
and certain other religious figures.

Nevertheless non-Islamic attitudes could
not be so easily overturned. In areas under
Turkish rule, the tombs of rulers were sometimes very splendid, in a clear continuation
of pagan or shamanistic Central Asian practice. The 13th century turbes or tombs of
Saljuq princes and princesses at Erzerum in
eastern Turkey clearly show this. Even more
unorthodox was the playing of music at
funerals by some dervish sects, though this
was most characteristic of countries where
the Christian influence persisted.

wine at home. Illegal brews, fermented for
four months were alcoholic and needed
straining before consumption. Indeed, Imad
al-Din Zangi, the first successful Muslim
leader against the Crusaders, was murdered
while drunk in 1146. Drinks made from
raisins were considered legal as they were
virtually alcohol-free.

Public and private entertainment

Public entertainment tended to be associated
with religious or political celebrations, ranging from the end of the fasting month of
Ramadan to the proclamation of military victories. Annual military displays provided a
popular spectacle in a culture where most
armies were made up of professional soldiers
rather than by feudal levies. Shadow-puppet
shows introduced from Central Asia were a
form of entertainment that enabled ordinary
people to poke fun at their supposed betters,
who had the same love of hunting as practically every other political or military elite.
Arabic books on hawking influenced comparable books written in 13th century Europe.

It was a small step from hawks and hunting dogs to peaceful pets. The love of cats had

A CIVILIZATION OF RANKS AND GRADES

Chinese society was highly stratified and several ranks existed even amongst the peasantry. The poor led a precarious existence, often slipping into debt, while the status of female slave-concubines was often better – the more there were within a household, the wealthier the family which owned them. The size of the family could also influence its wealth, particularly amongst the peasants where three generations often worked the land together in a labour-intensive system.

In Korea the status of the old 'true bone' hereditary aristocracy was officially abolished by the 11th century, though the principle of hereditary status remained deeply engrained. Theirs was an aristocracy of service based upon the Chinese model, which included civilian and military elements, while the core of Korean society consisted of the free 'yangmin' or 'good people' consisting of farmers, merchants, craftsmen and soldiers. Like China, Korea was not isolated from outside influences and, during the 13th century, Korean customs, language, dress, music and dance were influenced by Mongol Central Asia.

Mongol society was more fluid, though the deference and loyalty shown to leaders astonished the Mongols' western neighbours. It was normal for a defeated tribe to be accepted as part of the conquering people though there was, of course, a clear pecking order amongst such tribes, clans and families. These were often denoted by giving the tribe a 'colour coded' name, from Golden or Blue at the top, to Black at the bottom.

Chinese costume ranged from the coarse and almost uniform dress of the peasantry to that of the ruling elite so opulent that it astonished visitors from other civilizations. As elsewhere, clothing denoted social status, but it also indicated age in a society where the elderly enjoyed enormous respect. The single, most distinctive element of a

A Turkish nomad with his horse in a painting by Siyah Qalam made in the late 14th–early 15th century, probably from Transoxania. This is one of several studies of Turkish nomads done by an artist who not only had a sense of humour but who really understood the hardship of the steppe nomad's way of life.

21

Chinese costume was, of course, the silk fabric which lent itself to an elaborate weave. The most expensive Chinese silk was called ice-white and was so delicate that it could not be worn in direct sun or rain. Costumes in Korea and Japan owed a great deal to imported Chinese fabrics, though both also had their own distinctive elements. But it was in Central Asia that the biggest differences could be found. Amongst the Mongols and Turks, both sexes wore long straight tunics over loose trousers, with thick but flexible boots. Women of the tribal elite also had a remarkable ceremonial headdress made of tree bark, covered in silk and decorated with feathers. Woollen winter clothes were often heavily padded, while thick capes and quilted hats gave protection against rain and snow.

From the beginning, the traditional Chinese house had been built around a courtyard and sometimes had an inner section serving as a flower garden. The main living quarters were rarely more than two storeys high and were usually distinguished by an outside staircase, slatted windows and a low-pitched tiled roof. The Japanese took their love of gardens to greater extremes than anywhere else and formal gardens became the centre of domestic arrangements for the ruling elite. Running water in a garden was a great asset to the owners as they could give Winding Water Banquets, where wine cups were floated from guest to guest.

Each unit within a house or complex normally consisted of a large room with flimsy walls built on a platform on stilts in order to avoid Japan's acute humidity. Movable screens lent a certain mystery to the women's quarters in Japanese houses, which otherwise lacked privacy and even the bedroom consisted merely of a curtained platform in the middle of the main room.

Compared to this, even a Mongol ger or tent could seem comfortable. It was normally made of a sheets of felt laid over a complex wooden frame, though in high summer only the roof might be covered. The interior was divided into two compartments, with men receiving visitors in the western part while the women lived in the eastern. A hearth was placed in the centre, beneath the smoke hole, the head of the family sleeping on a couch behind this hearth. Work was allocated by sex, women driving carts, setting up tents, milking cows, making butter, repairing clothes and looking after the children, while men made the carts, the frames of tents, horse-harness, looked after the horses, milked mares and hunted.

Education in the service of the state

In China, education was structured to serve the state and was theoretically open to everyone. In fact many members of the vast bureaucracy were talented men from humble origins. In local schools, pupils first learned literacy, then began studying the classical texts written by the philosopher Confucius in the 6th century BC. Each school also had a small Confucian temple. Colleges in the main or capital cities trained pupils who had passed lower exams, the study of classical texts remaining on the curriculum up to the highest grades. The whole system revolved around fiercely competitive written examinations, so much so that professional clerks made copies of each entrant's papers so that examiners could not recognize someone's handwriting, thus becoming vulnerable to bribery or corruption.

The Korean system of education was similarly designed to provide the government with high-quality civil servants, though it retained a foot in the aristocratic past. Here government and privately sponsored schools and academies taught Confucian classics, poetry, letters, mathematics and medicine. By the 12th century Korea's private academies had earned a particularly high reputation.

Polygamy and a stiflingly protective attitude towards the women of the elite characterized sexual relations in China and, by extension, Korea and Japan. Amongst the

period, partly because it was believed to have healing properties. At the same time the wealthy elite had a love of peculiar delicacies. Public restaurants could be found in every town and city and the menus were very varied. There were also bars serving alcoholic drinks, though the poor made do with streetside awnings where they could buy bean soup and shellfish. Far to the west the little that is known about medieval Mongol eating habits indicates that they consumed practically anything available and had a reputation for drunkenness.

The highly structured and almost stylized ideal of Chinese civilization manifested itself in various forms of entertainment; theatre, for example, flourished – there was no scenery and actors relied on mime to evoke a location, while elaborate costume and makeup indicated character. Plots provided exciting action and humour, whereas medieval Japanese theatre focused on the dramatic life of the samurai class.

Everywhere religious festivals provided a focus for general jollification, and, within the home, wealthier families were entertained by jugglers, acrobats, professional dancers and fencing displays. There was a game called 'liu-po', which involved a dextrous manipulation of sticks, cups or counters. The Chinese were also addicted to gambling. The 13th century Venetian traveller Marco Polo was astonished by the Chinese habit of keeping fish as pets while the Japanese took this fascination with ornamental fish to even greater extremes.

Chinese attitudes to death were based on Confucian ideas. The role of the family was so central to Chinese life, and respect for elders and ancestors so extreme, that the Chinese fear of being buried away from the family plot caused the government problems in recruiting soldiers. Attitudes to death amongst Central Asian people varied. Most Mongols, for example, still clung to a shamanism that was common throughout northern Asia. As a result the burial of leaders, such as Genghiz Khan in 1227, could include the sacrifice of horses and even humans.

Left top: Boys sit next to their teacher and learn to write on a Vietnamese paintings of the 14th–15th century, from Nam Giang. One piece of work is apparently being checked for mistakes. Correct calligraphy was extremely important in a Chinese-style bureaucratic state like medieval Vietnam.

Left bottom: Fun in the countryside, with boys flying a kite while a man and woman ride towards a platform where some sort of boardgame seems to be ready for them. The style of this 14th–15th century Vietnamese painting from Nam Giang is very Chinese but some of the more stylized features of Indo-Chinese art can also be seen.

Mongols, marriage was also polygamous though the children of wives and concubines were considered equal. One remarkable aspect of Mongol marriage was the tradition of a son 'taking over' his father's wives, naturally with the exception of his own mother. This was acceptable amongst many Altaic peoples and was just a means of ensuring the survival of women and children in such a harsh environment. The situation in Tibet was different again, with both polygamy and polyandry being common.

China is often believed to have the oldest surviving culinary traditions, the oldest Chinese cookery books dating from the Southern Sung period (1125–1279). Few people ate meat because of the difficulty of storage and in southern China the basic diet was rice, fish and vegetables. Tea had become the universal drink during the early medieval

INDIA AND SOUTH-EAST ASIA – THE WORLD OF CASTE

Traditional Indian society was based upon the Hindu caste system in which religion and social organization reflected an ideal whereby each individual adhered to rules governing status, behaviour and economic activity of his or her caste. Change came only with the soul's reincarnation to a superior or inferior caste, dependent on the individual's behaviour in the previous life.

In southern India, peoples such as the Cholas, who dominated southern India from the late 10th to early 13th centuries, the Hindu caste system was less rigid and there were cases of successful bandit leaders 'winning' their way into the dominant 'kshatriya' ruling or warrior-caste. Other variations were found in parts of south-east Asia which had converted to Hinduism. In Indonesia, for example, individuals and villages could be rated as kshatriya, 'priyayi' or 'refined', and had certain occupations reserved for them.

The social structure of the Khmers, or Cambodians, who developed the most sophisticated Indianized civilization in Indo-

China, was only superficially based on caste and was, in reality, a deeply entrenched class system. The Khmer aristocracy owned large numbers of slaves, including those whose families had fallen into debt bondage.

Northern Vietnam fell within the Chinese cultural orbit, while the south was more Indianized. Further east in the Philippines the bulk of the population lived in isolation from the outside world. Closer to India itself, Buddhist and Hindu culture dominated Malaya and Burma until Islam rose in Malaya in the 14th and 15th centuries. Yet many aboriginal peoples clung to traditional social patterns, with family units headed by an elder or father-figure, while fields, trees and streams were largely under joint family ownership. Some peoples, like the Negri Sembilan, had an even more ancient matrilineal family structure as was also found in Sumatra, southern Vietnam, Melanesia and even parts of India itself.

Costume in south-east Asia again shows various cultural influences. While ordinary people, wore little more than a waist wrapper or loincloth, the Khmer aristocracy dressed in imported Chinese silks, had elaborate hairstyles and used perfumes abundantly.

Domestic architecture remained equally resistant to outside influences. Khmer peasant houses were wooden, built on stilts away from humidity and unwelcome animal guests, and thatched with palm leaves, while the houses of the aristocracy were also of wood, but roofed with tiles and furnished with Chinese rugs. Cleanliness was reportedly a source of communal pleasure as well as a hygiene amongst all classes of the Khmer; foreign observers were often shocked by the way men and women bathed together.

India had an ancient system of education. Hindu religious education was based on the Vedas, or religious texts, and theoretically all three 'twice born' or elite Aryan castes were supposed to have some Vedic knowledge. Attitudes were not, however, fixed and the Hindu philosopher Ramanuja wrote his famous treatise on the importance of devo-tional worship around 1050. Of course the brahmins had most knowledge of the Vedas, a student becoming part of his teacher's household, leading a rigidly regulated life in which his dress, cleanliness and daily routine were strictly supervised until he himself qualified as a brahmin priest. By medieval times a great deal of such teaching took place in monasteries. Practical skills taught to the elite included phonetics, ritual behaviour, grammar, astronomy, military skills and the use of poisons. Upper caste women also received some religious instruction, but mostly were taught the fine arts.

Extra-marital attitudes

Many outsiders were shocked by Indian and south-east Asian sexual attitudes. Amongst the Khmer, for example, girls were allowed pre-marital liaisons, whilst married women were allowed extra-marital sex if their husbands were away for longer than a certain time, particularly in time of war. In fact the Khmer regarded sexual union as a spiritual act as well as a means of reproduction. Some early attitudes survived the coming of Islam to Malaya, with the continued acceptance of certain forms of Hindu marriage, including stylized abduction.

The culinary arts of south-east Asia were an obvious mixture of local traditions combined with Indian and Chinese influences. While the Khmer aristocracy reportedly ate off gold and silver plates, the peasantry ate their daily rice with scoops or spoons made from palm leaves. The diet of ordinary people appears to have been healthy, with rice, fish, plenty of vegetables and fruit with pork or venison for special occasions. Alcoholic drinks were brewed from honey, sugar-cane and rice.

A passion for gambling and cockfighting mirrored Chinese culture, as did the Thais' addiction to fighting fish. Amongst the neighbouring Khmer, elephants and pigs were also set upon one another, while men competed in boxing, wrestling, archery contests and a local team game rather like polo.

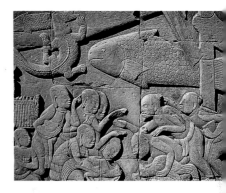

Above: On this late 12th-early 13th century Cambodian carved relief a group of men watch a cock-fight. A huge number of such carvings cover many of the Buddhist temples built by the Khmer civilization.

Opposite: The birth of Jaina on a 15th century Indian manuscript about the 'ford finders', who helped mankind find the way to truth. Though it comes from Madyha Pradesh in central India, one of the figures at the top may carry the reverse-curved sword found in several sorts of southern Indian art.

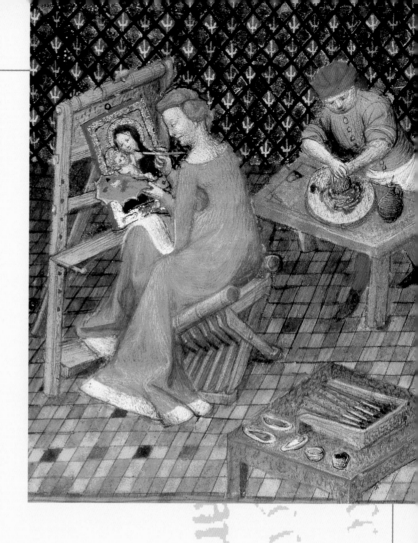

2 | THE ARTS

Scholars of the Italian Renaissance invented the name 'Medieval', meaning the 'age between' or 'middle age' to describe the period between Graeco-Roman 'Classical' Art and their own supposed rediscovering of Classical art in the 14th and 15th centuries. In fact the name 'Medieval' was intended to suggest that the arts of this 'middle period' were inferior. To some extent such attitudes survive today, but a glance at Medieval Art shows just how wrong they were. In other parts of the world, the arts of what Europeans call the Middle Ages undoubtedly saw a Golden Age.

A GOLDEN AGE OF RELIGIOUS ART

The Church was the main patron of artists and craftsmen throughout the Middle Ages, and in some backward areas this increased its importance. At the same time, however, some of the fringes of European civilization such as Scandinavia and Ireland played a less prominent cultural role after the 11th century than previously. Yet the Church was by no means the only patron of art and music. The cult of Courtly Love, which flourished in the 12th and 13th centuries, as well as the greater wealth of the aristocratic elite and the growing mercantile middle class provided other sources of funds for those willing to produce secular as well as religious art.

The early Renaissance in Italy during the 14th and 15th centuries produced even more varied patronage, as rival rulers competed to attract the best artists and craftsmen available. As a result even inferior artists had little trouble finding work and as a result did more to spread the ideas of Renaissance art than their more famous compatriots. By the 15th century in Italy, for example, patrons came from very varied backgrounds, some of the most enthusiastic being professional soldiers who had clawed their way up the social ladder as 'condottieri', or mercenary leaders.

Federigo da Montefeltro (1422–1482) was just such a professional soldier who became Duke of Urbino and, for a while, Urbino was the most important centre of art, literature, science and philosophy in Europe. While all this flowing of Gothic and Renaissance art was going on, the bulk of the ordinary European people were untouched except, perhaps, for the addition of some new styles of statuary or wall-painting in their local church.

The status of artists would not change for many years and, even in Renaissance Italy, the ruling elite tried to 'possess' artists as

they had done before. In most countries, artists were still regarded as superior craftsmen to be hired as servants. However, by the end of the medieval period, some had earned wealth in their own right, although many were still prepared to wear the 'livery' or uniform of the household of their current patron.

What changed most between the 11th and 15th centuries was the subject matter which inspired artists, poets and craftsmen. Even in the 12th century most subjects were still religious, but, with the cult of Courtly Love, came a renewed emphasis on heroic adventures not seen since the Dark Ages (5th–7th centuries), as well as a new set of romantic ideals. All this had a huge impact on art. It could be seen in book illustration, wall-painting and tapestries, as well as jewellery and other luxuriously decorated objects, as part of a flowering of civilization known as the Twelfth Century Renaissance. A new interest in the individual human being, pioneered by Gothic art, was then taken much further in Renaissance Italy, which also added the ideal of absolute realism, unhampered by a fear of idolatry.

Another characteristic of the medieval Renaissance was an idealization of the ancient Roman past. Scholars seemed to believe that classical ideas were better than anything else, merely because they were Roman, while the artists happily copied decorative motifs and entire compositions in the belief that the ancients had all the answers.

Meanwhile in other parts of Europe Gothic art continued to flourish well into the 15th century, reaching a degree of delicacy which the Renaissance itself never achieved. At the very end of the Middle Ages, Renaissance ideas suddenly burst beyond the frontiers of Italy, yet practically every new

Opposite: A lady makes a panel painting of the Virgin and Child while her assistant grinds pigment for paint. All paints had to be made by hand. This illustration from *The Story of Thamyris* by Giovanni Boccaccio was painted in the 15th century.

Below: In this Italian manuscript examples are shown of various sorts of pigments used by medieval and Renaissance artists. It was probably made as a sort of instruction manual or colour-chart. All pigments were made from plants, animals or crushed minerals.

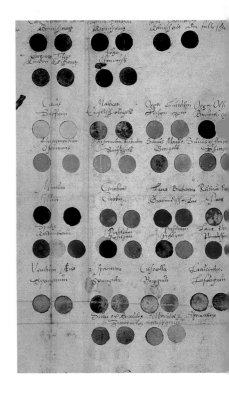

Notation and motets of the Mass in a book of music made for the Chapel Royal in the reign of King Henry V, around 1420. By this date musical notation was almost the same as used today.

Italy finally provided a technological link between large and small-scale art with the invention of portable oil-painting on canvas rather than on clumsy old wooden panels. It is said to have been invented in Venice around 1500, perhaps as a result of the Venetians' knowledge of Asian painting on silk and cotton.

The birth of western music

Music had huge prestige in the Middle Ages, being regarded as a science as much as an art, and again the Church was the most important patron. Christian religious chant developed out of Jewish cantillation, but it had also been influenced by Greek musical theories. Gregorian Chant dominated the early centuries, without instrumental accompaniment and without part-singing harmony until the 11th century, when Guido of Arezzo (c.990–c.1050) introduced the set of horizontal lines still used in sheet music today.

Over the next hundred years, most new developments stemmed from Paris. Meanwhile secular minstrels rose in prestige as they provided the main channel whereby the ideals of Courtly Love spread throughout the knightly elites of western Christendom and to some extent the wealthy merchant class. Of course their music changed over the years. At first it was played on simple instruments until new ones, such as the lute and viol, arrived from the east.

The best songs could also be understood in several different ways. Hildegard of Bingen, who wrote her *Liber Divinorum Operum* in around 1160, produced verses which were written as examples of Christian mysticism, but included ideas which worried the Church because they were similar to Islamic mysticism. Meanwhile the elite minstrels were joined by many itinerant musicians who played similar, though often much cruder, songs for ordinary people.

There were parallel developments in the range of instruments available. In the early Middle Ages the harp, lyre and zither were

development in what is called the Northern Renaissance still owed its origins to Italian influence, though it was often expressed in a very different way.

A similarity in style between different art forms was one of the main characteristics of medieval art. Large-scale sculpture in stone and even little figures in golden reliquaries or jewellery were similarly designed, whether the subject was secular or religious. The same was true of enamel-work and textiles, which had much in common with painting, from a tiny miniature in a book to a wall-painting in the main hall of a castle.

probably the most common for playing secular music. The psaltery also evolved from the simple zither and, when beaten with sticks rather than plucked by hand, became the dulcimer, which reached western Europe from Byzantium in the 15th century. The portable pneumatic organ had already been introduced from Byzantium in the 10th century, developing into the great church organ.

New instruments from the Muslim world arrived via Spain or the Crusades during the 12th and 13th centuries. They included plucked and bowed instruments such as the lute, from the Arabic 'al-oud', and its short-necked northern European version, known as the 'mandora' or 'gittern'. Meanwhile the modern guitar evolved from similar roots in Spain and Italy, as did an early form of plucked, rather than bowed, viola. The bowing of stringed instruments again came from the east, though probably via China and Central Asia. A distinctive bowed lyre became the English crowd or Welsh crwth whereas, somewhat confusingly, the modern viol did not develop from the early instrument with the same name but appeared independently in late 15th century Spain. Woodwind instruments developed from equally varied routes, as did the drums. Brass instruments only appeared at the end of the Middle Ages.

Following the troubadour age of the 12th and 13th centuries came a new flowering of sophisticated music called 'Ars Nova'. Modern western music, however, had its origins during the 15th century Renaissance. New forms of music also developed, along with what could be described as comic 'operettas'. The first known was a story of Robin Hood and Maid Marian, performed in southern Italy around 1285. By the 15th century this sort of entertainment was extremely elaborate and put on for the aristocracy. Throughout the centuries, ordinary people retained their own simpler folk music which, though influenced by that of their feudal superiors, included 'rounds' for several singers in chorus or canons, where one singer began and others gradually joined in. Many of these songs welcomed the coming of spring or celebrated the beauty of nature.

The domination of Latin

The impact of religion on literature was felt in several surprising ways. The existence of so many different languages was itself seen as a sign of God's anger since the days of the Biblical Tower of Babel. Meanwhile Latin was not only the language of the Church and of scholarship, but also virtually the only tongue to unite the peoples of western Christendom.

Furthermore the use of a single language was believed to hasten the arrival of God's Kingdom on earth. Within the babel of European tongues, there was a clear pecking order, with French as the language of the aristocracy. Even in the 15th century, it remained the true language of chivalry, though it was no longer used in everyday life by the ruling classes of England, Germany or Italy.

Other languages were persecuted for cultural, religious or political reasons. The Celts suffered and as a result, the Gaelic literature of the Scottish Highlands virtually dried up by the 12th century; but of course Scots-Irish Gaelic had itself obliterated the ancient Pictish dialect for similar reasons some centuries earlier.

As languages rose and fell, the Middle Ages remained one of the richest sources of stories in the history of European literature, and almost every country still has folk heroes dating from this period. Some are knights who fought for their king, country, Christianity or simply for justice. Others, like Robin Hood, were outlaws defending the weak peasantry against the exploitation of an unscrupulous aristocracy.

A young chorister sings and a monk plays an organ while a servant pumps the bellows, on a 15th century earthenware plate. The dog on the right also adds his voice in a typical example of medieval humour.

Sigurd killing the Dragon on the 12th century carved portal of the wooden stave church at Hylestad in Setesdal. Several of the early churches of Scandinavia were decorated with scenes from pagan Viking mythology, though here the ancient hero is armed much like a knight from France.

At the same time medieval Europeans were fascinated by their non-Christian neighbours and rivals. The mixed feeling of the chivalric elite towards their Saracen foes, for example, comes across clearly in 12th and 13th century 'chansons de geste', for example in the beautiful *Aucassin and Nicolette* love story written in the late 12th century. Here Muslim soldiers were frequently described as knights, comparable to those of Europe, just as brave and just as honourable but doomed to defeat because they were not Christian. Minstrels who sang such epics carefully included accurate details about the weapons, armour and horses which were their knightly patrons' pride and joy.

Other tales describe the sense of obligation and even fear which the feudal elite felt towards the mass of toiling peasants who almost represent the forces of nature itself. This is nowhere better seen than in the *Story of Sir Gawain and the Green Knight,* the earliest English version of which was written in 1386, and formed part of the epic tales of King Arthur and his Knights of the Round Table. The Green Knight turns out to be immortal and, like life itself, returns after a bleak winter to have his revenge on Gawain. But, given the overriding importance of honour in such stories, Gawain survives because even the primitive Green Knight or Green Man recognized the young knight's worth and spares him.

A fundamental change came over European literature during the Italian Renaissance and survived almost to modern times. This was the fascination for and idealization of Latin, and subsequently Greek, literature. The styles of medieval 'Gothic' writing came to be ridiculed by the educated elite. Paradoxically, however, the Renaissance and late medieval period also saw far greater status being given to literature in local languages, even in Italy, where assorted Italian dialects emerged from the shadows of Latin and French domination as the 'Stil Nova' or 'New Style' developed by poets like Dante Alighieri (1265–1321).

A lady and her maidservant stand between the Lion and the Unicorn on a 15th century
French or Flemish tapestry. This is not only an example of the extremely luxurious
fabrics which decorated noble palaces, but illustrates the late medieval aristocracy's
fascination with everything concerned with tales of chivalry.

BYZANTINE ART –
THE FOUNTAINHEAD

Byzantine art was overwhelmingly religious in subject and inspiration. Most secular art was reserved for textiles, jewellery, ceramics, some metalwork and small luxury items for the ruling elite. Though deeply Christian, Byzantine art was also rooted in the previous civilizations of the Eastern Mediterranean and Persia, while the Graeco-Roman elements tended to be rather self conscious, inserted as a sort of affirmation that the Byzantine Empire was descended from ancient Rome. Nevertheless Byzantine religious art remained the fountainhead for most western European religious art until the Renaissance. Meanwhile Byzantine minor arts absorbed ideas from an even greater variety of sources as the Middle Ages progressed.

Byzantine art's biggest influence was, of course, on fellow Orthodox and eastern Christian cultures such as the Orthodox Balkans and the Christian Caucasus, though here Armenian and Georgian arts were themselves sources of ideas for Byzantine craftsmen. The biggest and most important cultural colony of Byzantium was, however, Russia, which had been at least officially converted to orthodox Christianity in 988. Its arts, crafts and architecture were directly inspired by those of the Byzantine world, though they were modified to suit local climatic and cultural conditions.

At the same time Russian folk art continued to flourish, exerting a powerful influence upon the otherwise Byzantine arts patronized by the ruling elite and the Russian Orthodox Church. Other even more disparate artistic influences were also at work in Russia, though largely in the secular arts – those of Scandinavia and Germany in the north and those of the Turco-Mongol steppe peoples in the south.

Large-scale sculpture never flourished in the Orthodox Christian countries and stone carving was almost entirely limited to decorative patterns executed with supreme craftsmanship. Secular and religious scenes were carved on the exterior of churches in Georgia and Armenia (for example the Church of Aght'amar on Lake Van) and the appearance of similar carvings on a few 12th century Russian churches has posed interesting questions for art historians. Were they inspired by the faraway Caucasus or was there more Byzantine carving than is generally realized?

Most surviving Byzantine figurative art consists of traditional manuscript illustrations and even more traditional mosaics or wall-paintings. This vigorous art had a huge impact on neighbouring Christian cultures, where the entire interiors of medieval Georgian and Russian churches were sometimes covered with religious scenes. In what is now Romania, and particularly in the northern province of Moldavia, this spread to the exterior church walls at the end of the Middle Ages.

From the 12th to 15th centuries, just when the Empire entered its final decline, Byzantium enjoyed its own artistic renaissance. This was seen in minor arts as well as larger works, though Byzantine ceramics never achieved the standards seen in the Muslim Middle East and nowhere near the craftsmanship of Far Eastern potters. But Byzantine ivory carving could compete anywhere while other eastern Christian craftsmen earned reputations in various minor arts; Georgia, for example, became famous for its cloisonné enamelware.

Music and literature in the Orthodox world

Much of medieval western music stemmed directly from the Byzantine world, where musicians used a variety of ancient Graeco-Roman, as well as recently adopted Middle Eastern instruments. There was in fact a very strong Muslim influence where stringed instruments were concerned. Much of the music still used in Orthodox religious services has survived virtually unchanged since medieval times, but whereas it used an eight-tone system, secular music tended to use a more complex sixteen-tone system, perhaps inspired by the extraordinarily complex music of the Muslim world.

Most Orthodox countries based their 'art music' upon that of Byzantium, though Russia also developed its own distinctive musical tradition. The same was true of Georgia, which still has an incredibly ancient

tradition of polyphonic singing. Meanwhile the secular music of the Caucasus was amongst the richest in the world, with instrumental music using cymbals, lutes, tabors, flutes, pan-pipes and bagpipes in a remarkable synthesis of the region's own ancient traditions, as well as newer influences from the Byzantines, Persians, Arabs, Turks and practically every other passing conqueror or civilization.

Literature was the most self-consciously 'classical' aspect of Byzantine culture, but not much secular Byzantine literature survives. Heroic epics were written for recitation, probably by the poets who played a major role in secular festivals. One of the most famous examples was the *Epic of Digenes Akritas* written near the Syrian frontier in the 11th century. Rulers also employed professional panegyrists to praise them, while other

Opposite: The deeply spiritual character of medieval Russian Christianity is clear in this Head of Christ, painted on an early 14th century Russian icon. Realism has been abandoned in favour of a sculptural quality which gives great power to Christ's face.

Below: Late 14th–early 15th century Russian icon of St. John the Divine of Patmos, from the Trinity Sergiev Monastery. Russian religious art grew out of the late Byzantine style, but became more intense and unrealistic.

A late 12th century Byzantine enamelled gold icon of the Archangel Michael brought back to Venice as loot by the Fourth Crusade. The wealth and sophistication of Byzantium came as a shock to the rough western warriors of the Crusade. It also inspired their greed and envy.

Catholic churches to dominate Balkan Christianities. From the start, the Russian Orthodox Church used a Slavic language, rather than Greek which, like the Latin of the western Church, was unintelligible to the vast mass of its followers. Moreover, the written version of the language in question was based on that of southern Bulgarian and so remained beyond the reach of most Russians, even when read aloud.

The situation in Georgia and Armenia was different. Georgia had been firmly placed within the ancient Persian literary tradition and even after the country's conversion to Christianity, Georgian secular literature had more in common with that of Persian-Islamic peoples than that of Byzantine Greeks. This remarkable tradition is best seen in the country's national epic, *The Man in the Panther's Skin*, which is a 12th century Georgian version of the much better known Persian *Shahnamah* written almost two hundred years earlier.

A great deal of oriental writing was also translated into Georgian during the Middle Ages, including the remarkable *Story of Barlaam and Josaphat*, which includes a story of the Buddha and probably reached the Caucasus via the Manichaen Turks of Central Asia and the Arabs of Iraq. It then travelled west where it is said to have had a profound impact on various heresies, including that of the Albigensians in southern France who gave their name to the Albigensian Crusades of 1208–1255.

This period of cultural splendour was, however, short-lived and did not survive the Mongol invasions of the 13th century. Meanwhile surviving versions of the Armenian national epic *David of Sassoun* are quite late and have been strongly influenced by Turkish literature. The arts of the Orthodox Christian world sometimes seem to lack variety compared to medieval Western Europe, but this was not really the case. While variations may have been small in religious subjects, they were much greater in secular art, music and literature.

writers wrote savage satires about those in charge of the Empire. Literature for the ordinary people tended to be humorous and considerably influenced by Middle Eastern tales such as those in the *Thousand and One Nights*.

Linguistic struggles in the Orthodox and Catholic worlds

As in western Europe, language, literacy and literature were used as powerful weapons in the struggle between competing cultures. Two Slav scripts, for example, were developed early in the medieval period, the glagolitic and the cyrillic, and these got caught up in the struggle between the Orthodox and

THE BIRTH OF ISLAMIC ART

The role of artists and the arts in the Muslim world was different from that in western or even eastern Europe. The iconoclasm, or deep-seated dislike of representational religious images which had convulsed Christianity in the early Middle Ages, remained a feature of Islamic art. Even so the Muslims' fear of realistic representation on the grounds that it could lead to idolatry was not as pervasive as is often thought. There was plenty of representational secular art, even some three-dimensional sculpture, and in some unorthodox parts of the Muslim world there would always be a small amount of realistic religious illustration.

Nevertheless Islamic religious art developed a sophisticated repertoire of decorative motifs based on abstract patterns and stylized plant life, as well as the Arabic script which was often used in such a stylized manner that it was almost impossible to read. This varied decorative repertoire of motifs was then used on surfaces ranging from the margins of book pages to the domes of mosques. Meanwhile secular patrons continued to demand illustrated books of heroic or humorous stories, superbly carved ivory panels, huge wooden doors covered with scenes of courtly life, and assorted forms of ceramic, glass and metalwork where little human figures often seemed lost amongst a mass of floral or abstract decoration.

Like that of all other cultures, Islamic art evolved over the centuries and reflected the tastes of new political or military elites. For example, the Seljuk Turks, who took control of most Muslim lands from the 11th to 13th centuries, brought with them a love of human sculpture dating from a time before they converted to Islam. As a result people, animals and mythical monsters were carved on buildings, including some religious ones. A few almost life-size statues of Seljuk rulers or court officials survive in direct contradiction to the belief that there was no realistic sculpture in Islamic art. The Turks and Mongols similarly stimulated textile design with new ideas for rugs and wall-hangings

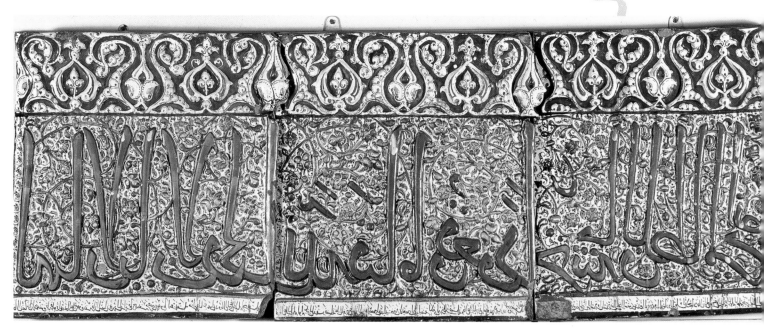

Lustre tiles from Mashad, 13th century Iran.
The technique of metallic glaze or lustre-ware ceramic was invented in Muslim Iraq or Egypt in the early medieval period.

فقال إمام الله للجواز أن ينبغ وللصدق أن ينبغ وحقين أن ينبغ أنه بأنهم ليحكم ملك اليوم فكان الجماعة

أن بأبنت بعوبة وأبت تصديق يدعوته فنوجس نوجس ما هجن في أفكارهم ونطن لما بطن من أستكارهم دخا ذ ان

فقال أدى نظر بعض النظر أثم ثم ثم قال أزواة النفض وأشاة لقول المربن أطاشة الجوهر

الشك وقد أقبل بها عز من الزمان عندالامتحان يكم بخل أو بجان

brought from as far away as China. The Seljuk period also saw a remarkable degree of similarity between realistic illustration on widely different scales. The ancient east Iranian and Central Asian school of wall painting was now mirrored in often tiny book pages as well as in new forms of ceramic decoration.

The Islamic religious establishment is said to have been almost as suspicious of music as it was of 'idolatrous' representational art on the grounds that music was so powerful that it could lead people away from religion. Arabic and Persian literature is certainly full of references to men and women going into raptures over some particularly effective performance while talented musicians, poets and singing girls clearly had a power and influence to be envied by modern pop stars.

By the 11th century, a new 'art music' had emerged from a blending of the Arabs' own musical heritage and that of the Turks, Persians, Berbers and European Andalusians. Performers came from every corner of Islamic civilization, including Africa, to find patrons amongst the wealthy political and mercantile elites of the Middle East, but, although the Middle Ages were a golden age in Middle Eastern music, little is known about how it

actually sounded. Music was learned by ear, not by written notation, yet there were plenty of books on musical theory. The basic modes were different to those in European music, having more in common with that of India, Persia and Byzantine Greece. Yet the musical instruments were not so different, even though they were tuned differently. Many are used to this day and include the plucked harp, zither, oud, sahin and later the Turkish saz, the bowed nabab and rabab, various woodwind instruments, the distinctive stringed qanun played with small hammers, and assorted drums.

In general, Islamic music tended to be soft and plaintive to western ears, with singers being famed for trilling sounds and vocal gymnastics as found in modern opera, while words tended to be simple and repetitive, but sung in innumerable ways. Although Shia Muslims developed an emotional form of religious 'passion play', it seems to have been under Turkish rule that music was more widely introduced into unorthodox forms of Muslim worship. This was particularly apparent in Anatolia, where continuing Christian influence may have prompted various sufi religious brotherhoods to introduce

Above right: Aristotle and a pupil discuss philosophy in an early 13th century manuscript by Ibn Bakhtishu. Many ancient Greek scholars were lost to western Europe following the fall of the Roman Empire. In the Middle East, however, they were translated and written about.

Above left: The story of the knave and the fool in a 13th century manuscript. This kind of humerous moral tale was extremely popular in the medieval Islamic world. The illustration also shows the 'qadi', or judge, riding a mule.

Opposite: Men discussing literature in the library at Basra, Iraq, in an early 13th century manuscript painted by al-Wasiti. As in medieval European libraries, the books are laid flat on the shelves though in this case they are also grouped in sections.

music and even dance into their celebrations. The most famous of all these brotherhoods was, of course, that of the Mevlavi or Whirling Dervishes.

The world of the word

There was no concept of 'literature' in medieval Islamic civilization as writing involved almost every aspect of culture and a great deal of everyday life as well. As the untainted and direct word of God, Islam's holy book, the Koran, was regarded as being far above mere literature. But the Koran was also the fountainhead of perfect language. The Arabs' ancient poetry came second, and although this was rooted in an epic desert tradition it evolved far further during the Middle Ages with new poetic forms and new themes such as verses on love, wine and war.

Each form was strictly governed by its own conventions and the poet was admired not so much for what he said as the way he said it. From the 10th to 12th centuries, literary centres also flourished in more distant Arabic states. Andalusian poets, for example, became famous and, in turn, had a big influence upon the troubadours of southern France.

The ruling elite was expected to support poets and writers, and literary skill was so highly regarded that a rather tedious form of rhymed prose was used, even in official government documents. Meanwhile Arabic literature embraced the same heroic tales found in medieval European literature but, being an urban civilization with a flourishing middle class, the medieval Arabs developed a new genre in which clever but powerless heroes outwitted those with political or religious authority.

Medieval Persian literature followed a different path. It really began in eastern Iran during the 10th and 11th centuries as a reaction against centuries of Arabic cultural domination. Like other aspects of this Persian revival, literature harked back to the glories of the ancient Persian empires, most obviously in Firdawsi's great *Shahnamah*,

completed around 1010, and which recounted the seemingly eternal struggle between Iranians and Turks. From the later 11th to 13th centuries, Persian literature continued to flourish under Seljuk Turkish rule, producing a series of political and military treatises, including those known as Mirrors for Princes, which provided good advice for the ruling class. Persian, in fact, became the language of administration, while Arabic remained that of religion, even in areas where Turks formed the bulk of the population. This, in fact, remained the case in the Ottoman Turkish Empire almost up to modern times.

Turkish literature has rarely been given the status extended to that of Arabic or Persian, but the later medieval period did see the writing of exciting warlike tales and perhaps the funniest stories in Islamic literature. Those concerning the escapades of Nasraddin Hoja were typically Turkish, often rude and disrespectful, but at the same time deeply moral. The 'sufi' religious brotherhoods, which had become a characteristic feature of Turkish Anatolia, were largely responsible for the survival of Turkish during the disastrous Mongol invasions, and from then on Turkish literature began to flourish in its own right.

The other languages of the medieval Muslim world did not achieve the same literary status. Some never became literate, in the sense of being written down, until modern times. Berber dialects, for example, were spoken by the majority of people in North Africa throughout the medieval period, but produced no Berber literature. Other almost forgotten languages survived in odd corners of the Muslim world, even within Arabia where the Qara people of Dhufar spoke Shahari. This language was similar to those found in Ethiopia, in Africa, and their own legends state that the Qara originally came to Dhufar 'from the west'. In fact the Qara's distinctive culture is probably a survivor of those cultures which dominated most of Yemen and southern Arabia in ancient times.

THE WORLD'S LONGEST CIVILIZATION

China was, until the 20th century, the longest uninterrupted civilization in world history. This was certainly reflected in its arts, which were characterized by continuity of style and inspiration. Under the Sung dynasty (10th–13th centuries), however, China was much more inward looking and resistant to outside artistic influences than it had been under the previous T'ang rulers (618–909), despite continuing wide ranging trade contacts. At the same time, Sung China's flourishing economy and cultural life provided artists, writers and craftsmen with plenty of patrons. Although this patronage changed under Mongol rule, the Mongol or Yüan period (1237–1387) was one of the most original in Chinese history, compared to the highly traditional Ming era which followed (1368–1644).

Korea was distinguishable from China by language and by its now deep-rooted Buddhist religion, whereas in China, although culturally influential, Buddhists remained a minority. Nevertheless Chinese influence had an enormous impact on all forms of Korean art.

Japanese art, along with most other aspects of its culture, owed a similarly large debt to strong Chinese influence. But the main period of learning from outside ended in the 10th century, to be followed by centuries of cultural and political isolation during which most foreigners' ideas were despised and Japanese civilization expanded from within. The 10th and 11th centuries were also characterized by a city or metropolitan-centred culture which was, in turn, followed by a period of political instability, contributing to a decentralization of both culture and patronage in what became known as the feudal age. The 12th and 13th centuries saw a flowering of Japanese art and

literature, the Kamakura period (1185–1392), though it took time for this brilliant culture to reach more distant provinces.

Meanwhile, a culture had developed in Central Asia, along the Silk Roads which linked China to the Middle East. Between the 4th and 14th centuries, some little trading towns seem to have consisted almost entirely of Buddhist monasteries, stupas and temples cut into cliff faces. They were filled with wall painting, clay or wooden sculpture, textiles and religious books. Though inspired by Chinese and Indian art, they also retained their own vigorous Turco-Mongol character and would play a major role in spreading east Asian artistic and cultural ideas at the time of the vast Mongol 'World Empire' of the 13th and 14th centuries.

Above: A carved wooden sculpture of a wrestler in a Japanese Zen Buddhist temple, built in 1450. The martial arts were closely connected with Zen Buddhism in Japan.

Part of a Japanese painting on a Shio riverbed screen showing public entertainment at Shijo Gawa in Kyoto. It was made in the late Muromachi period from the mid-14th to 16th centuries. The contrast between the graceful movements of the dancers, the dignified behaviour of their educated audience, and that of the ordinary people down at the front is typical of Japanese art. Kabuki classical drama developed from this sort of performance.

The cultural wealth of these centres, although perhaps artistically inferior, probably mirrored that of Tibet's Buddhist monasteries, which remained virtually untouched treasure-houses of Central Asian art until the devastating Chinese occupation of this century. Tibet was, in fact, not as culturally isolated as was once thought and during the medieval period its art, administration, literature and, of course, religion were influenced by several neighbouring civilizations. Under Mongol domination in the 13th and 14th centuries, Tibet played its own vital role as a centre of northern Buddhism.

As a result, the Mongol ruling elites of Central Asia, China and even Iran sent presents to these monasteries, including astonishing pieces of laquered armour, horse-harness and other objects which are only now coming to light.

Artists with a different eye

China was the fountainhead of east Asian art, most obviously in the area of painting and ceramics. There was a renaissance in Chinese painting under the Sung dynasty, the finest being done on silk, with paper relegated to more everyday art. The basic inspiration of Chinese painting was, however, different to that of western art. Artists were trained to depict things accurately and with great insight, but from memory rather than from life. In fact the Chinese artists were supposed to rely on what they found within themselves rather than what they saw outside.

Chinese ceramics were exported across a vast area and fragments have been found in Europe, Africa, most of Central Asia and even Australasia. Nevertheless Chinese potters did not go unchallenged, with Koreans making excellent celadon-ware, while Muslim potters made greater technical advances as they struggled to imitate the finest Chinese imports.

Far Eastern music and literature were similarly based upon aesthetic values which differed from those of Europe and the Middle East. Yet there were clear connections between Chinese musical instruments and those of the Muslim world. Chinese musicians, for example, made considerable use of zithers, pan-pipes, drums, bells and assorted woodwind. This inevitably had a profound impact on neighbouring Korea and Japan and, in the former, dance was extremely highly regarded, particularly when performed by young women.

A standard form of pictographic character writing had been developed in ancient times in China by the Han dynasty (206BC–AD220) in ancient times and consisted of some 9,000 characters, although only a fraction were in regular use. By the 11th century, the 'authorized' versions of ancient or classical Chinese texts had also been established by scholars working in the Imperial libraries, which also included political, technical, scientific and military works as well as religious and literary texts. In 1054 Chinese astronomers even recorded the creation of the Crab nebula in the night sky.

Some of the greatest developments in Chinese literature took place during the early Middle Ages and a great deal of Chinese literature was written by civil servants who had both education and spare time. Poetry in praise of rulers was well paid and popular, as were works praising the beauties of nature. Other literature was written by those who had had an education, but had opted out of China's rigid bureaucratic system, many being poets

who found their inspiration in alcohol. These literary elites influenced the oral literature of the rest of the population and the old travelling storytellers are known to have started using notebooks to help them remember details of plot or characterization. It was the birth of the Chinese novel, which reached its finest form during the Ming period.

Paper had been invented long before this and was widely used for literature as well as official documents. Similarly printing, though known earlier, was being used on a wide scale by the 11th century, and this all contributed to the spread of literary styles amongst the educated elite. Meanwhile perhaps the greatest piece of medieval Japanese literature, *The Tale of Geni*, was completed by Lady Murasaki in 1020.

Female dancers leading what is probably a wedding procession on a late 14th or early 15th century manuscript painting, probably from Transoxania. The style of both the painting and the dancers' costumes is a mixture of Chinese, Central Asian and Muslim Iranian styles.

INDIAN ART – FOOD FOR THE MIND

The classical Indian attitude regarded art as 'food for the mind' to be consumed and appreciated. Above all, it was the quality of workmanship which counted while the artist was considered a superior craftsman who 'knew how things ought to be done'. Indian aesthetics also included the concept of 'angelic' prototypes for all things, a concept close to the Platonic ideal which later inspired much of the art of the Italian Renaissance. Using living models as a source of inspiration was frowned upon because it ran counter to the belief that art should lead the mind heavenward, and not focus upon this imperfect world. The artist was, in fact, supposed to help the spiritual enlightenment of people as a whole, not pander to the whims of one patron.

Within India most tribal peoples of the jungles and mountains adopted their own versions of the basic Indian cultural pattern and only in the remotest corners of neighbouring Sri Lanka did the aboriginal Vedas avoid assimilation by the Ceylonese settlers. This deeply spiritual but conservative aestheticism was also found throughout the Indianized cultures of south-eastern Asia and proved so attractive that in many areas indigenous cultures were virtually extinguished by Indianized, Hindu or Buddhist civilizations. In other areas conquerors were taken over culturally by those they had defeated. This happened, for example, during the 11th century in Burma where the Burmese absorbed the culture of the Indianized Mon. The attraction of Indian culture similarly led many Indonesian peoples to adopt many, though not all, aspects of Indian art in preference, for example, to those of China.

Music had a particularly high status in Indian culture. It was thought to have divine origins and was associated with female rather than male creativity. As a result Hindu temples and Buddhist monasteries were important patrons of music and musicians, though in the Middle Ages the secular aristocracy took over much of this role of patron. Nor was Indian 'art music' unchanging, since there was a profound Persian and Arabic influence on the music of northern India during the later medieval period. In contrast, earlier and perhaps more classical Indian traditions survived in the south where the Muslim conquest remained very superficial

Seated divinity on a 15th century Jain manuscript from Madyha Pradesh. The religion of Jainism grew out of Hinduism in the 6th century BC but took the ideals of asceticism even further.

or did not reach. Dance was seen as the daughter of music, Indian traditional dance being characterized by a highly stylized repertoire of movements, gestures and themes. These enabled dancers to tell complex stories through mime, and to express the whole range of human emotions.

Medieval Indian literature, like that of China, was heir to an ancient tradition of epic and religious writing. The most refined was written in Sanskrit for court circles. However the 'Kavya', or adventures of Hindu princes in love, war and the pursuit of justice, had declined since the 7th century. Even more distinctive was the tradition of Sanskrit drama which, unlike European theatre, had virtually no interest in the passage of time or space. Instead it focused almost exclusively on the emotions and of its characters. Nor was there much interest in tragedy, Indian drama being much more concerned with love.

The earliest known Indonesian literature appeared in 11th century Java, where the poetic form of 'Kakawin' was based on Indian themes. The local Javanese script died out around 1400, but Indian Vedic epics continued to provide subject matter for puppet dramas performed for ordinary people. No literature survived from the medieval Khmer culture, though the earliest surviving Thai works, dating from the late Middle Ages, are thought to have been based upon a lost Khmer tradition.

In contrast, the literature of Vietnam, or at least of the northern heartland of Vietnamese culture, was in Chinese. No Malay literature seems to have survived from the medieval period of Hindu cultural domination, but early fragments were embedded

in 14th century Muslim sources. Old stories, several of which are based on the ancient Hindu or early Javanese tales, also survive in the shadow puppet plays which still entertain Muslim Malaysian audiences. The varied and cosmopolitan literature of Malaya also incorporated Arabic and Persian tales, most remarkable of all being the popularity of Alexander the Great's largely mythical adventures which reached Malaya via Persian-Islamic writing. Finally the Malays started to record their own history in the 15th century. Further north, in Burma, the earliest literature dates from the late 12th century and included religious, administrative and legal text books made for the ruling Pagan dynasty, though the first works in the Burmese language itself were not written before the late 15th century.

Gigantic heads of the Bodhisattva Lokesvara carved on the Temple of Bayon of Angkor Wat in Cambodia in the late 12th or early 13th century. They are believed to represent the Khmer king, Jayavarman VII, as the Lokesvara or Lord of the World.

3 | ARCHITECTURE

THE SKYLINES OF SOME PARTS OF THE WORLD ARE STILL DOMINATED BY BUILDINGS ERECTED IN THE MIDDLE AGES. IN WESTERN EUROPE, SOARING GOTHIC CATHERDRALS REMAIN THE GLORY OF DOZENS OF CITIES. MANMADE DISASTERS SUCH AS INVASIONS, AND NATURAL ONES LIKE EARTHQUAKES, HAVE MEANT ONLY A FEW MAGNIFICENT RELICS REMAIN IN REGIONS LIKE THE MIDDLE EAST. SIMILARLY, AS SO MUCH ARCHTECTURE WAS MADE OF WOOD IN INDIA, LITTLE NOW SURVIVES.

FROM CASTLES
TO CATHEDRALS

Until the present day, domestic architecture reflected the availability of local building materials. Only the rich could import stone into areas which lacked it, or choose to build in brick where there was plenty of timber. As a result the homes of ordinary people, though they varied in size, sophistication and even splendour where rich merchant families were concerned, varied even more from country to country and region to region.

In the south-east of England, for example, almost every building was of timber, as was also the case throughout Russia and much of Scandinavia. In parts of the Iberian peninsular, stone dominated, but in others there was a well-established architectural tradition of brick. Much the same held true in Italy, while in France there was a clear dividing line between the wooden architecture of the north and the stone of the south.

This did not mean that everything was made of timber in an area where timber dominated. By the 14th and 15th centuries, most English manor houses had brick or stone chimneys built as a precaution against fire as well as a way of removing smoke more efficiently. Much of the interior would also have been covered in decorated plaster while the floors might have been tiled.

Meanwhile the poorest people in a village made do with inefficient, leaky smoke-holes in their roofs, rushes strewn on bare earth floors and wind howling through cracks in rickety wooden walls. In winter, even the local lord's chamber would have been dark and chilly, despite a roaring fire in the grate at one side of the room

In the sunnier south, winters were shorter, though not necessarily warmer, and greater wealth meant that the urban middle classes, and even some peasants, had more comfortable homes. Similarly, several features of Roman domestic architecture survived, at least amongst the better off whose 'villas' still had aspects in common with those of earlier centuries. The crowded urban tenements of ancient Roman cities had their descendents not in the cities of western Europe, but in the teeming cities of the Muslim eastern Mediterranean and Byzantium.

In the far north, however, primitive domestic architecture remained much as it had been in the early medieval and Viking periods (5th–10th centuries). The low stone, wood and turf longhouses of places like the Scottish islands normally consisted of one or two rooms, with cattle byres being added in the 11th century and, later in the Middle Ages, assorted subsidiary rooms. However, these unimpressive dwellings were probably very efficient in retaining what little heat was available – they were certainly found throughout the Scandinavian north as far as Iceland and Greenland.

Making a castle comfortable

Up until the 11th century, fortifications reflected the availability of local materials, which in turn led to a widespread and effective use of timber, turf and earth. From then on, however, a stone-built castle became the symbol of a new political order and the means whereby it was imposed, the most famous example being the White Tower of the Tower of London, built in the 1070s by William the Conqueror after conquering England.

Not all 12th century castles looked like the so-called 'Norman keeps', but in each area stone and brick fortifications were either improved or imported into new areas. Within the heartlands of western Europe, an

Opposite: The oldest of the conical roofed 'trulli' houses at Alberobello in Apulia, southern Italy, date from the 12th century. They were made this way because the area is so full of stones and they may also be related to the 'sugar-loaf' houses of central Syria. A short-lived Muslim Arab state was established in this part of southern Italy during the 9th century while the ruling family of 12th century Apulia were related to the first rulers of the Crusader Principality of Antioch.

astonishing number of small local fortifications had been thrown up during the 10th and 11th centuries in response to invasions and raids from several directions. They mirrored a growing fragmentation of political influence and authority.

Throughout northern France, the Low Countries and England, many of the wood and earth 'motte and bailey' castles of the 11th century were gradually replaced during the 12th century by stone structures, often in much the same design as went before. Further to the south, the castle architects of Mediterranean Europe could draw upon their own distant Romano-Byzantine heritage, as well as more advanced ideas from their close Muslim neighbours.

The descendants of those Crusaders who carved out short-lived states in various parts of the Middle and Near East in the 12th and 13th centuries drew upon Islamic ideas to an even greater extent, erecting some of the most impressive castles within supposedly 'European' architectural style, most notably the Krak des Chevaliers in Syria dating from the early 13th century. The Celts had meanwhile developed their own form of passive defences in the form of tall, windowless and almost chimney-like towers with a single doorway in one side of the wall.

Political and economic changes within Europe led to some remarkable changes in castle design. In France, Germany and Italy the castles of kings, emperors and the most powerful barons became statements of wealth and power, as well as including great luxury and a fair degree of comfort.

In England this trend took a slightly different turn, with most castles becoming aristocratic homes rather than fortresses, so much so that, by the 15th century, most of their 'fortification' was a sham designed to impress rather than to protect. More businesslike fortifications could perhaps be seen in the defence of rich cities and strategic harbours, but even here the possession of impressive walls and towers was a demonstration of wealth and increasing independence.

Architectural splendour for the glory of God

The most decorated and sophisticated architecture was of course religious. The great cathedrals of medieval western Europe are some of the finest buildings ever erected. From the 11th to 13th centuries there were extraordinary advances in technique, size and decoration, while some unlikely corners of Europe, including the Orkney Islands north of Scotland, enjoyed their own era of architectural splendour. Here the magnificent Cathedral at Kirkwall was founded in 1137 because of local wealth and power generated as a result of being on one of the main north Atlantic trade routes.

Everywhere it seemed that church interiors were getting taller, their walls and arches lighter, their windows larger and with ever more magnificent coloured glass. In fact Gothic stained glass windows remain one of the glories of medieval art.

These developments continued into the 14th and even 15th centuries, with ever more elaborate stone and painted decoration being mirrored by wood carving of astonishing delicacy. There were, however, regional variations, even before the Italian Renaissance sent European architecture down an entirely different route. Many of the churches built for the Crusading Military Order of Templars, for example, were round, being based on the Dome of the Rock in Jerusalem, which was mistakenly believed to be a remnant of the ancient Jewish Temple. Abbey churches built for some of the newer monastic orders, such as the puritanical Cistercians, lacked the sculpture which abounded elsewhere, while in many parts of Iberia and southern Italy, Islamic forms had a profound influence on Christian religious architecture.

Much is known about the men who designed and built these amazing structures, and of the women who helped decorate them. Medieval Europe did, in fact, have a genuine building industry, though it did not develop its own guild system.

Right: The wooden stave-church at Fasgusnes, Norway, was built in 1150. A handful of wooden churches survive in Scandinavia and some late examples like this one have been called 'mast churches' because their central area was built to a remarkable height.

Below right: A 14th century ceiling in Gloucester Cathedral which has the earliest surviving fan-vaulting in England. The masons are believed to have been sent from London by King Edward III after his murdered father, Edward II, was buried in the cathedral.

Below left: The cloisters and Church of San Giovanni degli Eremiti were built in 1132. When the Normans conquered southern Italy and Sicily in the 11th century they created a new kingdom which incorporated Italian, Byzantine Greek and Arab Islamic cultures. One result was this remarkable church, built in the style of an 11th century Sicilian or North African mosque.

From the 11th century onwards, craftsmen became more specialized although much of the work was done by unskilled migratory labourers. Carpenters played a major role as so many buildings were made of timber, and even those which were of stone or brick included a great deal of wood. Most medieval carpenters had their own workshops where timbers were laid on the ground and joined into a framework, but not finally pinned together. These individual pieces of wood were then marked and taken to the building site where they were put together. The sawyers already formed a separate group or craft, since it was they who felled the trees and made them into manageable planks or timbers using pit-saws operated by two men.

'On site' the joiners formed another distinct group which was largely responsible for doors and windows. Thatchers or tilers covered the roof which could also be made of stone or wooden slates, according to the availability of local material. The use of clay roofing tiles increased from the 13th century onwards as a precaution against fire, particularly in urban architecture. In addition to the roofs, tilers were also responsible for chimneys as well as the daubing of walls. In the latter case, they normally used a mixture of

earth, cow-dung and mortar bound together with straw or hair, all of which was then plastered to give a smooth finish.

Sometimes daubers and wallers were listed as separate groups using different materials on different parts of the building. Stone masons built stone buildings, elite members of this craft group being referred to as hewers or freemasons. The settlers, wallers or layers who actually built stone walls had a more humble status than the freemasons, but all grades of mason could be involved in the construction of timber buildings because many of them had stone foundations.

Most workers were employed and paid on a daily basis. Unfortunately their pay depended on the number of daylight hours, so that they got considerably less in winter than in summer. In England the highest wages were found in the prosperous south-east, but skilled workers or craftsmen everywhere received at least twice that given to unskilled. Foremen were employed on a longer term basis, but some of the most specialized craftsmen might only be required for a few days. As a result, such men often moved around the country doing other work in winter to maintain their families, and even the most skilled could sometimes be very poor.

Louis Leidet builds a palace in a 15th century French manuscript illustration. The difference in status between architects and ordinary labourers is clearly shown in their clothing. A man of status would never let his hose or leggings hang loose.

FROM VILLAS
TO TOWER-BLOCKS

A great deal of Byzantine religious and military architecture survives, but far fewer domestic buildings. Nevertheless the houses of ordinary people were probably similar to those of the previous Roman period; at one extreme the poor either lived in small houses with rushes strewn on the floors or in tenements up to nine storeys high. Most homes were of brick, with only the wealthy using stone, though in forested regions such as the coast of the Black Sea, almost all were of wood. Houses of the rich had sloping tiled roofs, while ordinary homes were flat-roofed, at least in the drier parts. The villas of the Byzantine elite were given strong gates for fear of riots and banditry and a widespread collapse of law and order between the 14th and 15th centuries resulted in the fortified houses with their strong similarity to Italian urban architecture. A typical example is the Palataki House, dating from the 14th century.

Most of the downstairs windows looked inwards towards a central courtyard, though the higher rooms had external windows as well, often glazed with small panes of glass. Stables faced the courtyard where there would be a cistern or well. The homes of the well-off generally had toilets which, in some cases, were linked to a system which drained into the sea. There was often a small bath-house designed as a separate structure, while the wealthy also had small shrines or chapels in their gardens. The layout of the house

itself was of ancient origin and basically consisted of a central hall with other rooms leading off. Some of these formed smaller halls where the men of the household received guests, while the private family rooms were upstairs and had galleried windows overlooking the courtyard. Many had a special room which could be heated for use in winter, either by charcoal braziers or, in wealthier houses, by an underground hypocaust. Late Byzantine domestic architecture was inherited by the Ottoman Turks in the 15th century.

Byzantine palaces seem to have looked less magnificent than might have been expected, at least on the plain exteriors. But inside, these palaces were light and airy with a great deal of colourful decoration ranging from marble panelling to brilliant mosaics.

Above: Building work in the 1320s on the Cathedral of the Assumption in Moscow's Kremlin being blessed. This copy of the Russian Chronicle was made for Tsar Ivan the Terrible.

One of the carved capitals in the Cloisters of Monreale Cathedral in Sicily, Italy. It was made in the late 12th century and, like most carvings at Monreale, is a mixture of Byzantine, Italian, French and even some Islamic elements.

Opposite: The church in the Monastery of Moldovita in Romania was decorated in the early 16th century. Painting the exterior of churches reached its peak in the old principality of Moldavia. These images also include one of the earliest illustrations of the conquest of Byzantine Constantinople by the Ottoman Turks.

Balkan domestic architecture was very similar to that of the Byzantines but to the east, in Georgia, other traditions persisted, particularly in the countryside. Here a distinctive form of house was known as a darbazi. Its lower part was largely of stone, while the top half consisted of a central pyramid or cupola made of overlapping slabs of wood. These regions were also characterized by widespread cliff dwellings which consisted of either caves or completely new chambers cut from the rock. Russian domestic architecture all appears to have been of timber

Nevertheless, there was a considerable difference between north and south. In the Kievan south, an essentially Central Asian style of semi-sunken house predominated, with living and storage rooms being half-excavated out of the ground as a protection against the fierce climate, while the upper part and roofs were made of wood which was weatherproofed with clay. In northern Russia, however, the timber came largely from

straighter coniferous trees which, as much of the ground was frozen solid for part of the year, meant that northern Russian houses were built above ground with large straight timbers laid directly one upon the other.

With very few exceptions, medieval Byzantine military architecture was not on the same scale as that of many of its neighbours. Any exceptions, such as the massive walls of Constantinople, dated from earlier centuries, having been started by the Emperor Theodosius II in AD413. In fact, medieval Byzantine architects inherited so much from their Roman and early Byzantine predecessors that most of their work consisted of upgrading existing structures. Byzantine fortification was not very innovative, nor was the craftsmanship impressive.

Things were different in Armenia and Georgia, where the Armenians had been the most highly efficient military architects of the early medieval period. Again, the Georgians were heirs to several traditions, including Byzantine, Islamic, Armenian, Turkish and even Mongol. As a consequence of a struggle to maintain its freedom as an outpost of Christianity, Georgia became a land of castles. As already stated, Russian fortification was overwhelmingly constructed from earth and timber. A few stone defences began to appear in the north-west of the country as a result of western European influence and pressure, but elsewhere an effective tradition of wooden fortresses and city walls developed. Only in the 15th century, with the spread of Muscovite power, did massive brick 'kremlins' begin to appear. The oldest tower in the Moscow Kremlin dates from 1485.

Sensuous domes and glittering mosaics

Byzantine religious architecture was in many ways the most distinctive in Europe. It was a fusion of Graeco-Roman, Middle Eastern and Persian traditions which, by the 11th century, evolved into something new and remarkably complex The main patrons were, of course, the Orthodox Church and the Emperor, with little of the secular or corporate urban patronage seen in western Europe – at least not until the 14th and 15th centuries. Byzantine churches tended to have elaborate plans and abundant detailed decoration rather than a grand conception, and as the Empire weakened they also became smaller. Following the restoration of Byzantine power and the fall of the Crusader Empire of Constantinople in 1260, a new style of religious architecture emerged. It was based on existing building traditions, but was now characterized by small and almost intimate buildings, more thoughtful and reflective, but also narrower, with smaller domes set on top of tall cylinders.

Meanwhile the Orthodox states of the Balkans developed their own distinctive styles which, although based on Byzantine concepts, differed one from another, though all tended to use multiple domes and greater height. Georgian and Armenian religious architecture were different again, being based on several traditions. As a result, although the ground-plans of Georgian and Armenian churches and cathedrals were similar to those of Byzantine religious buildings, their grandeur and decoration seemed in fact to have more in common with Turkish and Persian architecture.

Russian religious architecture, on the other hand, was firmly based upon Byzantine principles, although even these were necessarily modified to cope with Russia's fearsome winter climate. The domes of churches became taller to shed the snow and, like the steeply sloping roofs, soon projected beyond the walls to shed rain and snow. Walls became thicker to insulate against the freezing temperatures and windows smaller. As a result, the dark but abundantly decorated interior of Russian Orthodox churches like the Cathedral of Santa Sofia in Novgorod built in 1052 had a powerful feeling of mystery and religious intensity which was lacking in the lighter, airier interiors of Greek Orthodox churches.

AN EMPHASIS ON PRIVACY

Muslim domestic architecture included a variety of traditions and ranged from vast and splendid palaces to simple cave dwellings, yet in each case Islamic religion dominated the domestic arrangements so that all these 'homes' had features in common. Above all there was an emphasis on privacy and an almost modern concern for peace and quiet.

Despite the wealth and the military background of almost all Muslim governments, Islamic palaces were rarely realistically fortified. Most palace buildings consisted of barracks, administrative offices, mosques, parade and training grounds, horse-racing tracks, gardens, cisterns and sometimes an enclosed game reserve, the largest having been the Caliph's 'palace city' of Samarra in Iraq, built in the 9th century. Later palaces were much smaller, but still followed the same pattern of main public reception halls and private residential quarters at the centre, surrounded by lesser buildings and gardens.

These decorated and impressive structures were largely of brick, including a great deal of unfired mud-brick, and as a consequence, very little survives.

Even fewer ordinary houses remain, though archaeological excavations show that in 12th century Cairo, most domestic housing was of mud bricks, often strengthened with sandstone columns. These could reach six storeys high and may have had much in common with the existing towering town houses of Yemen. Those in Cairo had lavatories on each floor connected to flues which ran through the walls to cesspits and were flushed with water. Every house, shop and workshop had cisterns for drinking water, which were topped up from reservoirs in each quarter of the city. Each tenement block had its own courtyard, from which the rooms of the ground floor opened into a public reception room and private harem quarters. Manuscript illustrations such as various

copies of the humorous Maqamat of al-Hariri made in 13th century Iraq and Syria suggest that there were other types of houses, some having their courtyard covered by a light wooden dome or pyramid which could be opened down one side to let in light and air. Almost all had ventilation ducts which turned to catch the wind and channel a cooling draught into the interior of the house. Fountains and small water channels also served as humidifiers inside the house.

Stairs tended to be external and, like the many open verandas, provided space where semi-porous water containers used small amounts of evaporation to give a refrigerating effect on drinking water. As in most Islamic architecture, the decoration of houses and even palaces consisted largely of surface textures and colour rather than the basic structure. An often harsh climate led to a love of idealized mini-landscapes such as gardens which aimed to be mirrors of Paradise with an emphasis on greenery, shade and, again, flowing water. Unlike most modern European gardeners, or those of medieval Japan, Muslims did not try to accentuate a welcoming nature, but to replace an often hostile one. This tradition continued even in the gentler climates of the Iberian Peninsula, Turkey and the Balkans. Everywhere water was an essential ingredient to create these mini-climates, as a decoration in its own right and to provide relaxing sounds.

In rural villages, of course, housing was much simpler. Written and illustrated evidence indicates that there were animals

Above: The Patio de los Leones in the Alhambra Palace at Granada, in Spain. It was started in 1377 and shows Moorish design at its most sophisticated. The use of water to cool the interior and create a soothing sound was also typical of medieval Islamic architecture.

Opposite: So-called 'sugar-loaf' houses at Khan Shaikhun in central Syria. These examples are clustered around the base of an ancient 'tel' or mound of debris caused by thousands of years of human habitation.

almost everywhere, though all but the most primitive hamlets had their own shops, pools of water and mosque. Syria was noted for a distinctive form of 'beehive' house whose rounded shape, though looking odd from outside, was efficient in reflecting heat in summer and retaining it in winter. Elsewhere, the peasants lived in caves, not because of backwardness, but because rock dwellings were again cool in summer, warm in winter.

Several changes to Islamic domestic architecture resulted from Turkish settlement in the 12th century. These not only reflected the Turks' own recent nomadic existence in Central Asia but may also have included some Chinese influence. Palaces built for the Seljuk dynasty (1037–1300), for example, tended to consist of scattered pavilions rather than one complex. A Seljuk love of gardens and fountains remained fully within established Islamic traditions and was inherited by the Ottoman Turks in the 14th century. Some of these new features could be seen in ordinary Seljuk houses, at least those of the wealthy, and these tended to be more Central Asian than the rulers' palaces were.

Citadels for the Sultan

Effective fortification was very advanced in the Muslim world and resulted from the coming together of military traditions from much of the known world. It included the machicolation, which enabled defenders to drop missiles on their attackers in almost complete safety, and the newer 'bent entrance' introduced from Central Asia in the 8th century which forced attackers to expose their unshielded right sides. A continued use of mud and fired brick might seem old fashioned, but in fact mud-brick walls effectively absorbed enemy missiles, tended to retain their shape when undermined and were cheap and quick to erect.

In Muslim Andalusia and North Africa a form of concrete, popularly called 'tabby', had developed in the 10th century, which enabled western Islamic architects to repair

damaged fortifications quickly and to erect others which were as cheap, effective, and almost as ugly as modern concrete defences.

Religious architecture remains one of the glories of Islamic civilization, yet the mosque was basically a place of communal prayer, lacking the consecrated character of a Christian church or the sacred quality of an oriental temple. Early mosques, such as the Great Mosque in Damascus built in the late 7th century, were based upon the traditional Arabian house rather than previous forms of religious structure, and this unpretentious character meant that the basic mosque could easily develop into more specialized structures such as schools or a meeting place for dervish brotherhoods, or even, by the 12th century, into what was essentially a non-religious hospital.

At the same time the elaborate tombs of political or religious leaders had mosques, or at least prayer-halls, attached to them. Amongst the most imposing was that built for the Turco-Mongol conqueror Tamerlane and his family at Samerkand, completed in 1434. This was widely considered to be a Turkish or Persian addition to the basic Arab concept of the mosque being merely a place set aside for prayer.

The little that is known about the men who built these mosques and palaces sheds interesting light on medieval Islamic civilization. The use of slave labour was, for example, virtually unknown, while, at the other end of the scale, the best architects formed a highly paid elite which travelled huge distances from one patron to the next.

STREETS OF LACQUERED BEAMS

Chinese domestic architecture was designed almost entirely from wood and although very little survives from the medieval period, there are plenty of highly accurate illustrations in manuscripts and other sources. These generally show wood-framed houses with remarkably large windows, at least where the homes of the well-off are concerned. The urban rich lived in multi-storey dwellings in which the main wooden beams were richly carved, painted and even sometimes gilded. Their walls were normally plastered, while interior walls were often covered with richly embroidered drapes and numerous movable screens to give some degree of privacy in what was otherwise a rather open system of rooms. Coloured illustrations indicate that ordinary domestic houses were given red tiles, while religious buildings, such as pagodas, had yellow tiles.

Compared with the rich decoration seen in many Chinese dwellings, medieval Japanese houses appeared much simpler. In fact the domestic life of even the Japanese elite seemed almost Spartan. The home of a rich or aristocratic family was called a 'shinden', and, although it largely developed from an earlier Chinese prototype, by the 11th century it clearly had several of its own distinctively Japanese characteristics. The architectural design of such wooden houses tended to be simple, even stark, with the floors raised off the ground to avoid excessive humidity at certain times of year. Unlike Chinese houses, very few Japanese private dwellings were more than one storey high. Nor did the medieval Japanese make much use of the Chinese system of tiled roofs as these were thought to make the buildings too hot during the summer months.

Instead, the home of an aristocratic samurai warrior in the 12th century or later was called a 'yakata' and consisted of several separate structures within a stoutly fenced courtyard. This in turn usually had fortified wooden gates on three sides and a water-

The Hall of Perfect Harmony stands at the centre of the Forbidden City, in Beijing, China. It was started by China's ruling Ming dynasty in the 15th century.

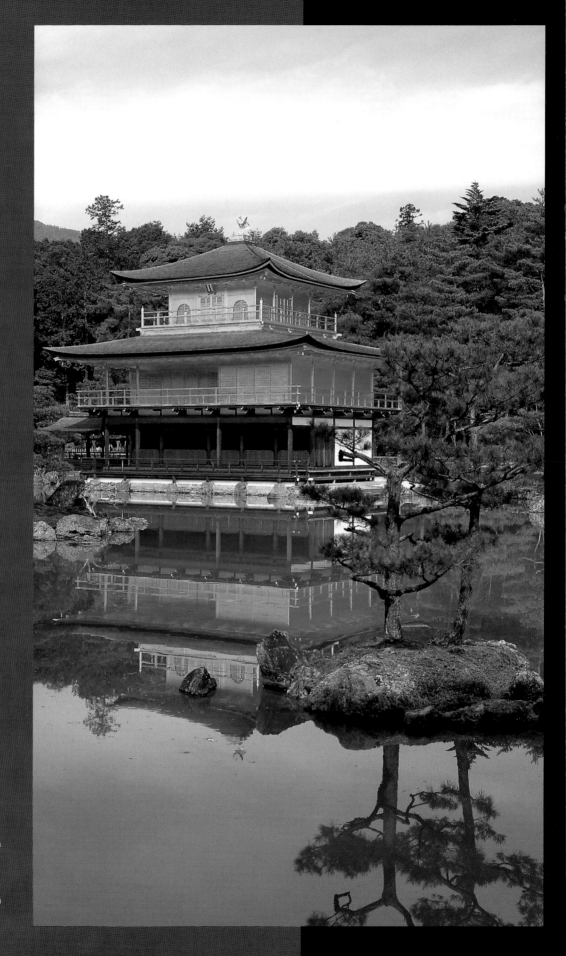

The Kinkanku-Ji Temple, which was also known as the Golden Pavilion, was built at Kyoto in Japan in the 14th century. The beautiful location of this building reflected the Japanese Buddhist belief that mankind must constantly learn from nature.

filled moat around the outside. Within this simple stockade there were vegetable gardens, storage buildings and one or more wells. Most of the domestic buildings in the compound were connected by covered walkways or corridors and each consisted of very light, almost flimsy panelled walls, a slatted or thatched roof and large open verandas.

China without a Great Wall

The popular image of Chinese fortification is dominated by the famous Great Wall of China. In fact, this was an abandoned ruin throughout most of the Middle Ages and was only rebuilt in the 15th and 16th centuries. The medieval Chinese frontier ran far to the north of the ancient Great Wall and for most of this period the main threats to the Chinese heartlands came from the west and northwest rather than the north – the Great Wall was redundant as a military defence. The northern and western frontiers relied for their defence on a chain of separate but powerful fortresses linked by watch-towers. Those furthest to the west were not even made of stone, but were constructed in a cheaper and simpler way by using layers of beaten earth reinforced with brushwood.

Within China itself, however, the main towns and cities were all strongly fortified in a style which proved so effective that there was little change in Chinese military architecture until the large-scale introduction of cannon in the late 14th century. Typically such fortifications consisted of an outer earthwork, a high main wall and a separate inner citadel, but in the 12th century the southern Sung dynasty (1127–1279) ordered that the main walls should be doubled in height, perhaps because of the appearance of counterweight trebuchets from the west.

Paradoxically it was medieval Korea rather than China which attempted to defend its northern frontier with a 'long wall'. This was built by the Koryu dynasty (935–1392) to seal off the entire Korean peninsula from troublesome northern neighbours in Manchuria and Mongolia. In Japan the system of earth, timber and plaster forms of fortification, which had been developed in China as the upper parts of most urban defences, were refined into a system of military architecture which was as beautiful as it was effective, though this was more a characteristic of the 16th and 17th centuries rather than the Middle Ages.

As in all the finest Chinese architecture, religious buildings were designed in terms of colour as well as shape and plan. Basically, however, temples and monasteries built for China's many tolerated religions all tended to have a great deal in common, features which were also shared by religious buildings and many secular ones as well. For example, particularly close attention and scope for imagination seems to have been given to the shape and intricacy of roofs, which sometimes achieved fantastic forms.

One type of building did, however, stand out as being distinctively Chinese. This was the 'pagoda', a tall tower-like structure with wide projecting roofs at each of its many storeys. One of the oldest surviving Chinese pagodas is the White Pagoda at Pai-t'a-ssu in Inner Mongolia built shortly after 1031. Such structures may have developed from, or been influenced by, the basic Buddhist stupa. This itself had originated as a domed burial mound, which then evolved into a chamber for religious relics. Stupas eventually became the ritual centres of Buddhist monasteries and were usually erected on a square mound also serving as a surrounding walkway. On top there would be a mast or pole topped by several symbolic ritual parasols or umbrellas.

In Japan, the mast with its umbrellas evolved into such a dominating feature that it became, to all intents and purposes, a form of pagoda. Like most Japanese architecture, however, the temples, monasteries and pagodas were almost entirely of wood. In Korea there was more use of stone, including decorative marble, which enabled architects to show originality and to break away from the domination of Chinese architectural forms.

The Shariden or relic hall of the Enkakuji Monastery at Kamakura, was built in 1285. The use of traditional materials such as wood and thatch were part of the Japanese desire for harmony with nature but also reflected the classical style of Chinese architecture introduced to Japan by Zen Buddhist monks.

HOUSES ON STILTS

The vast majority of domestic Indian houses would have been of simple wood and mud-brick construction, but even the basic layout remains largely unknown. Early illustrations of palaces show forests of columns, ornately carved balustrades and early forms of dome. Regional variations in the foothills of the Himalayas included steeper roofs and a greater use of wood in rainy Kashmir.

Houses in the Indianized states of south-east Asia were raised on stilts to keep the floors away from ground which could be awash with monsoon rains, as well as snakes and other unwelcome visitors. Most buildings in the similar coastal regions of Indonesia were almost invariably made of wood, bamboo and thatch, but some of the

more important inland structures were of stone. Nevertheless, even here many buildings were constructed of wood, including temples and palaces described by 13th century Chinese visitors as having gilded, brightly, carved timbers.

The simple fortifications in south-east Asia were also made of wood, though some cities had brick walls. India, on the other hand, was strongly fortified, the most impressive defences being of dressed stone over a rubble core. Detailed descriptions by visiting 6th century Chinese pilgrims refer to Indian villages having fortified gates, walls of mud and fired brick in addition to ramparts of wood or bamboo. Later Arabic and Persian writers suggest that little had changed, but by the late 14th century the most distinctive feature of Indian defensive architecture had appeared. This was a ceremonial 'chatris', or kiosk, above the main gate where a ruler could see and be seen.

Within Indian and Indianized civilization, religious architecture was intended to enhance the status of the ruler as well as be designed for spiritual reasons, since kings were to some extent divine or stood as links between the gods and ordinary mortals. Within India, especially in the south where many medieval Hindu, Jain and Buddhist structures largely escaped the ravages of Muslim invasion in the 11th to 14th centuries, the exuberance of Indian architecture showed itself in fantastic shapes and an abundance of decorative and figural carving. On the 13th century Temple of Siva at Amritapura, for example, there are small statues in decorative niches over almost the whole roof. Even here, however, most subsidiary buildings were probably of wood. The same fate overtook the majority of Buddhist

religious and other forms of architecture in Sri Lanka to the south. Here brick and stone only began to be used in sizeable quantities in the 12th century. Thereafter the styles of Sri Lanka remained very conservative. Monasteries, for example, continued to consist of residential halls raised on platforms along with stupas for relics, other shrines, eating rooms and kitchens.

The 8th to 14th centuries saw a remarkable outburst of truly monumental architecture in several parts of south-east Asia, most notably at Borobudur in Java (8th century) and Angkor in Cambodia (late 12th century) where huge structures almost covered in carvings still stand surrounded by dense jungle. Here the planning of entire cities often reflected the Hindu concept of the cosmos as a series of concentric circles, with a

huge temple in the middle representing Mount Meru, the mythical centre of the universe. In some cases this primary temple was surrounded by artificial lakes and canals representing the oceans which separated the encircling continents. Though based on earlier Indian models, these huge south-east Asian temple complexes were built by local craftsmen. In purely architectural terms they were very simple structures consisting what was really only vast piles of carved stones. Once the basic structure was completed, the sculptors started work, decorating the uppermost layers while the surrounding earth was gradually removed.

Yet it is the sheer size of some temple cities which makes them unique: Angkor Wat in Cambodia remains the biggest single religious complex ever made by man.

Above: The vast Buddhist temple complex at Angkor Wat in Cambodia consists of tower sanctuaries, pavilions, access galleries and gates. It was the most remarkable achievement of Khmer architecture, spreading outwards and skywards at the same time.

Opposite: The Sun Temple in Orissa, India. This remarkable building is a typical example of how a complex tower structure came to dominate Hindu religious architecture during the medieval period, originally representing the mountain home of the gods.

4 | COUNTRY LIFE

Agriculture provided the basis for all medieval civilisations, even the most urbanised and mercantile. At the same time, agricultural technology developed quickly from the simple systems used in classical times. New tools, machines and crops had a huge impact on the way rural people lived and worked. They would also lead to increased food production and new patterns of trade, with produce being exported over remarkable distances.

THE FOUNDATION OF MEDIEVAL SOCIETY

The climate of western Europe changed during the Middle Ages. It got milder from the 11th to 12th centuries then began to get cooler and wetter again in the 14th century. In several countries previously marginal areas such as woodland, moorland and heavy clay lowlands were brought into cultivation, leading to greater food production and increased population during the early centuries. These also saw an expansion of politically dominant peoples into more backward territory such as the German thrust into Slav areas and the Anglo-Norman push into Celtic lands of Wales, Ireland and Scotland in the 12th to 14th centuries. The latter only really came to end with Robert the Bruce's defeat of the English at the battle of Bannockburn in 1314.

This was, however, often done in a structured way with specific areas being seized and defended, followed by colonization and regularly planned settlements like modern 'new towns'. Even areas which remained unsuitable for agriculture were still used profitably. Cattle were pastured on rougher grassland, pigs herded in the forest fringes despite the continuing menace of wolves, while only the most sterile heath and marsh were left alone. But as the climate cooled in the 14th century some of this newly cultivated land was again abandoned, particularly the now waterlogged clay lowlands.

Nevertheless it has been estimated that roughly the same proportion of England was under cultivation in the 14th century as at the start of the 20th century. The image of a land still covered with mighty forests full of outlaws was, in fact, another medieval myth.

The basic administrative unit throughout western Europe was the parish whose boundaries were largely set by the start of the 12th century. The rural or feudal manor was the next most significant, along with lands belonging to monasteries and other church land-owners. In most of medieval Europe the local 'fief-holding' knight and his family were the leaders of rural society, with ordinary villagers looking to them for protection and advice, while one of the knight's sons or relatives might be the local parish priest. It was not a democratic society but the old concept that a privileged position had to be earned by accepting the responsibilities of leadership and of serving social 'inferiors' would survive for many centuries to come.

In more peaceful parts of Europe the rural knights were already turning away from their old warlike ways by the 13th century; becoming more interested in farming, the current price of wool and maintaining local law rather than fighting battles.

Nevertheless younger sons who could not inherit their father's manor often stuck to soldiering as a career. One such example would be William Marshal, younger son of a relatively minor noble family who rose by courage and ability to become Earl of Pembroke, guardian of the young King Henry III and the most powerful man in England in the early 13th century.

Opposite: Manuscript painters loved adding details of everyday life to their pictures and this is a typical early 14th century example. Two women milk sheep in a pen made of wattle screens while two others carry away the milk in a pitcher and a churn.

Below: Peasants often worked in the fields under the supervision of their lord's representive. Here they reap the corn with sickles while the bailiff looks on. Women would come along later to collect any grain that had been left or dropped.

Opposite: Bees return to their hives, in a 12th century English Bestiary or Book of Beasts. Bestiaries were popular in the Middle Ages and included real creatures as well as mythical monsters. The texts are full of moral lessons, for example about the bees' hard work and obedience to their queen.

The open field system of agriculture was normal in France, England and neighbouring regions. Here large fields were divided into strips, each worked by peasant families with different crops grown using a rotational system. Beyond these strip-fields were large meadows where the animals grazed. The lord's bailiff also ensured that each peasant worked several days a week on the lord's land. At busy times of year a peasant might have to work additional 'gift days' for which he could be paid with wheat, butter, cheese or seeds. He might then join in a village feast put on at the lord's expense.

By the 14th century many local landowners rented out their land to others and accepted money instead of labour from their peasants while a new class of more prosperous 'peasant farmers' appeared. In England the scarcity of agricultural labour and the steadily rising price of wool encouraged many to turn their fields over to sheep farming which was also viable on more marginal land. As a result many peasants moved out of their villages into isolated farmsteads to tend sheep while the Black Death plague in 1348 led to the desertion of villages in less fertile areas as the survivors moved to successful villages and the towns.

At the end of the 15th century the enclosure of large open fields also began as landlords and wealthier farmers divided up the land at the expense of poorer peasants which in turn led to the appearance of many more hedgerows throughout the English countryside. Meanwhile a scarcity of labour and a general increase in prosperity as a result of

the flourishing wool trade meant that those who survived the Black Death could demand higher wages. Along with increasing taxation, a sense of injustice heightened by the aristocracy's extravagant lifestyle, declining respect for authority and a feeling that ordinary people could now make their voices heard, all contributed to the peasant revolts which erupted across Europe.

Medieval new towns

Of course the life of ordinary people differed considerably outside the heartlands of medieval Europe. On the other hand several of these fringe areas also saw substantial colonization by newcomers including Anglo-Normans, Flemings and others. Specialists known as 'locatores' were hired by the authorities to establish new villages, ranging from the village of Tancredston 'planted' in Wales around 1100 to the town of Bruck an der Leitha planted close to the Hungarian frontier in Austria between 1236 and 1239. They divided up agricultural land into standard plots, built houses, a church and mill, found new settlers and if necessary supported them for the first year. In return the locatores got a larger plot of the best land and commercial privileges such as a market.

Meanwhile there were changes within Celtic rural society. The people of the Scottish Islands, for example, were descended from Celtic tribesman and Viking settlers, living as farmers, fishermen and by raiding distant shores. The most prosperous farmers were called 'odelars' but they did not own the farms, merely held them in trust for their extended family.

Other variations were seen elsewhere. In northern Germany and the Danube basin the most effective 'colonizers' included wealthy and powerful Monastic and Military Orders, who, like the Teutonic Knights, were often invited in by Hungarian and Slav rulers. In rural Scandinavia earlier Viking forms of society persisted, though under increasing Germanic influence.

The 13th century barn at Ter Doest in Belgium is one of the biggest surviving examples of medieval secular architecture in Europe and originally belonged to a neighbouring abbey. The walls are brick but the vast timber roof and columns are made of oak.

arte componunt. et ex uariis floubz condi
mumera ple castra replent. Exercitum et
mouent. Fumum fugiunt. tumultu exaspa
epta sunt de boum cadaueribz nasa. Ham
culoum occisoum carnes liberant ut et

In this late Anglo-Saxon Calendar, made around 1030, peasants are ploughing with a team of oxen. The plough is a large and complex mould plough designed to turn and break the soil rather than merely scratching a furrow for seeds. The fact that four oxen are needed suggests heavy soil.

As elsewhere, land was inherited by elder sons while a steady increase in population meant that there were plenty of younger men to fill the armies, merchant classes and urban craftsmen. This also meant that the early medieval Viking tradition of settling distant lands continued, though now often in the guise of Crusades against Finland and Estonia.

Within Italy things were again different. During the 11th and 12th centuries much of the rural aristocracy moved into the towns and soon joined the merchant class investing in agriculture as a purely business exercise. Together they bought up the best land, drained swamps, irrigated dry areas, terraced hillsides and built new roads. These business landowners also provided cash so that peasant farmers could invest in new crops and equipment, then shared their profits.

As a result Italian agriculture led the way in advanced techniques, distribution and marketing systems. Nevertheless the peasants' side of the story is rarely heard. Instead early Italian Renaissance records from the 14th–15th centuries say only what the sophisticated urban elite thought of rough peasants. On the other hand, the Italian countryside produced many of the most successful mercenary commanders at a time when the 'condottieri' system dominated. For the urban elites, meanwhile, possession of a country villa was a sign that they had made it in Renaissance society.

Medieval village life

Villages themselves differed according to climatic conditions and culture. In England and France the local lord usually owned the dovecote and the mill where his peasants had to grind their corn. Most villages also had a potter, blacksmith, carpenters and a wheelwright to make and repair wheels. A hayward ensured fair distribution of hay for the animals in winter, a dairy mistress supervised the making of butter and cheese and a miller operated the windmill or watermill.

Not until the 15th century did many villages have a rudimentary inn for travellers, while the typical village consisted of houses along a main street or clustered around a village green. The homes of poor villeins tended to be single-roomed thatched cottages made of 'wattle and daub' – wood and clay – those of the better off having more rooms, wooden shutters on their windows and some furniture.

Castles and manor houses were administrative centres and home to household knights and servants who formed the lord's retainers. In times of tension knights and sergeants would train in the courtyard while scouts would scoured the countryside and sentinels listened for suspicious sounds at night. A beacon on a nearby hill might form part of chain which sent warning of an attack to the king, local baron or city. Even in peaceful times there were outlaws or bandits in the forests or mountains, pirates around the coasts, and occasional public disorder or political disturbances.

The most obvious variations on this pattern were seen along the fringes of Europe. In the Scottish islands, for example, local crafts included tanning various forms of leather, fine quality wood carving and shaping pots from soft soapstone. Further afield in northern Scandinavia, Iceland and Greenland the cooling of the climate in the 14th century led to houses of sandstone and turf huddling together in complexes of up to twenty rooms for people and animals. A massive drystone storehouse might also be built next door to keep wolves and bears away from food supplies and the furs ready for export.

European agriculture had been revolutionized during the early Middle Ages, by the invention of a new form of plough, probably in Germany, a century or so after the fall of the Roman Empire. This turned over the earth with its mouldboard rather than scratching a furrow like the traditional Mediterranean plough. The ridges and furrows made by deep medieval ploughing can still be seen, sometimes with large turning areas for the ploughman's oxen at each end. This new plough was not, of course, suitable everywhere; certainly not in many parts of the south where the soil was too shallow. Here the Mediterranean plough still proved the most useful.

Further south the great island of Sicily escaped the chaos which undermined European agriculture following the fall of the Roman Empire in the 5th century. It remained under Romano-Byzantine rule until conquered by Arabs and Berbers in 827–901, after which Sicily shared in the agricultural boom enjoyed throughout Islamic civilization.

Finally, in the 11th century, Sicily's thriving agriculture was taken over undamaged by the Norman conquerors and thereafter Sicily remained the main source of wheat for the booming economies of central and northern Italy. Here agriculture also revived in the 12th and 13th centuries, only to suffer from the overpopulation and plagues until a second Italian agricultural expansion accompanied the Renaissance in the late 14th and 15th centuries. It was characterized by new crops such as mulberry trees for a flourishing silk industry around Lucca, saffron from Aquila grown as dye for ladies' hair and to flavour food, rice introduced to the Po valley by the 15th century, and the vast olive groves of the deep south.

Animal husbandry was of secondary importance in most of medieval Europe, although peasants normally grazed their beasts on common land open to all villagers. Sheep and goats were kept for milk as well as meat and wool, along with a smaller number of cows. The peasants' biggest problem was, however, keeping animals alive through winter. Some were needed as next year's breeding stock but the bulk were slaughtered and their meat salted or smoked. The number of sheep greatly increased, of course, with the booming wool and cloth trades of the 14th–15th centuries, and even in Italy good agricultural land was turned over to sheep though their wool was never as good as that from England and Spain.

Men pressing grapes for wine in a 12th century Psalter. It seems unlikely that the person treading the grapes would really work naked, but perhaps the artist was trying to draw attention to the dangers of drunkenness.

THE DECLINE OF THE BYZANTINE PEASANT

Rural life in the Byzantine Empire had continued virtually uninterrupted since Roman times, but there were some significant changes. Huge loss of territory to Muslim conquest in the 7th century – particularly the 'bread basket' of Egypt – had caused food shortages, particularly for the army and in the cities, so the imperial authorities tried to increase food production by improving the conditions of their remaining peasantry.

Nevertheless it still remained illegal for a peasant family to change its place of residence and special documents were required for travel near the frontier. The gulf between landowners and rural labourers remained vast and taxes largely fell on the peasantry, most of those who tilled the fields being paid labourers, serfs or slaves.

By the 11th century there were few small freehold farmers left, and their status slumped still further. Meanwhile the aristocratic elite started to move out of the Byzantine cities into the countryside, buying up the best land. The entire Byzantine world was then shattered by the Fourth Crusade's seizure of Constantinople and the heart of the Empire in 1204. Thereafter, the surviving fragmented Byzantine states went their own ways. The 'Empire' of Trebizond, for example, was based in territory that was very different to that of other Byzantine states. Here the Pontus mountains and southern coast of the Black Sea were lush and in places almost subtropical. Land-holding was on a very small scale whereas in the mountains and small parts of the Anatolian plateau still controlled by Trebizon, large-scale ranching replaced arable farming.

Despite this, unlike most other remnants of Byzantine territory, a free peasantry flourished to the end. A peasant 'gonikeia' or small family farm could, for example, be inherited, mortgaged, sold or farmed but it could not be abandoned. Even Trebizond's aristocracy remained relatively small landowners or archons who were more like rich peasants than minor noblemen. The only great barons seem to have been from the semi-independent ranching areas of the southern frontier.

Contrary to the popular image of the oppressed Russian serf, the medieval Russian peasant may even have been freer than much of western Europe's peasantry. From the 11th to 13th centuries the rural Russian population largely consisted of free farmers, though agricultural slaves often worked the fields of the local 'boyar' or lord. The main problem faced by medieval Russian peasants appears to have been paying taxes in years of bad harvest. In such cases their families might slip into the ranks of the despised 'zakupi' who were like temporary serfs, bound to work the land until their debt was paid off. If, however, they attempted to run away and were caught they became the permanent slaves of their creditors.

Villages differed considerably in such varied climatic conditions. In many parts of the Byzantine Empire they were associated with an aristocrat's villa as had been the case in Roman times. Apart from the local priest, other essential members of the community were the blacksmith, potters, brickmakers and those operating watermills for irrigation and power. Many of the larger villages also had shops. Fruit groves outside the village were owned by individual peasant families, as were the fields beyond, but the more distant pasture land was held in common by the village as a whole.

Landscapes without change

Agricultural implements consisted of simple hand tools and wooden ploughs pulled by oxen or mules. Byzantine crops were largely unchanging, and irrigation probably declined as a result of invasions and the general disruption of rural life.

In fact, Byzantine agricultural technology was backward when compared to the advances in the neighbouring Muslim world or the developments seen in western Europe and the only large areas of intensive agriculture were near the coasts. Silk manufacture had been introduced from Asia in the mid-6th century, supposedly by two monks returning from China with silkworm eggs hidden inside a bamboo stick, but rice was not grown until the very end of the Byzantine

era. Windmills were not adopted despite being widespread in both Islam and Europe, while watermills and ploughs were unchanged. Yet several parts of the Byzantine world remained major exporters of wine, olive oil, cereals, dried fruit, nuts, timber, cattle and sheep. Trebizond, for example, was fertile and well-watered though the slopes of some valleys were so steep that men had to tie themselves to trees for safety while working terraced fields.

Most agricultural work was heavily labour intensive, August and September being the busiest months. Cereals were reaped with simple hand-sickles, threshed and ground in local watermills. A remarkable manuscript on the 'Labours of the Month' was, in fact,

Opposite: Christ and a shepherd on 14th or 15th century Byzantine or Serbian icon painting. The figure of the angel is entirely traditional while the shepherd with his broad-brimmed hat and heavy wooden club is realistic.

Below: A hunting scene in a 12th century Serbian manuscript. The art, costume and daily life of the peoples of the Balkans had features in common with both the Byzantine and western European worlds.

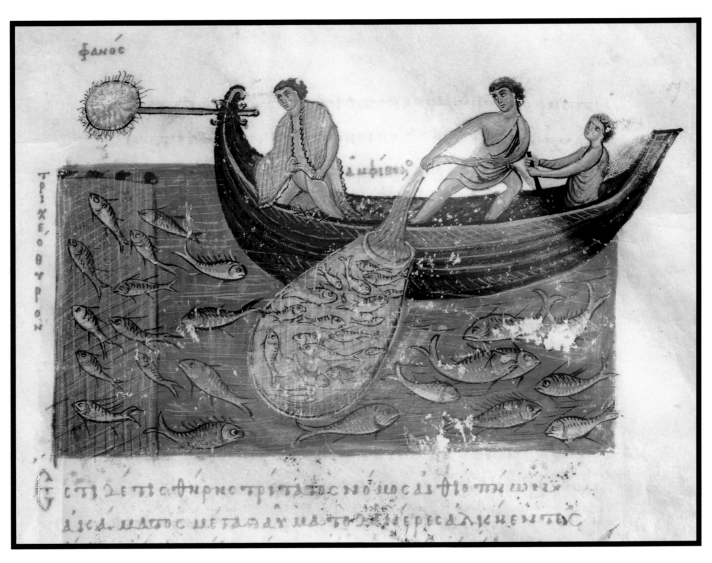

Above: Fishermen using a lamp to attract fish at night in an 11th century Byzantine manuscript illustration. This method of fishing was shown in ancient Greek art and is still used by fishermen around the Aegean Sea today.

Opposite: A physician watches peasants at work, in an Arabic translation of a Greek medical treatise made in Iraq at the end of the 12th century. On the top row men dig a field, another cuts weeds while a fourth brings food and drink. On the lower row a team of men thresh and winnow the wheat.

made for a Trebizond aristocrat named Prokopios Chantzames in 1346 and in it the artist John Argyros shows late Byzantine rural life in great detail.

The growing of cereals was also important in southern and central Russia. In the north, however, Russian colonists faced different problems. Around Novgorod the soil consisted of a thin fertile layer of boulder-clay. As a result, both the Russians and the indigenous Balts and Finns continued to use a shallow plough which scratched the surface rather than covering the fertile layer with sterile boulder-clay. Some of the Russian settlers even adopted the primitive slash and burn agriculture of the Finno-Ugrians, moving in a nomadic style from one clearing in the forest to another to give the rapidly exhausted soil time to recover.

The animals found in the Byzantine countryside remained similarly traditional. Mules were the most common beasts of burden, oxen being used for threshing, pulling carts or ploughs and pumping water. In upland areas raising cattle was associated with a transhumant way of life, as in parts of Turkey. Flocks wintered in the valleys or then grazed the mountain pasture in summer. Down on the coasts fishing was an even more important activity, also being done at night with the aid of lamps attached to boats. Some places like Crete earned additional income by breeding hunting dogs while elsewhere peasants caught singing birds which found a ready market in towns and cities. Annual fairs or markets were another vital aspect of Byzantine rural life where peasants could borrow from money-lenders if they got into difficulties.

ISLAM'S GREEN REVOLUTION

An agricultural revolution began in the Middle East in the 7th and 8th centuries then spread rapidly across the entire Muslim world, having a profound impact on life as far west as the Iberian peninsula by the 11th century. This agricultural revolution also led to a massive increase in population size in almost all areas as a result of a general improvement in diet and in standards of health. On a more personal level, the Islamic agricultural revolution changed methods of cooking as well as the food crops available. New crops also enabled the development of new industries.

The phenomenal expansion of irrigation in what was an essentially dry part of the world meant that more abundant and newer systems of raising or moving water were needed. Perhaps the most visible were the sometimes enormous nouria vertical waterwheels which spread from Iran and the

Middle East to Portugal in the west. Rather less dramatic was the gradual evolution of a complex and sophisticated legal system to ensure a fair distribution of irrigation water. These laws grew out of those which already existed in Syria and Yemen in the pre-Islamic period and they were based upon the principle that the closer a farmer was to the source of the water, the greater were his rights. Any apparent unfairness in this concept was balanced by the fact that larger and wealthier landlords tended to be found in the fertile lower valleys rather than in the poor, backward and often still tribal upland regions.

Mongol invaders and agricultural decline

Of course there were exceptions to this flourishing and somewhat idyllic picture of medieval Islamic agriculture. In Anatolia, following the Turkish conquest after the battle of Mantizert in 1071, the new Seljuk rulers tried to reverse the agricultural decline which had characterized the previous Byzantine years. They encouraged a revival of irrigated agriculture as a tax base if for no other reasons, but their success was short-lived. The Mongol conquests of the mid-13th century had already devastated much of the eastern Islamic lands as part of a Mongol policy of returning large areas to pastoralism so as to maintain their own nomadic way of life.

Elsewhere in the Middle East the Mongols did not destroy agriculture in such a conscious manner but the wars which came in their wake dispersed the peasantry who maintained the irrigation canals. Once these delicate systems declined beyond a certain

Right: Two fishermen in a manuscript from Mamluk Egypt or Syria, *c*.1350. The net used by one man is the same as those still cast by fishermen in the Middle East, though shown much smaller than a real net. The second man has a water container made from an animal skin over his shoulder, perhaps so that fish could be kept alive and fresh for market.

point it became virtually impossible for the peasantry to return since they could no longer grow enough food to maintain themselves; thus a cycle of decline which started in the 13th century continued into the 20th century.

Other examples of invasion and population movements had a similar, though usually less dramatic, impact in the western Islamic lands of North Africa and the Iberian peninsula. Here a remarkable form of coexistence had developed between the largely settled Berber communities of the coast, oases and mountains, their nomadic Berber cousins and various nomadic Arab tribes which moved into the area from the 11th century onwards. Unlike the earlier Arab conquerors who had become a ruling elite largely confined to the towns, the arrival of entire Arab tribes, such as the Banu Hilal and Banu Sulaim who captured most of Tunisia in 1057, led to a localized decline of agriculture comparable to that caused by the Mongols in the east. But it was not as widespread, nor as devastating. Berber

tribes ranged the highlands and the deeper desert while Berber communities farmed fertile areas closer to centres of power or tended palm and olive groves around such urban areas.

The most fertile agricultural areas were also dominated by the estates of a resident Arab aristocracy. Elsewhere autonomous Berber tribal communities lived under the authority of their own chieftains who in turn represented the authority of a distant Sultan.

In almost all regions sharecropping was the most common form of agriculture. The landlord's tenants generally had a contract to grow grain on unirrigated land for only one season. Four-fifths of the crop then went to the landlord. Sharecropping contracts tended to be for longer periods where fruit-growing land was concerned while irrigated fields were, of course, the most valuable of all.

The distribution of land was even more complex. In some tribal areas it consisted of freehold farms belonging to individual members of the tribe. Most land ownership was agreed on the basis of established custom and written documentation was only kept by government for high-value estates immediately around towns or cities. Perhaps as a result these fertile groves tended to be the subject of endless litigation, intricate deeds of sale, gift and inheritance.

Much the same was true of the Middle East, though in some more barren, outlying or war-ravaged regions the condition of the local peasantry could be desperately poor. Consequently these were the areas which responded most eagerly to unorthodox religious teachings. Wandering dervishes and various Shia sects found a ready audience and although most governments tried to crush heretical movements they generally failed.

New crops, new food, new farms

In more favoured regions new food crops and agricultural techniques often permitted double cropping where only one had been possible earlier. The extensions of existing irrigation systems also enabled land to be cultivated which had lain idle for decades if not centuries. Nowhere was this more obvi-

Left: A Mamluk horseman killing a boar in a mid-14th century cavalry training manual. Unlike the knights of western Europe, the elite cavalry of the medieval Muslim world were paid professional soldiers who underwent constant and highly structured training courses. Nevertheless this still included hunting.

ous than in Iraq before the Mongol conquest. Meanwhile oranges and lemons spread westward from India to Spain, along with sugarcane, the growing of cotton, rice and mulberry trees for the new silk industry.

Bedouin woman looking after a herd of camels in a manuscript made in Baghdad in 1237. The painter, al-Wasiti, is one of the very few early medieval Islamic artists whose names are known. He was at his best when illustrating everyday scenes involving ordinary people.

The spread of bananas from south-east Asia to Morocco and Spain was perhaps the most remarkable of all. This plant could not be taken from one place to another in the form of a seed, but had to move as a living plant, a relatively small step at a time, generation by generation. Not surprisingly books on the science of agriculture were in great demand; one of the most important being the *Book of Farming* by the Andalusian Ibn Bassal who, in 1085, put his knowledge into practice by constructing a botanical garden for the ruler of Seville.

Existing cash-crops like almonds, figs and cork from the cork-oak also became increasingly important. There were even new vegetables such as aubergine and asparagus. As in the Byzantine realm the basic

Mediterranean plough changed little, since it remained suitable for most shallow and light Middle Eastern soils. New technical and theoretical books were, however, written on farming and botany, drawing upon knowledge from India and even further east. These discussed different kinds of soil, their manuring, watering and most suitable crops as well as more advanced methods of grafting trees and moving living plants over long distances.

Market forces and livestock

There were fewer changes in animal husbandry but the importance of meat, above all mutton, to the Islamic diet, way of life and religious practice meant that the economies of even the remotest peoples became market orientated. Partly as a result, perhaps, the wool and skins from these animals prompted further developments in the textile industry.

The firmly established patterns of long-distance trade which characterized medieval Islamic civilization similarly contributed to the market orientated nature of its agriculture. Large quantities of basic foodstuffs as well as smaller volumes of high-value herbs and spices were transported over huge distance by land and sea. Within the Middle East, for example, dried fruits, honey and nuts were carried from country to country while snow to cool the drinks of the elite was packed in lead containers and carried on camel back before being stored in efficient 'ice-houses' throughout the year even in the hottest parts of Iran and Iraq. Ice was even used to transport fresh water-melons from Central Asia to Baghdad in the 9th and 10th centuries.

Cattle were far less important, except in odd corners of the Muslim world where ancient customs persisted. The Qara of Dhufar were again an example. Here cows were central to their way of life, having an importance almost comparable to that seen in India, though of course the Qara were Muslim rather than Hindu. Women looked after the animals but only men were permitted to milk the cows.

THE CLASH OF THE PASTURE AND THE SOWN

The early Mongols had straddled the border between the vast east Siberian forests and the easternmost Central Asian steppes and mountains but were a poor, backward people compared to Turkish neighbours who controlled the Silk Roads to the south. Meanwhile the peoples of the Siberian forests and bleak sub-Arctic tundra held little interest for Turks or Mongols, since they were poorer still. China was the main target of any Turkish or Mongol raiding and its wealth was built on agriculture.

For over a thousand years Chinese governments had a major role in irrigation, flood control and the transport systems which permitted agricultural produce to move around the vast Chinese state. But despite these efforts, natural disasters had an appalling impact on China's rural population, leading to massive disruption and the displacement of entire communities. Similarly the authorities recognized that it was in their interests to settle such people as quickly as possible and to get tax from their revenues going again.

In better times the authorities encouraged improvements to irrigation techniques and there was a general, though not uninterrupted, increase in the land under cultivation and in yields from cultivated areas. A similar increase in agricultural production was seen in Japan, particularly from the later 13th century onwards. This resulted from a more intensive use of wet-rice cultivation in paddy fields, double and even triple-cropping being possible in favoured areas, and with an improvement in the control of water resources.

The overwhelming majority of the Chinese population was engaged in agriculture and the peasants' year revolved around religious festivals which were often associated with the agricultural cycle. As in the Muslim world, books on farming matters and related festi-

vals, were available to the literate land-owning class. These books often included advice on proper conduct, control of the family and the education of sons. The lack of grazing and the ferocity of winters in many parts of China also stimulated particular ways of keeping valuable animals alive until the following year. Where horses were concerned winter feed of wheat-bran was stored in special sealed containers.

The Japanese countryside was dominated by an aristocracy which owned much of the best land by the later decades of the Heian period (794–1185). A great deal of good land was also held, tax-free, by religious foundations and monasteries. Meanwhile the main rural economic unit was the private manor owned by a minor aristocratic class which strove for the official rank and government office which would exempt them and their property from tax.

In other ways, however, this Japanese rural elite was more like a middle class and, like the peasants, suffered from the snobbery of the urban elite. Nevertheless these same despised provinces became the seat of economic and military power in the 12th–13th centuries as Japanese central authority fragmented into what is known as the feudal age or Kamakura period (1185–1392). The old

Mongol 'gers' or tents in the mountains of Mongolia. The word 'yurt' applies to the region of grazing claimed by this family. Such a scene would not have changed since the days of Genghiz Khan.

73

distinction between free and slave similarly disappeared within the mass of rural poor. Even in good times this peasantry suffered from the elite's efforts to maintain social distinction by restricting the forms of clothes

Scientific agriculture in the east

Agriculture was, of course, most highly developed in China. Here the standard measurement of land was the mou, a theoretical strip

A prince riding out with his hawk on a late 14th or early 15th century manuscript painting, probably made in Transoxania. His costume is an elaborate version of the clothing shown in Central Asian art since at least the 8th century. Much the same applies to his horse harness, while his sword is a straight Chinese weapon rather than a curved Turkish sabre.

and even the types of food the 'lower orders' were allowed. The status of the peasantry was so low that the military authorities who dominated later medieval Japan did all they could to stop members of the military class getting into debt and thus slipping down the social scale.

A similar though by no means identical process took place in Korea under the Koryu (935–1392) and Yi or Li (1392–1910) kingdoms. Here large areas of agricultural land passed into the hands of the state which redistributed it to government officials via a complex system of land grants. In later centuries this same land tended to become concentrated in the hands of a few very powerful aristocratic families while free farming families sunk to the status of serfs.

two hundred and forty paces long by one wide; there being an estimated fourteen 'mou' per registered head of population. Chinese agriculture was characterized by a careful use of all available manure, including animal and human excrement with crushed bone as fertilizer. An elaborate system of crop rotation also maintained the fertility of the soil with a 'double-mou' or long strip of earth divided into three narrow furrows separated by ridges. The seed was then carefully planted by hand in the furrows; the position of each ridge and furrow being changed each year as a form of small-scale crop rotation.

Farmers were concerned primarily with growing enough to feed and clothe their families. In addition to ploughs and wheel-shaped seed distributors, farmers also used mechanical rice mills with hammers and rollers, though the biggest task was lifting irrigation water from canals or wells. Rice was the staple diet of southern China, with wheat and millet in the north, and barley in the far

This was done by riders using lassos on long poles. In total contrast to the Chinese, the Central Asian peoples relied on meat and milk as a primary source of food though they also imported grain and rice from settled

north-west. A better strain of drought-resistant rice was also introduced from Vietnam in the 11th century. Compared with Chinese agriculture, that of Japan was poorly organized though perhaps equally intensive. Meanwhile in Tibet each isolated valley attempted to be self-sufficient in barley and vegetables.

Fish farming and pasturing animals for meat provided a small source of income for Chinese peasant farmers but animal husbandry was far more important for the nomadic peoples of Central Asia. It was, in fact, the means of survival for most Turkish and Mongol tribes who kept cattle, goats, sheep and horses which were sold at considerable profit to the Chinese. The horse herds themselves ran half wild until it was time for them to be gathered together and tamed.

neighbours. A similar way of life was found amongst Tibetan nomads, though their special ecological circumstances on the roof of Asia meant that yaks replaced cattle.

Hunting was essential to all the peoples of Central Asia, but played a very minor role in China, Korea and even Japan. Mongol and Turkish tribes on the fringes of, or deep within, the Siberian forests also trapped animals for furs which fetched huge prices amongst settled peoples. The primary sources of profit for Chinese farmers came from timber groves, fruit orchards and vegetable plots. The growing of mulberry leaves for silk worms and lac trees for the gum used in lacquer work were important in some areas, though tea and sugar only rose to importance in the later Middle Ages.

A study of a sheep and a goat by the Chinese artist Chao Meng-Fu, 1254–1322. Few artists have matched the Chinese when it comes to observing the character of animals, particularly the artists of the Yuan period when China was ruled by a Mongol dynasty. This was not only for aesthetic reasons but also reflected the medieval Chinese way of looking at man's place in nature.

THE GIFT OF MONSOON RAINS

Agriculture in India and south-east Asia was dominated by the seasonal monsoon rains. Nevertheless there was plenty of variation in crops and village organization ranging from the dry north of India to the lush islands of Indonesia. Even in areas with abundant rainfall the control and distribution of seasonal water resources remained vital; in Sri Lanka there were 800 kilometres of canals by the reign of King Parakrama Bahu I in the 12th century. The soils of Indo-China were mostly poor with wet-rice cultivation only possible in the river valleys and deltas while the people of the mountains relied on slash and burn cultivation. In Malaya, agriculture was largely confined to the river banks whereas Java was much more fertile, though volcanic eruptions could lead to major population shifts.

The predictable cycle of monsoon rains and intense drought led several medieval south-east Asian states to build huge water storage and distribution systems which permitted rice to be grown on a far bigger scale than before, though these were mostly concentrated around the capital cities. Meanwhile rural life in many parts of south-east Asia was dominated by powerful rulers and strict adherence to Hindu or Buddhist religious customs. In these Hindu and Buddhist kingdoms, temples and monasteries owned a great deal of land and employed great numbers of landless labourers. Most farmers do, however, appear to have been free. Amongst the Cholas of southern India (10th–13th centuries), for example, they formed a warlike group which frequently clashed with the aboriginal peoples of jungle areas.

There may have been fewer such clashes in Indonesia where villages appear to have been virtually autonomous under the authority of village elders called 'ramani dusun'. Here ordinary people paid taxes to the king's officials or his regional vassals and did enforced corvee labour on irrigation systems or religious buildings. The little that is known about village life in the Khmer kingdom

(9th–14th centuries) indicates that the peasantry were again obliged to maintain shrines and hermitages established by the ruling elite. Each family seems to have had enough land to sustain itself, with women doing most of the hard agricultural labour. The same was seen amongst the Champa of southern Vietnam during the 11th to 15th centuries. In less developed areas there tended to be a greater difference between coastal and inland peoples. The interior tribes of Malaya rarely formed part of the coastal states while in the Philippines inland people often spoke a different language to the coastal settlements.

In most areas the main function of irrigation was to make wet-rice cultivation possible between rivers rather than simply along their banks. Rice was the most important crop throughout southern and south-eastern Asia but there were others. In southern India coconut palm and banana groves were often sited in clearings within dense forest. In Indonesia full use was made of the rich volcanic soil of mountain slopes for rice cultivation, whereas in less favoured Indo-China millet, bananas, oranges and pomegranates supplemented the basic rice crop. Surviving

inscriptions and late 12th century carvings show that south-east Asian peasants also let pigs forage in the paddy fields, these being their most important farm animal. Such inscriptions also show that ginger and honey, perhaps from wild bees, were used to make ritual food for religious festivities.

Amongst the most primitive peoples were Sri Lanka's aboriginal forest dwellers, the Veddas, who hunted giant lizards and grey apes for food, while also gathering wild betel nuts. The little that is known about the hunter-gatherer life of these peoples suggests variation in their social organization. They lived in caves and slept on rocks rather than the damp earth. Their Singalese neighbours believed that these Veddas were the only people on earth who never laughed whereas the Veddas believed themselves to be 'the sons of Kings'.

Hunting could also be very profitable for more sophisticated peoples. The Khmer collected exotic forest produce for export, including scented wood and brightly coloured feathers. The plumage of the male kingfisher was in such demand in China that Khmer birdcatchers used caged female kingfishers as lures along the riverbanks.

Opposite: The god Krishna milks his cows on a 7th century Pallava-style Indian relief carving in the caves of Mahalibalipuram near Madras. The cow had great religious significance to the Hindus, but at the same time the way the animal is encouraged to lick its calf to stimulate the flow of milk adds an element of everyday realism.

Below: A late 12th or early 13th century carving of peasant men and women with an ox-cart and an elephant. They are apparently going to a building site, perhaps to erect a temple, since one of the men at the front has a spade and the cart carries a heavy block of stone.

5 URBAN LIFE AND COMMERCE

THE MEDIEVAL WORLD WAS CRISS-CROSSED BY ALMOST AS MANY TRADE ROUTES AS THE MODERN WORLD AND IN SOME REGIONS, BUSINESS FINANCE WAS NEARLY AS COMPLEX AS IT IS TODAY. BUT THERE WERE OTHER REGIONS, EVEN IN EUROPE, WHERE THE LOCAL ECONOMIES STAGNATED AND PEOPLE KNEW VIRTUALLY NOTHING OF THE OUTSIDE WORLD. ATTITUDES TO MONEY AND TRADE WERE SIMILARLY VARIED, THOUGH VERY FEW RULERS COULD RESIST THE DESIRE TO MAKE AS MUCH OUT OF TRADE, INDUSTRY AND BUSINESS AS THEY COULD. SOMETIMES THIS MEANT TAKING PRACTICAL STEPS TO IMPROVE MARKETS AND COMMUNICATIONS; IN OTHER CASES, IT SIMPLY MEANT DEMANDING EVER BIGGER TAXES.

BOOMING CITIES AND AN EXPLOSION OF TRADE

The Vikings of the 9th–10th centuries are usually portrayed as destroyers rather than builders but, in fact, they founded many new towns, not only in Scandinavia but also in the British Isles and Russia. For example the Irish capital of Dublin really dates from a Viking settlement of 841. By the 11th century existing towns were expanding in most parts of western Europe; for example in 11th and 12th century Germany, the Jewish merchant population grew in parallel with central Europe's economic growth. By the 12th century the space within the fortified walls of many cities was filling up with businesses and housing, so the gardens and orchards were pushed outside the town walls.

Meanwhile the growth in urban population provided new markets for the milk and meat produced by surrounding villages. Inside the walls of medieval towns and cities, it was not always as filthy and squalid as is popularly thought. Many streets were cobbled and each householder was responsible for cleaning the road in front of his own property; with flocks of animals daily coming in and out of the city, this was clearly necessary. Meanwhile their new wealth enabled cities to build impressive cathedrals, not just for the glory of God, but also for their own glorification, and the town-halls, which were the centres of urban administration and justice, could be almost as magnificent.

Medieval towns may have been places of opportunity, but not everyone grew rich. In fact, by the 14th century the poor were sometimes worse off than they had been before. Meanwhile there was a distinct pecking order between merchants, artisans or skilled craftsmen, and unskilled labourers, and, more often than not, the latter could only make their voices heard when they gathered as a mob.

Right: Italian bankers, representing Avarice, in a late 14th century treatise on the Seven Deadly Sins. The success of the banking houses of cities like Florence gave them great power.

People living in urban centres were, of course, more vulnerable to plague and other epidemics, yet the towns almost always quickly revived and continued to grow after each disaster, attracting more people from the surrounding countryside who hoped for a better, more comfortable existence. The widespread wars, rioting and particularly severe Black Death plague of 1348 may even have frightened surviving rich merchant families into doing more for the poor.

Opposite: The Bishop's Fair at Sens in France, on a 14th century French manuscript. This market was held for two weeks every June on the Plains of St. Denis. Here sheep are brought for sale, merchants sit in their tent-like booths while another tent serves wine or beer, all under the watchful eye of the bishop.

The unlikely combination of a travelling tinker and a mermaid admiring herself in a mirror was probably an early 14th century artist's way of warning how a woman's vanity could cost her husband a lot of money if a travelling salesman arrived at the castle door. On the other hand most medieval households probably had a dog to chase the tinker away.

As a result, many of the prosperous merchants in the 15th century spent huge sums on charitable works such as building poor houses, libraries as well as providing hospital treatment and better jails.

Yet it was in southern Europe where urban life first came to dominate the life of the surrounding countryside. In other areas, such as the shrinking Crusader States in the Middle and Near East, loss of territory to reconquering Muslim or Byzantine forces meant that the knightly class retreated into the remaining coastal cities until these also fell. Acre, the last Crusader outpost on the Middle Eastern mainland, was retaken by the Muslims in 1291.

In Italy and parts of the Iberian peninsula much of the ruling elite had either always lived in towns, or had recently moved there as a matter of preference. At the same time, increasingly rich merchant families bought themselves aristocratic status by lending money to rulers who were temporarily short of cash, but still had the authority to offer increased social status through knighthoods.

The urbanization of Italy

In Italy these urban knights became a significant political and military force. They commanded city militias and dominated many town councils until the merchant class got rich enough to challenge their power. These urban knights tended to have money fiefs instead of, or in addition to, their landed estates. These money fiefs could consist of the right to levy taxes on a weekly market, collect tolls for the use of a bridge or ferry, or might simply be the revenue from a factory or business.

In these flourishing Italian cities, many noble families lived in fortified houses rather than castles. Some owned tall towers, or torre, inside the city walls, from which rival families fought the street battles described in Shakespeare's play *Romeo and Juliet*. At one time there were so many of these torre that Italian cities were compared to forests.

Italy's wealth also made it the banking centre of Europe where many of the richest men of the 14th century founded their fortunes by borrowing money. In fact, there were very few 'merchant dynasties' in the 15th century.

One thing that all cities wanted was greater freedom to run their own affairs. In the 11th century, for example, many towns and cities were under the patronage of a local baron or the Church to whom they owed feudal fealty. Gradually, however, the towns bought charters of liberty for cash or earned them by loyalty during a crisis, giving them a lucrative degree of independence where internal or business affairs were concerned. Such cities and towns also had their own administration, employing a council, mayor and sheriff to maintain law and order and organize defence.

By the 14th century many urban citizens owed feudal dues to no one outside the walls of their city, which was a considerable privilege in a world where feudal obligation was still considered the normal way of structuring society. Civic pride, as well as the need to combat the constant threat of plague epidemics, encouraged city councils to do all they could to clean dirty streets or markets and reduce the risk of fire.

Villages near a town could buy and sell at its market or fair, though they might have to pay tolls to cross a bridge or use a ferry, and, if they were bringing produce for sale, the owners of markets would charge some kind of rental fee for space to erect a stall or booth. Expensive exotic goods were normally sold in permanent shops where, for example, oriental spices were offered whole, ground or even ready mixed into hot 'powder fort' or sweet 'powder douce'.

Craftsmen often owned the shops where they sold their goods, and these were open to the back so that customers could see the craftsmen at work. To avoid unfair competition and quarrels, however, shops were often closed on market day. Meanwhile, small towns across Europe were buying, or earning, the right to hold these money-spinning local fairs; for example, the little Leicestershire town of Loughborough in England was permitted to hold its own market in 1221.

Guilds and urban careers

Guilds played a vital role in urban life. The earliest were frequently those of the most influential merchants and theoretically had to be licensed by the king or ruler. Later, the general merchant guilds split into specific trades and crafts, the less prestigious, and thus poorer, businesses forming their guilds last. Boys would start out as apprentices to a master craftsman or merchant, working unpaid for a specified number of years in order to learn the business. They would become journeymen, or 'day-men', paid a daily wage until the guild of their craft considered them good enough to rate as master-craftsmen. If they had enough capital, both master-craftsmen and journeymen could also set up their own business, at which point they would become a member of the relevant guild.

Young apprentices might make an unruly crowd, but they also provided their city, or at least one of its competing political factions,

Sigurd and the Dwarf making a sword, on the carved portal of the wooden stave church at Hylestad in Setesdal. This church had several such scenes from Norse mythology and this one provides a clear picture of metalworking techniques during the 12th century.

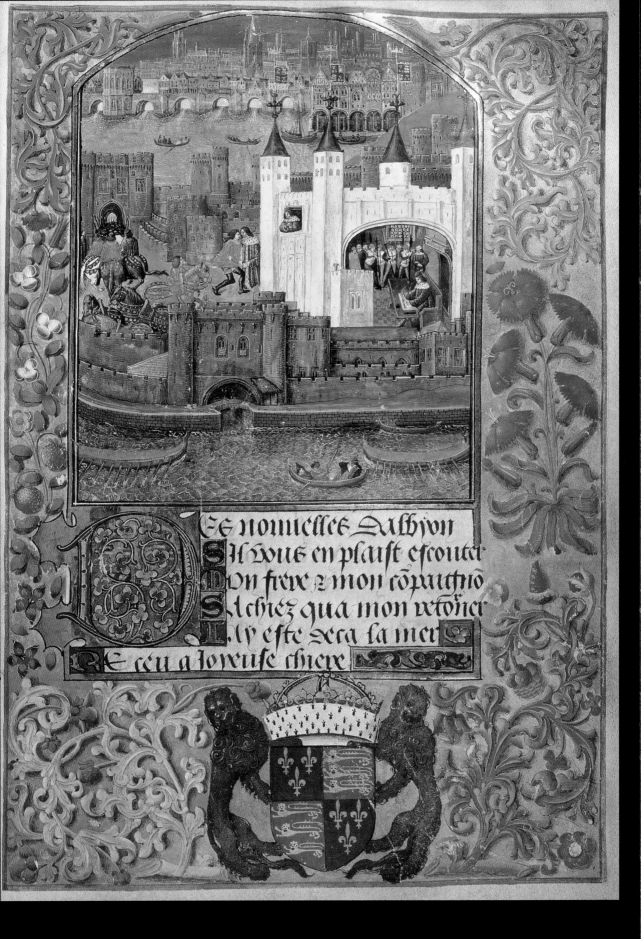

Es nouuelles Dalbyon
Sil vous en plaist escouter
Mon frere z mon compaignio
Lechez qua mon retoner
Ay este deca la mer
Et ceu a ioyeuse chiere

with military manpower. By the 14th century, many guilds even had their own livery or uniforms for ceremonial occasions. Guilds also played a cultural role, paying for and eventually performing religious mystery plays as well as maintaining roads, bridges or chapels. Outside Italy, comparable organizations in Europe appeared without the need of cities. In the northern Scottish islands, for example, the crews of trading ships seem to form temporary commercial associations for mutual support and profit.

'Unicorns' from Greenland

Western Europe was much more industrialized than it might have appeared. Although most coal was sea-coal, washed up in places like the north-eastern coast of England, it was also mined, but not used for domestic heating nor even much in the arms business since this produced inferior iron. The iron industry had existed for centuries, though the volume of metal involved increased dramatically from the 11th century onwards. Lead was used for roofing, drainage and various alloys, while tin, copper, silver and gold also had specific uses. The quarrying and transport of building stone was, like timber-cutting, a major medieval industry. Clay was also needed for roof tiles and pottery.

The export of leather hides played a significant role in the economies of several parts of Europe, whereas glass production remained more localized. The wool trade and cloth industry witnessed the most dramatic expansion and were particularly important in England, which, along with Spain, produced some of the best wool. However, Italy was the centre of the cloth trade, which peaked in the 14th and 15th centuries.

In fact western Europe was part of an almost world-wide trading network stretching from Greenland to Japan, and including much of Africa. Cloth and iron of medieval Scandinavian origin have even been found in Inuit (Eskimo) archaeological sites throughout north-eastern Canada. It seems likely that these indigenous peoples were an important source of the sealskins, walrus tusks, polar bears and hunting falcons that went to the royal courts of Europe and the Middle East. In 1341, a commercial agent was, in fact, sent from Baghdad to Norway to buy more of these exotic northern items, which included soapstone and narwhale horns, believed to have come from unicorns.

Although warfare sometimes interrupted maritime trade, it was more of a problem on land and even in times of peace travel was difficult. Most roads were muddy or dusty tracks, although some of the more important bridges and passes were maintained in reasonable condition. In England a royal decree stated that roads between the country's main fairs must have a broad space on each side as a precaution against ambush by outlaws and only in the 15th century were a few roads paved. In the 12th and 13th centuries merchants tended to find lodgings in the houses of business colleagues or at a monastery, though a few inns started to appear in major towns and cities. Carriages and covered litters were only for great ladies or invalids and riding in a cart rather than on a horse or donkey was seen as a great indignity by those with any status. Carts and pack animals were, in fact, to carry goods.

Rivers were much more important when it came to moving large quantities and were also cheaper. Seagoing ships were getting bigger and in some parts of southern Europe, most obviously Italy, knights were as likely to find themselves serving aboard ship as on land. In fact Venetian and Genoese knights played a major role in protecting merchant fleets while experience of foreign ports could prove useful if a knight thought of entering partnership with a merchant. Some important ports were fortified, with inner harbours defended by walls and towers while their narrow entrance could be closed with a chain. Both Venice and Genoa also had trading outposts in the eastern Mediterranean, Aegean and Black Seas; this gave them better knowledge of Asia than any other European traders.

Above: The beautiful village of Perouges, north-east of Lyons in France, is so perfectly preserved that it has often been used as a film-set in European film or television costume dramas. Many of the streets are virtually unchanged since the 15th century, having been rebuilt after a siege in 1468. Those shown here probably originally had shops underneath.

Opposite: A view of the Tower of London in a collection of poems for Charles, Duke of Orléans, and other works. London was the busiest port in medieval England and here some boats are moored in the river Thames while another appears to be heading for the castle's water gate, now called Traitor's Gate. In the distance the artist has added Old London Bridge and some of London's buildings.

CITIES OF PARKS, GARDENS AND SLUMS

Romano-Greek civilization survived in the towns of what became the Byzantine Empire, and after centuries of decline, a modest urban revival began in the 10th century. Yet the Byzantine world never witnessed the remarkable explosion of cities, trade and industry seen in western Europe. Instead the towns remained pleasant, sleepy places, with plenty of gardens and open spaces where men, though not women, could relax in public and meet their friends.

The wages of ordinary people seem to have remained very low, though. Some worked for themselves, others were employed by the Church or the powerful monasteries, or in government factories. In fact there appears to have been considerably more state control than in the west, with the government able to stop merchants or craftsmen from leaving the Empire for fear that they might establish rival industries in neighbouring countries. Perhaps this was a wise move, since the Norman king of Sicily was so keen to establish his own silk industry that he kidnapped specialist weavers from the Greek city of Thebes in 1147. In contrast, the very poor or unemployed were constantly being moved on from the shanty towns they erected around relatively prosperous cities.

Unlike western Europe, the Byzantine world was wholly dominated by its capital city, Constantinople, the 'Great City' to which the eyes of all Orthodox Christians turned. It was far larger than any other town in the Empire, although its vast walled enclosure was not filled with buildings until long after Constantinople became capital of the Ottoman Sultanate. Instead its amazing fortifications enclosed gardens, orchards, allotments and waste ground. The only area of dense habitation was at the easternmost end,

around the Imperial Palace, the Cathedral of Santa Sophia and the Hippodrome. Elsewhere seven monastic and secular suburbs stood separately within Constantinople's walls.

Despite these open spaces the great city constantly needed to import food, which was brought ashore under close government supervision at several small harbours in the sea walls – the cities knew that any interruption in grain supplies from Russia, the Balkans or southern Italy could cause serious rioting. The government also tried to control the trade in salt fish, which was another basic foodstuff, and iron, which was needed for weaponry. Constantinople was dominated by the Byzantine Court and did not develop separate civic institutions. Nevertheless, here, as in most Byzantine towns, each quarter had its own recognized headman, while hospices were provided for the poor and elderly, each partially supported by charitable donations.

The situation in medieval Russia was different, despite the fact that the Russians attempted to model their state administration on the Byzantine Empire. Towns were

Below left: A bread stamp or marker from 12th century Constantinople. All bread sold publicly had to be marked in this way in the Byzantine Empire as a way of ensuring it was pure and of the correct weight. The baker of any bread that did not come up to the required standard could therefore be easily identified.

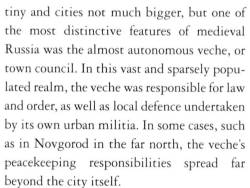

Right: Builders at work on a 13th century mosaic in Venice. Though made in northern Italy, the mosaics in the Cathedral of San Marco in Venice are almost entirely Byzantine in style. The men working here are probably using the same tools and techniques seen in most parts of the Byzantine Empire.

tiny and cities not much bigger, but one of the most distinctive features of medieval Russia was the almost autonomous veche, or town council. In this vast and sparsely populated realm, the veche was responsible for law and order, as well as local defence undertaken by its own urban militia. In some cases, such as in Novgorod in the far north, the veche's peacekeeping responsibilities spread far beyond the city itself.

Furthermore, Russian history offers several examples of a city throwing out a ruling prince who, for one reason or another, annoyed the merchant class which dominated such towns. The famous Alexandre Nevski, who defeated invading Crusaders on frozen Lake Peipus in 1242, was thrown out of Novgorod more than once before he eventually became Grand Duke and ruler of the whole of Russia. Another feature of Russian urban history was the steady shift of population from the declining south to the expanding north, a process which began even before the Mongol invasions of 1237–40.

Byzantium's failure in trade

Trade was the Empire's staple currency which underpinned its prosperity and, once this declined, so did the Empire itself. The Empire's relative lack of mineral resources also hampered economic development. However, it became known for fine craftsmanship in high-value goods such as silk, gold, silver, ivory and works of art, most of which were made in Constantinople. Less prestigious industries like pottery and leather-working were pushed outside the city walls altogether.

Other Byzantine cities had their own specialized small-scale industries. Trebizond, for example, exported fine cloths and silk, as well as skins, furs and the produce of local mines. Perhaps for this reason it remained rich right up to its final capture by the Ottoman Turks in 1461.

For most of the medieval period, the main role of Byzantine merchants and artisans was to provide luxury goods for the Court, Church and aristocracy. Guilds evolved out of

Saints Boris and Gleb on a Russian icon, painted on wood in Moscow around 1340. They are often shown as armed warriors, but here they appear dressed as members of the aristocracy. If it was not for their spears, they could be wealthy merchants.

the old Roman collegia and each industry had at least one to control wages and quality, although artisans were not obliged to join. Every guild had a president elected by the members and then approved by the local government, and it seems to have been difficult for citizens to change their family profession.

Although Byzantium was a vital link in the network of trade routes which linked China and India to Europe, Constantinople did not capitalize on its magnificent location until the late 12th century, when its foreign trade had largely been taken over by Italian merchants. Similarly Trebizond on the Black Sea coast, often called the 'gateway to Asia', depended on local commerce, possibly as a result of the high tolls they demanded from foreign merchants, who, as a result, preferred to use ports owned by Genoa or Venice.

Trade in other eastern Christian countries varied considerably from place to place; the rulers of Georgia are said to have sold their own people as Mamluk slave soldiers in various parts of the Middle East. Russian trade flourished in the Middle Ages, even under Mongol domination. The country was rich in natural resources, ranging from the furs of the Arctic to beeswax and honey from the forests, wheat from the south and fish from the biggest rivers in Europe. The small towns which grew up as a result were very rich. There were no roads except for infrequently paved portages between the main rivers, which were the lifelines of Russian trade. Here trading vessels ranged from longships, developed from earlier Viking designs, to large dugout canoes.

Roads were hardly better in Byzantium. Decorated carriages pulled by mules may have carried the elite around town, while noble women rode in litters carried by slaves, but beyond the city walls the old Roman road system had collapsed. Women as well as animals were employed as beasts of burden so, not surprisingly, maritime transport was preferred. Even so Byzantine ships lost out to their Italian rivals and eventually Italian sailors dominated the Black Sea as well.

A BUSINESS-MINDED CIVILIZATION

From its start, Islamic civilization was city-based and its expansion of population and agriculture was mirrored in a huge extension of trade. Most of the Muslim cities also grew organically, thus accounting for their narrow winding streets and separate quarters inhabited by different religious groups. At the time this proved an efficient way of getting goods in and out of the commercial centres while preserving that privacy central to Islamic family life. Such cities could not function without the suburbs beyond their walls, and these included prosperous residential areas for the wealthy, as well as semi-slums for casual workers. Rubbish dumps were also found outside the walls, as well as clearly defined cemetery areas often inhabited by vagrants and criminals. Beyond one of the main gates, a large open 'place of prayer' was used for religious festivals, and possibly for public executions, while one or more of the military training grounds were similarly sited outside the walls.

The appearance of a city could differ according to its climate and local traditions, yet Islamic cities were invariably dominated by the merchant middle class. People had a loyalty to their own quarter, which tended to reflect their religious affiliations and ethnic origins, but there was little sense of citizenship. The extended family formed the foundation of social organization, business dealing

Another picture by al-Wasiti in the Maqamat, made in 1237, shows merchants sleeping in the 'caravanserai' in Wasit, the artist's home town. Caravanserais or 'khans' were rather like medieval Middle Eastern 'motels', along the main trade routes and in every city.

Stories about the great Caliphs of the Abbasid period, particularly those about Harun al-Rashid, were popular throughout the medieval Muslim world. This late 15th century Persian illustration, in a copy of Nizami's Khamseh, shows the Caliph Harun al-Rashid visiting a barber's shop in Baghdad. Next door other customers retrieve their clothes.

even large tenement blocks, had an elected leader to deal with the authorities. Each quarter also organized its own young men into a militia to defend its interests and, if necessary, the city as a whole.

Meanwhile, the head of the family was undisputed master in the home, though the family went to the local 'qadi', or judge, if it had internal problems. The qadi and the 'muhtasib' were the two senior representatives of municipal authority. The muhtasib's responsibilities covered many things, including the quality of drinking and bathing water, the width of public streets, outbreaks of disease and the prompt burial of the dead. The urban authorities had virtually no jurisdiction beyond their walls, which was why cemeteries often became dens of thieves. The muhtasib also supervised the markets.

Another characteristic aspect of Islamic urban life was the 'waqf', a religious charity which dealt directly with the qadi and the religious authorities. The waqf often owned, through gifts and endowments, many of the public baths and factories in a town and used the revenue to support educational establishments and even provide irrigation systems for orchards outside the city. This system was extended into eastern Europe in the wake of the Ottoman conquests from 1348 onwards.

and relations with the urban authorities. A wealthy householder's tenants could also form part of this economic and social unit.

The role of the state tended to focus on the 'Dar al Imara', the local governor's office in a city's citadel. A typical example is the 13th century Citadel of Aleppo which towers over the city from the top of a mound of debris caused by thousands of years of human habitation in ancient times. The governor's primary role was that of defence, law and order, often leading to a mixture of autocracy and autonomy within the city. Each quarter, and

New towns on Byzantine soil

The new towns which the Seljuq Turks established in conquered Byzantine territory were more Central Asian than what had been built before, tending to be very spread out with scattered gardens, markets, running water and fountains. The Turks also increased the number of hamams or public baths. These differed from the Romano-Byzantine type in lacking a large immersion or 'swimming' pool and having instead constant hot and cold water flowing into smaller basins. The Seljuks and their Ottoman successors changed the face of what had been the Byzantine Empire, building mosques, 'madrasahs' or 'teaching mosques', hospitals for physical and mental disorders, soup kitchens and public accommodation for the poor. Many of these were again financed and administered by the waqf.

Although religious foundations of all faiths were exempt from taxation in the Muslim world, townspeople paid taxes to the urban authorities, military fief holders to their superior officers, users of waqf land to the administrators of the waqf, freehold landowners to the state treasury, while unmarried men paid an additional levy until they found a wife.

A special area outside the city walls was reserved for animals brought to market as food. Most smelly industries were either just outside or just inside the walls. The more valuable or prestigious the goods it sold, the closer a market would be to the centre of town. As a result, goldsmiths and booksellers tended to cluster around the main mosque in the very heart of the city.

There were no officially recognized guilds in a medieval Islamic city, but each trade was supervised by a man recognized by the government. Each trade also developed a sense of shared identity, attending the same mosque and serving together as a militia to defend the city walls. Slaves were rarely employed in industry or agriculture, except in some salt mines and sugar plantations, since slavery in the Muslim world was seen primarily as a source of trained domestic servants or elite professional soldiers.

Technology and the industries of Muslim civilization were in many ways very advanced. Distillation techniques supported a flourishing perfume industry, while new chemical ceramic glazes were a result of the constant attempt by the Muslims to compete with imported Chinese ceramics. A scientific approach to metallurgy also made it easier for Muslim smiths to adopt new steel technologies from China and India. Relatively rapid, long-distance communications helped the spread of such technologies and lay at the very heart of the Muslim world's flourishing commercial links with China, south-east Asia, India, east Africa, sub-Saharan west Africa and Europe. Islam's main exports were manufactured luxuries, including wood carving, metal and glass, textiles, lustre ceramics and tiles. The disruption of the Mongol invasions of the 13th century led to a serious industrial decline, although the peace which the

Ships are often shown in a very stylized way in medieval art, yet they often include interesting details. This vessel in a storm is on a picture by al-Wasiti made in Baghdad in 1237, illustrating the Maqamat of al-Hariri. It has two masts, a hinged stern rudder and a hull which is stitched rather than nailed together. Such a form of construction was still used in the Arabian Gulf until modern times.

وكــان اخبــب ســيظ طرشـرراك ويـغلـى الـمـدك عـلـى واحلـق الـك الجـت جلـف مالـغلـف
لـن قال ان الـعـبـد اذا اروم نـه وخفـت مـوته مـوتـك لـه مـولاه والـحـف علـيه مـولاه وانـى

لؤ تريتبهم هدا الـغلام الـبـك بـاخفـن نـتـه علـيكـم نـتـه وهـوان سـنـب
واشـكـرنـى ماجـتـه فـفـلـت المـبـلـغ فـمـا انـفـدرنا الاخـضـر الـغـال ولم

Above: Some of characteristic bustle of a Middle-Eastern market comes across in this little manuscript painted by the 13th century Iraqi artist al-Hariri.

Opposite: In this 14th–15th century Vietnamese painting a man and a woman go out riding. Neither appears to be using stirrups. The woman carries a large parasol while a servant on foot carries their luggage.

of kinship enabled trade links to be made over huge distances. Each time trade items passed through one of the cities which formed nodal points in this extraordinary trading network, the local government imposed a tax, which resulted in very high prices when goods reached their final destination. Yet the Muslim world never became completely reliant on foreign markets either for exports or imports, in fact remaining self-sufficient throughout the whole of the medieval period.

Transport was simple, but effective: each town had areas outside its gates where pack animals assembled, the main markets within the city often had large secure warehouses, while 'khans' or 'caravanserais' provided accommodation for merchants in the cities or on the major trade routes. Surviving 13th century examples on the high plateau of central Turkey tend to be around thirty kilometres apart, representing nine hours walking time for loaded pack animals.

Apart from the Nile, Tigris and Euphrates, navigable rivers were few, so transport by sea was important. The science of navigation was very advanced; navigational instruments included the 'kamal', a rudimentary sextant to calculate the altitude of stars, and the Chinese magnetic compass. When combined with detailed geographical knowledge, Muslim sailors could sail across oceans rather than skirt round the edges.

Muslim Arab sailors also reintroduced large three-masted merchant ships to the Mediterranean and developed a specialized horse-transporting galley called a 'tarida'. It is also worth noting that the caravels which took Christopher Columbus to America were developed from an earlier Muslim Andalusian vessel. There was even an artificial canal linking the Nile with the Gulf of Suez – and thus by extension the Mediterranean with the Red Sea – though this silted up several times. All this could not, however, alter the fact that by the 12th century Mediterranean trade was dominated by western Italian sailors.

Mongol 'World Empire' brutally imposed on most of Asia led to a rapid revival in trade with the rest of the world, if not a re-expansion of industry.

Contractual negotiations

The systems of contract on which such trade relied remained virtually unchanged throughout the medieval period. Merchants bought and sold on commission, often with capital borrowed from a rich lender or jointly invested by several merchants, who could be Muslim, Christian or Jewish. In fact the remarkable collection of documents found in an Egyptian synagogue not long ago include numerous business contracts which shed a detailed and very human light on the life of medieval Middle Eastern merchants. Business partnerships tended to be made for one commercial venture only, though bonds

CITIES OF THE
CELESTIAL EMPIRE

During the medieval period, China's economic centre of gravity shifted from north to south. The southern Sung capital and main port of Hangzhou became by far the biggest city in the world while the populations of nine other 11th century Chinese cities also topped a million.

Cities themselves were characterized by broad streets, tree-lined avenues and, often, wide canals. Fire-watching towers kept an eye on each quarter of the towns; fire was a serious hazard in cities built almost entirely of wood, and fire-fighting soldiers patrolled the streets. People were awoken at seven in the morning by temple gongs; monks and novices walked through the streets to alert any who overslept. The gates which separated each quarter of town were then opened, when street vendors began crying their wares and officials made their way to their offices.

Places for buying and selling ranged from the main markets remaining open from dawn to gone midnight, to small bazaars selling flowers and sweets, to street vendors who might sell only hot water.

The tea-houses, which were another feature of medieval Chinese cities, seem to have served as 'job centres' and, perhaps as a result of a growing gap between rich and poor, the poorest could enlist in gangs paid by one of the more powerful citizens to intimidate business or political rivals. Some were even armed and had their own rudimentary uniforms.

Despite the official Chinese bias in favour of agriculture, China's cities became some of the most important commercial centres in the world. Nor did a superior attitude towards commerce prevent the authorities from getting maximum revenues from it. They also encouraged wealthy merchants to

Top: Chinese art of the Sung period is often full of amazing details of everyday life, but few pictures compare with a large scroll painting by Zhang Zeduan called 'Going up the River at the Spring Festival'. This is one small section, showing a busy street corner in Kaifeng with people going about their everyday tasks.

Above: Another part of the amazingly detailed scroll painting by Zhang Zeduan shows some of the inhabitants of Kaifeng watching a barge whose crew are having some difficulty lowering their mast and sail fast enough to get under the bridge.

use their money for the benefit of the whole community, but when it came to looking after the most needy, Buddhist monasteries provided orphanages, hospitals, old-people's homes and even graveyards.

The transport of bulk grain from rural areas to the main cities was particularly well organized, but had such low profit margins that the authorities subsidized merchants involved in this business. The building of granaries to guarantee urban food supplies had been developed in the early medieval period. The rice in these stores was ear-marked, however, for government employees and the army, while 'voluntary granaries' were supposed to be sufficient to feed the ordinary people.

Industry and infrastructure

The most famous Chinese industry was silk, most of which was made in eastern China, though gilded silk became a speciality of some western provinces. Officially recognized guilds were highly developed, each craft being distinguishable by its special clothing, while many artisans were employed directly by state factories. In fact the Chinese government played a very prominent role in industry and mining, even imposing a state monopoly on certain strategic trades, including the highly lucrative tea trade.

State control of industry reached a comparable level in Korea. Here industry was concentrated around the capital, most manufacturing being in the hands of government factories which were often manned by government slaves. A variety of industries were involved, including cotton which became a major state concern. In stark contrast, the simple technologies seen amongst the nomadic peoples of Central Asia were kept in the hands of individual families. Here, control of transit trade remained an important source of revenue.

An old Chinese proverb said, 'In the north take a horse, in the south take a boat'. Many of the main cities were linked by canal to agricultural regions which supplied them with food and such canals were of considerable benefit in the movement of goods. Canals and roads were built and maintained with enforced corvée labour extracted from the peasantry as a form of tax and the roads themselves came in various sizes. Imperial highways were mainly for government officials, with a central lane reserved for the Emperor, while other roads were essentially for the military.

Major roads also had government checkpoints manned by officials for contraband and fugitives. Large wagons were pulled by oxen, small carts by donkeys, while poor farmers relied on two-wheeled handcarts. Mule trains were more efficient than wheeled transport in mountains and deserts, while horses were too valuable to be used as draught animals, except to pull carriages of the elite. Korea had a similar system of roads, and trade between Korea and China was so important for Korea that it set up special hostels for foreign merchants.

Rivers were vital for China's internal communications trade, the north–south canals linked only the main east–west rivers. The boats used in both canals and rivers ranged from large vessels with sails of bamboo matting to rafts punted up or drifted down river. China's significant advances in maritime technology during the medieval period were largely based on earlier discoveries and included stern rudders operated by wheel and windlass. Some of the ships involved were also remarkably big. The remains of a late medieval rudder on the site of a Chinese shipyard indicated that it was part of a vessel around 150 metres long, perhaps one of the ships which reached east Africa in the 15th century. The Koreans also took part in this flourishing Pacific trade, though on a smaller scale, and their government similarly promoted the construction of ports, secure warehousing and ferries over the main rivers.

Japanese urban life was transformed between the 11th and 15th centuries. The old Imperial capital had been planned on a grid system, but as central authority collapsed, smaller provincial cities took over as political, administrative and economic centres, growing in an unplanned manner and with much narrower streets. Their expansion stimulated regional economies and, as a result, increased trade. These cities also became centres of money-lending, often organized by sake brewers, who had readier cash than most people.

Japanese control of rice production

Although they flourished, Japan's smaller cities could never compete with the great Chinese centres in terms of trade. In fact control of rice-producing land remained the foundation of power in medieval Japan, with trade and commerce playing a minor role. In fact, Japanese trade continued to rely on bartering with little use of money and even luxury objects, art and medicines were exchanged for rice.

Nevertheless the 12th century saw an increasing formalization of crafts and manufacturing centres in Japan. 'Za', or mutual support guilds, appeared even at village level and there were an enormous number by the 15th century, forming closely knit communities of merchants or artisans, often with monasteries or aristocratic families as patrons. In Korea, guilds known as 'po' fulfilled much the same function.

Japan's geographical position on the fringe of the known world left it out of the main trade networks and, even in the 14th and 15th centuries, overseas trade was often in the hands of wako pirates rather than peaceful merchants. Japanese roads were notoriously bad, but there was sudden improvement as a result of the increasing importance of provincial centres of power in the 13th–14th centuries. Even so, the size and decoration of remarkably cumbersome ox-drawn carriages continued to indicate rank, and only the highest elite rode in elaborate sedan chairs.

THE HINDU RETREAT FROM THE SEA

During the early medieval period, Indian civilization was more outward looking than it was in later centuries while the main cities were huge sprawling centres of industry and commerce. But Hindu civilization steadily turned away from maritime trade and several of the Indianized Hindu-Buddhist civilizations declined when their peoples were attracted to the more commercially oriented civilization of Islam. In fact, by the 13th century most long distance trade seems to have been in the hands of Arabs, Persians and Chinese. In south-east Asia, foreigners inhabited the ports where they and local commercial communities formed a very mixed and mobile population. These coastal cities also tended to rise and fall in political and commercial importance and were still in this state of flux when European explorers arrived at the start of the 16th century.

Commerce in neighbouring Indo-China was influenced by Chinese as well as Indian practices. Amongst the Khmer, for example, women played a very prominent role ranging from village market level to large-scale trading enterprises. Payment was usually made in quantities of rice or other grain, while money was reserved for larger transactions. An even more primitive form of exchange existed in Sri Lanka, where the Sinhalese would leave cloth and food outside their homes at night, which was taken by the aboriginal Veddas of the jungle, who left lizard-skins and other trade items in return.

Guilds did not develop to a great extent in India. Associations existed of wealthy merchants who paid ruler tolls on the items they traded and sometimes hired private armies to defend their interests. The bulk of medieval Indian trade consisted of metal goods, salt, wood and luxury items. India's part in the iron and steel industry was particularly important and the country imported large quantities of iron ingots from many regions, including east Africa. Trade goods usually passed through several hands, enriching several entrepots along the way. Outlying islands and tribal peoples far from the sea could also be involved in this remarkable trading network, exchanging their own produce for basic things like iron, salt or cloth. The expansion of cash-crop economies in Java and Sumatra was also intimately connected with the spread of Islam in the 14th–15th centuries.

Overland communication

Land communications played a major role in India, but were not highly developed, the only exceptions being an ancient trunk road across northern India and a road down the western side of the country. In earlier times, powerful Indian rulers had planted fruit trees along main roads to provide both food and shelter for travellers, dug wells and built rest-houses, but it is unclear how much of this remained in the medieval period.

The most important forms of commercial transport were caravans of bullock carts or camels, but movement virtually came to a halt during the monsoon rains. In Indochina, the huge mountain ranges of the north-west remained virtually impenetrable, but its central plateau was easier to cross. Here, in the 12th century, the kings of Khmer built roads, rest-houses and bridges, some of which had more than twenty arches.

India's ancient trading connection with Socotra, the 'Island of Dragon's Blood' off the Horn of Africa, may account for the island's apparently Indian name, while the medieval Chola state in southern India conquered vari-

Left: The barely changing character of everyday life in medieval India is well illustrated in this carving from the Great Stuppa at Sanchi-Bopal. Although it was carved in the 1st century BC or 1st century AD, the houses, costumes, the horseman who does not use stirrups, the elephant and even perhaps the elaborate chariot could still be seen in 11th century India.

Below: Another carving on the north gate at Sanchi-Bopal shows people fishing in a river surrounded by waterfowl. Their boat is stitched together, just like the river craft of Iraq and the great ocean-going ships which sailed between India and the Middle East during the medieval period.

ous islands in the Bay of Bengal in 1021 and even attacked Malaya in 1030. Yet by the late Middle Ages, sea travel was seen as a form of grave spiritual pollution by high caste Hindus and, as a result, Indian sailors were steadily ousted by their Arab and even Chinese rivals. Whoever sailed them, the main trade routes still converged at the Straits of Malacca and the Sea of Java where coastal states competed to control such important strategic waters.

To the north, Indochina's lack of deep-water harbours was not a problem since it had sufficient sheltered roadsteads. Further east, the Philippines largely remained outside this trading network, even though by the 12th century Chinese trading posts had been established. The greatest foreign impact on the Philippines came later, from the south, with the arrival of Muslim south-east Asian and Indian merchants in the closing decades of the medieval period.

6 SCIENCE, SCHOLARSHIP AND MEDICINE

The idea that the middle ages were a time of ignorance, superstition and fear of new ideas is a myth. Although one people's Dark Ages could be another's Golden Age, it was the spread of new ideas that was one of the most astonishing characteristics of the medieval period. Naturally it was slower than in more recent centuries, but intellectual currents still reached Western Europe from as far away as India and China.

THE ROOTS OF WESTERN SCIENCE

One of the most obvious features of western European scholarship and science was the enormous respect, even reverence, with which ancient Greek and Roman scholars were held. Above all, Aristotle was seen as the fountainhead of secular knowledge. This was a time when established written authority completely dominated the experimental spirit which now characterizes the modern approach to scholarship and science.

At the same time, however, medieval scholars and alchemists were fascinated by scientific experimentation for its own sake. Nevertheless, this was often bound up with the quest for semi-magical elixirs of life and ways of turning one material into another, for example base metal into gold. Such apparently contradictory atttitudes can even be seen in the life of great scholars such as the English Roger Bacon (c.1214–1292).

The Middle Ages were also a time of great interest in mechanical devices. Sometimes these were little more than toys for the rich and powerful but other, more practical machines helped in the building of great cathedrals, the draining of marshes, or the digging of deeper mines. Seen from a modern perspective, medieval Europeans seem to have had a confused and almost childlike attitude towards scientific knowledge, ranging from enthusiasm to suspicion and fear.

Medieval scholars were themselves often very impressive, serious-minded men and could be found in some apparently unlikely places. For example, Gaelic Irish scholars, supported by various Scottish and Norse rulers of the Western Isles, translated Greek literary and medical texts at a time when the only other Europeans to do such things were Muslim scholars in Spain or Sicily. On the other hand, the impact of these Irishmen was

very localized, and western Europe's 'rediscovery' of ancient learning really began with the Italian Renaissance in the 14th Century.

An unhelpful result of their rediscoveries was the new cult of Humanism, whose followers tended to believe that the ancient Romans had the answer to every cultural, social or scientific problem. This infatuation with classical Roman civilization lay at the very heart of the European Renaissance.

The idealization of ancient Greece came later in the 15th century with the arrival of several Byzantine scholars in Italy who opened up a whole new field of study for westerners. These cultural refugees were fleeing the advancing Ottoman Turks and they

brought with them many Greek books which were then edited, copied and soon also printed for the increasing number of educated middle-class readers. The Renaissance Humanist belief that modern problems could be solved by studying ancient texts became so deeply entrenched in European culture that it survived long after the end of the Middle Ages and is even visible today.

Opposite: Wounded men being treated by doctors in a 15th century French manuscript of 'Le Bon Roi Alexandre'. Only the most senior men could expect such good treatment in the medical tent.

Below: Herb extracts provided the basic ingredients for most medieval medicine. Herb gardens like this one from the *Roman de la Rose*, made around 1400, were an feature of monasteries, and the gardens of doctors.

Those scholars who laid the foundations for late medieval and Renaissance Humanism came from many different backgrounds. Poggio Bracciolini (1380–1459), the great Italian manuscript hunter, was the son of a poor village chemist who climbed the academic ladder by sheer hard work, whereas his rival Niccolo Niccoli (1364–1437) came from a rich business family and used his inherited wealth to send other people looking for dusty old manuscripts. Like so many of the great characters of late medieval and early Renaissance Italy, such scholars could be a quarrelsome lot. They carried on long academic feuds, occasionally coming to blows.

Cardinal Johannes Bessarion (1395–1472), the founding father of Greek studies in Italy, was himself a refugee from Byzantium who donated his entire manuscript collection to Venice in 1472. The library is still there today. Because of Venice's close commercial links with the eastern Mediterranean and with the German Empire north of the Alps, this wealthy commercial city became not only the centre of Greek learning in Europe, but also of the printing of relatively cheap copies of newly discovered classics, which were then sold throughout Europe. The Venetians' willingness to seize on new ideas, such as the German invention of printing with movable type, may have been made easier by the city's long-established business tradition. Venetian merchants probably also knew about ordinary woodblock printing, as it had been used in the Middle East since at least the 12th century.

Medieval pragmatism

Throughout the 15th century, men of learning outside Italy remained more pragmatic and, in many ways, more medieval in their attitude towards learning. One aspect of knowledge which always remained brutally practical was medicine. Life was hard and much shorter than today. There were few doctors and, although priests did what they could, this rarely meant more than giving

comfort and the Last Rites to the dying. Some monks had a practical knowledge of herbal medicine which could, in fact, be remarkably effective. So did local 'wise women' who, nevertheless, always ran the risk of being accused of witchcraft.

The treatment of wounds remained very primitive, even in the best-run armies, although by the 11th and 12th centuries some Italian city armies did take surgeons with them to war. The Crusaders also had a chance to witness the techniques of their more advanced Muslim and Byzantine rivals.

One such meeting between a western and a Middle Eastern doctor was described in ghastly detail by the 12th century Arab soldier Usamah Ibn Munqidh. A Christian knight with an infected leg was brought to an Arab doctor, who put a small poultice on it. After a while, the infection began to heal, but then a European doctor came along and accused the Arab of knowing nothing. Instead he asked the knight whether he would prefer to live with one leg or die with two. Naturally the knight preferred to take his chance with one, so the western doctor ordered a strong soldier to cut off the knight's infected leg with an axe. This took two blows rather than the expected one, and the knight promptly died. The Arab doctor was not impressed, and nor was Usamah.

By the 13th and 14th centuries some barely trained barber-surgeons had learned to clean and bind up wounds, extract arrows and reset bones. Despite the crude medical facilities of the period, medieval people seemed capable of surviving atrocious injuries. Paradoxically this might have been because they lived in such an unhygienic world that they became resistant to everyday infections.

It was from the south and east that new medical knowledge reached most of Europe in the 11th to 14th centuries. Medicine was a field of study where western Christendom had no hesitation in learning from their Muslim Arab and Persian neighbours. Following the fall of the Roman Empire, Ancient Greek medical knowledge had been almost entirely

Opposite: This doctor is setting a broken leg in a cast apparently made of straw or wood. The illustration, made in Zürich around 1310–1340, shows Ulrich von Sachsendorf on his sickbed and the man at the back might be offering Ulrich a strong drink to help deaden the pain.

The gruesome business of dissecting a body for examination is shown in this woodcut illustration of an anatomy lesson, where a senior surgeon instructs one of his students. It appears in the Modena Manuscript of Anatomy made in 1493.

Right: A clockmaker winding up the weights of what appears to be a pendulum clock, the ancestor of more modern 'grandfather clocks'. Although this little drawing is in an Astronomical Treatise, made in England between 1350 and 1375, it shows how sophisticated medieval technology had become by this time.

forgotten by Europeans, but, along with Indian and Chinese medical knowledge, it had been translated into Arabic by the Muslims. Arab and Persian doctors went on to discover even more about how the body worked and their knowledge was eventually translated into Latin in Italy and Spain, most notably at the 'School of Salerno' south of Rome, which emerged in the 11th century.

As a result, by the 15th century medicine was flourishing once again in some parts of Europe, but more often than not this was for the benefit of the aristocracy. Since the Church still banned the dissection of human corpses for research, a battle offered surgeons a chance to study anatomy on the living, the dying and the dead. At the battle of Fornovo in 1495 it was more than coincidence that more than one of the most famous doctors of the day worked in the Italian camp. The wounded knight Berdardino Fortebraccio, who had several pieces of broken bone removed from his skull, and was walking around the streets of Venice only a few weeks after the battle, may not have been alone in owing his life to these men.

Everywhere in medieval Europe medical practitioners were highly respected and came in several grades of seniority. A master surgeon, for example, ranked above a mere barber-surgeon; by the 14th century there were also many women doctors. Blood-letting seems to have been regarded almost as a cure-all while certain phases of the moon were considered more suitable than others for surgical operations. Doctors could also fall back on thousands of years' worth of practical experience in the use of herbs. Some might even have had access to monastery libraries with a few medical texts, most of which would have been translated from Arabic.

Disease and epidemics

Nevertheless disease and epidemics remained a terrifying mystery. Leprosy was not as common as is sometimes thought, but those who suffered from it were isolated in special buildings. Although they had their movements strictly regulated, they were seen as 'Christ's Special Sufferers' and were well treated, even if greatly feared. Fevers were the most common complaints, and cities always remained vulnerable to epidemics.

By far the worst was the Black Death plague of 1348, though the reasons why it spread so suddenly remain unclear. Improved communications, increased trade and a much higher population must have contributed, although the crowding characteristic of medieval urban life was probably the main cause. As a result the Black Death wiped out approximately one third of the entire population of England. Even so, by the 14th century there were many hospitals in the main cities of western Europe, most of them founded by the rich and powerful as a form of charity.

Within western Europe veterinary science also advanced at least as fast as that of human medicine. The highly trained war-horses of the knightly elite were so valuable that the European military elite were eager to learn from Byzantine, Arab and Turkish vets whose knowledge was far in advance of their own. So it was not surprising to find that the earliest known books on veterinary medicine were again written in southern Italy, an area where Greek, Latin and Arabic knowledge came together.

BYZANTINE SCIENCE –
STUCK IN THE PAST

Constantine the African travelled throughout the
Muslim world learning medicine. He is shown
here lecturing students on uroscopy, one of the
basic skills of medieval medicine.

Reverence for ancient thought

Byzantine civilization was so conscious of its own classical Greek and Roman past that it held the ancient scholarly authorities in even greater awe than the western European scholars did. As a result, Byzantine scientists, and even doctors, added relatively little to what they inherited from their predecessors. Much more originality, however, was shown in religious philosophy than in secular scholarship.

Meanwhile, the practical aspects of applied science and technology were not rated very highly in the Byzantine Empire, and this had the paradoxical result of freeing practical scholarship from the shackles of the past. Byzantine engineers and technicians were in many ways advanced and highly practical in the way they went about solving technological problems. The magnificent architecture and above all the great domes of the Byzantine world, from the vast 6th century church of Santa Sofia in Istanbul to the jewel-like 14th century convent of Santa Sofia in Mistras, are perhaps the most dramatic witnesses to this practical technology.

The same went for water-collection and storage systems, siege engineering (both attack and defence), and, in its way, shipbuilding. The most famous of all Byzantine weapons, Greek Fire, was yet another example of how technology was turned to devastating use. This oil-based form of pyrotechnics invented in the 7th century became, in effect, a medieval flame-thrower which could be used on land and at sea, even continuing to burn on the surface of the water. Other devices, most obviously those used in siege warfare, also showed the Byzantine willingness to learn from eastern neighbours and included ideas that had originated in China, having reached Constantinople via the Muslim Arabs and Turks.

In complete contrast, Byzantine Greek geographers seem to have learned remarkably little from their eastern neighbours, despite close commercial links. It almost seemed like a conscious rejection of new information and a preference for clinging to an archaic, Mediterranean or even Greek-centred view of the world, and this was despite the fact that Arabic maps must have become available by the 12th or 13th centuries. Other Arabic books were translated into Greek, but had less impact than they would have had in western Europe. Even medicine remained firmly based on the ancient Greek and Latin authorities with minimal input from the Muslims.

Not surprisingly, therefore, Byzantine doctors and surgeons were steadily outstripped not only by their eastern rivals, but also even by the Italians and other western Europeans. This was not to say that the science of medicine was not taken seriously in the Byzantine Empire – far from it. The government provided a certain amount of medical services and hospitals in the main cities, but these were minimal and not as much as might have been expected in such a rich, sophisticated and urbanized civilization.

The most positive aspects of health care in the Byzantine world were, in fact, directly inherited from the Roman past and included the provision of adequate, secure and clean drinking water. The only new aspect of this concern with drinking water relied upon Byzantine engineering skills rather than medical science and resulted from the simple fact that the Byzantine Empire was so frequently invaded. The old Roman system of aqueducts which brought water from beyond the fortified walls into the cities proved too vulnerable to attack from invading forces, so instead they were largely replaced by huge underground cisterns from the start of the 11th century onwards.

The one area where Byzantine physicians do seem to have taken a distinctly modern view was in the field of mental health. For reasons which are not fully understood, the Byzantines were very aware of the problems of stress. They not only tried to provide help, but also believed that a house or hospital with an uninterrupted view of the sea was an excellent way of calming those suffering from psychological disorders.

Above: The greatest achievements of Byzantine technology and architecture dated from the early medieval period, but most were still in perfect working order well into the Ottoman period. The great 6th century underground cistern shown here was so impressive that it became known as the 'Sunken Palace'.

Opposite: Cardinal Bessarion was one of the leading scholars during the last decades of the Byzantine Empire. Following the Ottoman conquest of Constantinople, Bessarion remained in Italy where he founded Renaissance Greek studies. This portrait was painted by Joos Van Gent in around 1475.

A brilliant spark in the dying embers

The death throes of the Byzantine Empire saw a sudden flowering of Byzantine art, architecture and scholarship. Several figures stand out and the ferocity with which they disagreed with each other was astonishing. In the 14th century, the main debate had been between those who wanted to fight the advancing Turks and save the Empire, and those who advocated retreating into a world of mystical contemplation. By and large, the latter won the day.

Even in the final crisis of the 15th century the main issues remained religious, though they now had a sharper political edge. Above all there was the question of whether the Orthodox Christian Church should accept union with the Latin Catholic Church on the latter's terms. Three further names stand out. The first was John Bessarion (1395–1472) titular Patriarch of Constantinople and head of the Orthodox Church in Nicea, who was the leading advocate of union. The second was Gennadios Scholarion, who is said to have preferred domination by Muslim Turks to domination by Catholic westerners. He became Patriarch of Constantinople from 1453 to 1459, after it was conquered by the Ottoman Turks.

The third, and the most interesting, was George Plethon, who died around 1450. His solution to the problem of the dying Byzantine Empire was as radical as Bessarion's, but looked much further back into Greek history for inspiration. As a philosopher rather than a churchman, Plethon envisaged an agricultural utopia based upon ancient Sparta, with a citizen army maintained by serfs. But, despite being so backward looking, Plethon was aware of the need to use new technologies. Eventually he fled to Italy, where he lectured on Plato. He had a big impact on the development of Renaissance Humanism before returning to Greece, where he died about ten years before Mistras fell to the advancing Ottoman Turks.

BESSARION

THE GREEKS' MOST RECEPTIVE PUPILS

The contrast between the attitudes and achievements of Byzantine and medieval Islamic scholarship could hardly be most striking, despite the fact that both civilizations were dominated by religion. The only area where Islamic beliefs hindered new thinking was in philosophy, and here medieval scholars often got into trouble for putting forward unorthodox ideas.

Nevertheless, thinkers like Ibn Sina (980–1037) and Ibn Rushd (1126–1198) played a major role clarifying and commenting on the ancient Greek philosopher Aristotle, whose ideas dominated all non-religious thought in both medieval Muslim and Christian cultures. It was these men who, with various contemporaries, ware actually responsible for transmitting Aristotelian concepts back to western Europe and, as a result, became authorities themselves, their names being westernized to Avicenna (Ibn Sina) and Averroes (Ibn Rushd).

In relation to pure science, the Muslims have been called 'pupils of the Greeks', but this ignores the fact that medieval Arabs, Persians and even Turks also learned from their pre-Islamic Persian predecessors, as well as from the Indians, Chinese and others. Furthermore, as a result of their own research, Islamic scholars went on to add a huge amount of new information and several daring new concepts. Most Greek knowledge was translated into Arabic via Syriac or Aramean, the previous Semitic language of the Middle East, but because of its huge and flexible vocabulary, Arabic language was able to absorb ideas from as far afield as China and to cope with new scientific theories. Many scientific and mathematical words still used in European languages are of medieval Arabic origin. The greatest period of Islamic scientific progress was during the 10th and 11th centuries, when great strides were made in mathematics, medicine, geography and history.

Less acknowledged is the progress made by Muslim engineers, craftsmen and farmers in various fields of practical or applied technology: irrigation is the most obvious. Here surveyors developed various devices to check the level of canals and ensure a steady flow of water, including a simple form of astrolabe used as a theodolite. Technological advances also underpinned other industries, including the distillation techniques used in making

Right: One of the most notable features of technology in Islamic civilization was that, unlike western Europe, new ideas were not immediately used for military purposes. Most had an impact on industry, medicine or leisure. One such toy is shown in this picture from the *Book of Knowledge of Mechanical Devices*, written by al-Jazari in the late 12th century. It is a form of candle-clock where figures popped out of a small doors as each hour passed.

Opposite: The water-clock on the minaret of the Bu Inaniyya Madrasa in Fez, Morocco, dropped a heavy ball as each period of time passed. It dates from around 1350–1355 and may have been needed because this Madrasa served as a hostel for students at the nearby Qarawiyyin University Mosque.

scents from the essential oils of flowers or incendiary weapons from refined mineral oil. Soap was made for cosmetic and medical purposes, while glass-making was far more advanced than it had been in Roman times and included various enamelling techniques. Chinese paper-making technology reached the Middle East very early in the Muslim era, traditionally after some Chinese clerks had been captured at the battle of Talas in 751, and was soon accompanied by block-printing.

On the other hand, the cursive character of Arabic script did not lend itself to movable-type printing, which was invented much later in Germany. Sophisticated chemical knowledge did, however, permit the development of new textile dyes, ceramic glazes and decorative alloys used in metalwork.

The medieval Muslims inherited the pure science of several civilizations, while their own concern with precise time and place to established the correct time and direction of daily prayers led to notable advances in lunar calendars, astronomical tables and geography. Despite lacking accurate chronometers, Muslim geographers tackled the problem of measuring longitude by comparing the timing of lunar eclipses in different parts of the world. Their results were amazing, considering such crude methods. In pure mathematics, the Muslims translated Indian treatises and adopted India's numerical zero. As a result, the numbering system used today in the western world is called Arabic to distinguish it from the cumbersome old Roman numerals, which had no zero. The invention of algebra, from al-Jabr meaning 'restoration', analytical geometry, trigonometry and even spherical trigonometry were all new, invented in the 10th to 12th centuries.

Deep interest in light and optics led to an understanding of refraction, which enabled the depth of the earth's atmosphere to be calculated with great accuracy. A sun-centred, rather than earth-centred, solar system was suggested in 13th–14th century Persia, but, although books were written on this subject, the concept was not widely accepted. It may, however, have passed via the Ottoman Turks and Greeks to the great Polish scholar Copernicus by the early 16th century. There were fewer advances in zoology as the study of animals had little practical application, but it was very different with botany. Here Muslims could draw upon ancient Greek and

current Indian knowledge which, when added to their own traditions of painstaking observation, produced startling new results, which had a direct impact on both medicine and agriculture.

Hospitals, sanatoriums and stud-farms

Medicine was the field in which medieval Islamic civilization had its most notable scientific advances. These were based upon empirical observation; for example, the Arabs' interests in optics increased knowledge of how the eyes worked, while mental disorders were seen as 'mental sickness' rather than being ascribed to evil spirits, as in Europe. There were hospitals in all the main cities; for example the Hospital of Qalawun built in Cairo in 1284 was able to care for 8,000 patients, with staff which included physicians, pharmacists and nurses. Comparable advances were made in the understanding of contagious diseases and in many regions the charitable 'waqf' system financed the development of hot springs as free sanatoriums.

On the other hand, primitive belief persisted in many areas. There was, for example, a widespread belief in magic charms and talismans among uneducated poor or tribal peoples. Deep in southern Arabia, the Qara of Dhufar, for example, thought that cattle had healing powers. A cow would be sacrificed if a member of the family fell ill and at noon its blood was sprinkled on the sick person's chest in a clear relic of pre-Islamic paganism.

In stark contrast to such primitive survivals, Arabia developed a science of selective breeding which produced the Arabian horse. It would have a huge genetic impact on horse breeding across the world. Not surprisingly, perhaps, the first known example of artificial insemination in animal husbandry was recorded in the Middle East in 1286 and in fact veterinary medicine was more advanced in the Islamic world than anywhere else during the medieval period.

Preparing medicines was a highly skilled matter and was left to qualified pharmacists in medieval Islamic society. In this 13th century Arabic translation of the ancient Greek *Materia Medica* by Dioscorides, medicines are prepared over a fire while upstairs the pharmacist's assistants prepare the ingredients and store the resulting drugs.

CHINA'S SEPARATE SCHOLARLY TRADITION

Throughout the ancient and medieval periods, the Chinese attitude towards science was characterized by a deep belief in the power of reason, even in the concept of 'progress'. Like the scholars and scientists of Islamic civilization, those of medieval China never tried to dominate the world around them, preferring instead the ideal of harmony with nature.

On the other hand, Chinese scholarship from the 11th to 15th centuries tended to be very academic, its emphasis on self-advancement and self-knowledge in accord with the highly educated bureaucratic elite. The period also witnessed the emergence of the neo-Confucian philosophy which would then dominate Chinese civilization until modern times – it was basically a synthesis of the old Confucian rationalism combined with various aspects of Buddhist and Taoist mysticism. Given the number of merchants and invaders who entered China, and the Chinese soldiers, officials and ambassadors who ventured far beyond China's frontiers, it is not surprising to find that geographical knowledge was very advanced.

The spirit of invention

Although the great period of Chinese invention ended in the later 13th century with the fall of the southern Sung dynasty to Kubilai Khan's Mongol army in 1279, the subsequent Mongol period saw China being opened up to new ideas. This was particularly true in astronomy, where more advanced knowledge came from the Muslim Middle East. Not that the traffic was all in one direction; during the late 13th century, a Chinese astronomer named Fao-Mun-Ji worked with Arab scholars in the observatory established by the Mongols in north-western Iran.

The Chinese seem to have achieved more in technology and engineering than in pure science: for example, Chinese technicians led the medieval world in the fields of water-power, metallurgy, shipping and ceramics. Water often powered the bellows used in larger iron works, while complex systems of pulleys, cogs and ratchets helped drain water from mine-shafts. In the late 11th century, a complex gearing and escapement system comparable to that used by later European clock makers enabled an engineer named Su Song to construct a remarkable mechanical clock in the Sung capital between 1088 and 1092. The mechanism was inside a small pagoda-like structure with an armillary sphere on top which showed the movements of the stars, whilst a revolving drum indicated the time of day.

In the 10th century, control of water rather than water-power as such similarly led to the invention of watertight canal lock-gates, which meant that boats no longer had to be dragged overland between canals at different altitudes. Even so, large wooden capstans turned by buffaloes were still needed to haul river craft upstream in situations where the water flowed too fast for boats to be sailed, rowed or punted.

Medieval Chinese naval technology produced ocean-going ships whose size astonished the Venetian traveller Marco Polo when he arrived in the east in the 1280s. They were multi-decked, with stern rudders moved by capstan wheels and possibly even had watertight compartments. Some river-craft were even powered by teams of men turning paddle-wheels, while sea captains could navigate using the magnetic compasses which had recently been developed from an old fortune-telling device.

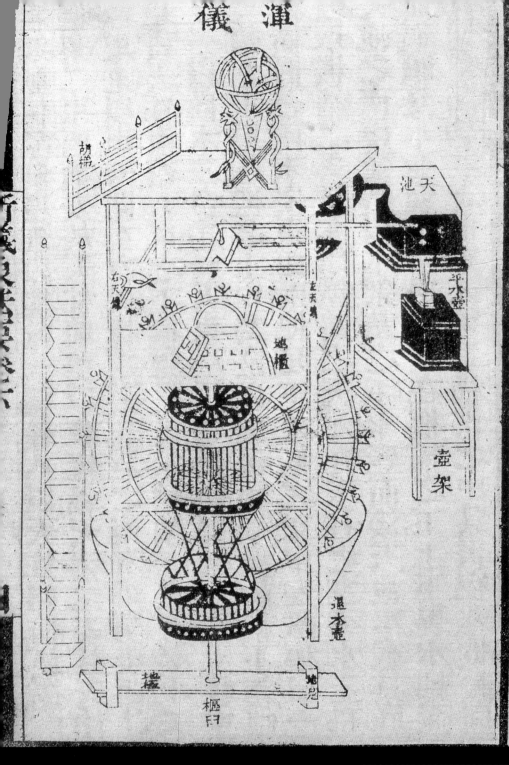

渾儀

Left: Chinese civilization was as fascinated by measuring time as any other in the Middle Ages. This drawing shows how the astonishing water clock made by Su Song for the Sung Emperor in the city of Kaifeng between 1088 and 1092 actually worked. It was nine metres high and contained three separate rotating mechanisms powered by a single source of water power.

Below: Unlike Su Song's remarkable water clock, the astronomical observatory in Beijing still exists in the south-east corner of the old Mongol capital. Much of it is believed to date from the period when the Mongols ruled China in the 14th century, and it included a spherical representation of the stars and a bronze armillary or zodiacal sphere.

Technological advances in the service of art

The craftsmanship which gave China such a far-reaching reputation was firmly rooted in practical technology. Improved high-temperature firing enabled potters to make superb porcelain in large quantities, while Chinese metalworkers copied decorative motifs and techniques from the Muslim west. In terms of technology and sheer volume of production, Chinese iron-workers led the medieval world, and they were also capable of casting steel as well as iron. Such technology enabled armourers to make superb blades and one-piece iron helmets, though Islamic armourers may have been the first to do this. When it came to textiles, Chinese weavers used new forms of spinning wheels and complex silk-reeling machines to cope with the great length of silk thread. Silk could also be waterproofed using an extract from the perilla mint plant.

Woodblock printing was so widespread that in the year 1005, the Imperial archives had around 10,000 printing blocks of official histories, commentaries and sacred texts. An inventor named Bi Sheng also produced a form of movable-type printing using individual Chinese characters made of baked clay, which were then set in soft waxy resin to set up a page. It could not develop much further, however, as there were so many different Chinese characters that Bi Sheng's system was impractical.

In 1234, however, the neighbouring Koreans took his idea one step further by making individual printing characters of metal. Other medieval Chinese inventions included gunpowder which was soon being used in flame-throwers, explosive grenades and rockets; the first bullet-shooting guns may, however, have been developed in the Middle East rather than China.

Alchemy and the effort to change one substance into another was taken very seriously and was a subject where Chinese ideas had a profound impact on several other medieval civilizations. But Chinese alchemists, unlike their Muslim contemporaries, never quite made the step from old-fashioned alchemy to the true science of chemistry. Another difference between Chinese and Middle Eastern alchemists was that the latter largely experimented with minerals, whereas Chinese alchemists largely concentrated on plants and, as a result, their work had a significant and lasting impact on medicine. Here medieval Chinese theories again had a visible influence on those of both India and the Middle East.

As with traditional forms of Asian medicine, Chinese doctors had what might now be called an holistic approach to sickness, whereby they strove to restore the 'balance' of all those influences believed to be working on an individual patient. This involved looking

Japanese sword-blades are justifiably regarded as being amongst the best ever made. The technology originally came from China, and some of the designs from Central Asia, but the finished product was purely Japanese. In this 16th century manuscript sword-grinders put the final edges to blades, just as they had done for centuries and would continue to do until modern times.

at the psychological, spiritual, physical and supposed magical influences which all had an effect on the patient. At the same time the Chinese had a complex and effective tradition of herbal medicine, which included, amongst many other things, the use of burweed to treat common colds.

INDIA, THE HOME OF ADVANCED MATHEMATICS

The roots of Indian scholarship, science and technology go back a long way and may have links with the ancient civilizations of the Middle East. Certainly the advanced study of astronomy characteristic of Hindu Indian civilization had much in common with the Babylonians who lived in what is now Iraq. The golden age of Indian science itself began at the end of the 5th century AD and led to an astonishing flowering of mathematics and geometry, achieving results in advance of those of ancient Greece and Rome. This in turn had a huge influence on similar studies in the medieval Islamic world.

History, meanwhile, was seen in terms of repetitive cycles rather than in terms of the modern concept of linear progress. This golden age is considered to have come to an end around 1200, perhaps because Indian scientific studies had been closely associated with Buddhism and the Buddhist influence went into steep decline around this time. Thereafter Indian science and secular, rather than religious, scholarship are said to have stagnated, but the capital cities of major states, such as the Cholas in southern India, remained centres of learning and medicine into the 14th century.

Astronomy had practical application when it came to religious festivals and predicting the sudden changes of India's monsoon climate. Mathematics underpinned India's remarkable achievements in architecture and engineering, yet the most remarkable form of applied science in Indian civilization was botany, closely linked to medicine and a field in which there was little or no stagnation. In fact the study and classification of plants continued throughout the medieval period and resulted in a system of scientific names for both species and sub-species.

Indian scholars also knew about the circulation of sap and took a very broad view of their subject, comparable to the modern concept of ecology. A belief in the 'dormant consciousness' of plant life also meant that

Indian scholars treated nature with greater respect than is usually found today.

Meanwhile, continuing detailed analysis of acids and alkalis contributed to India's already advanced metallurgy. Yet chemistry itself was regarded as the handmaiden of medicine and, like Indian botany and medicine itself, would have a huge impact on Islamic scholarship. The resulting knowledge also enabled Indian doctors to use metallic elements in medicines, in addition to traditional herbal remedies, long before this was attempted elsewhere.

Tropical diseases were, of course, common in India and the Indianized regions of southeast Asia, where the jungles were full of dangerous animals, insects and plants. This must have spurred the study of medicine which was known as Ayurveda or 'The Science of Life'.

As its name suggests, Ayurveda was a wide-ranging subject which dealt not only with symptoms and cures, but also with observation, research and even the 'transcendental intuition' of Rishis, or 'spiritually enlightened seers'.

Another feature which set Indian medicine apart from that of medieval Europe was an open-mindedness, elevating the pursuit of truth above all else. This in turn led to a liberal spirit, a willingness to learn from any source, and meant that the dissection of the dead was allowed for study. As a result the circulation of the blood was accepted, a vast knowledge of herbs and pharmaceutical drugs became available and ambitious surgery was successfully attempted. Even the concept of disease-causing microbes was considered, though it could not yet be proved.

Opposite: The ships which plied the eastern seas during the Middle Ages were sometimes very different from those seen in European waters. It was certainly true of this giant two-masted outrigger canoe on a late 8th century carving on a Buddhist temple at Borobodur in Java. Such vessels enabled the peoples of what are now Indonesia and Malaysia to move amongst the thousands of islands of south-east Asia.

Left: Some of the astonishing achievements of Indian technology remain a mystery to this day such as this amazing iron pillar made in the 3rd century BC. The way in which its fifty tons weight was transported from Topra to Delhi by Sultan Firuz Shah in the mid-14th century, and then re-erected, is better understood as the engineer's drawings still survive.

7 | LAW AND PUNISHMENT

MEDIVAL LAW AND PUNISHMENT OFTEN SOUND RUTHLESS AND CRUEL TO MODERN PEOPLE BUT THEY WERE IN FACT BASED ON CAREFULLY CONSIDERED PRINCIPLES. EVEN THE MUTILATION OF CONDEMNED CRIMINALS HAD ITS REASONS. IN A WORLD WHERE THE FAMILY WAS OFTEN A PERSON'S ONLY MEANS OF SUPPORT, IT WAS THOUGHT FAIRER TO INFLICT PAIN ON THE GUILTY THAN TO LOCK THEM AWAY, SINCE IMPRISONMENT COULD MEAN THAT THEIR INNOCENT FAMILY STARVED. SIMILARLY, PUBLIC SHAME WAS AN EFFECTIVE DETERRENT IN A SOCIETY WHERE EVERYONE KNEW THEIR NEIGHBOURS AND THERE WAS LITTLE CHANCE OF A LAW BREAKER MOVING TO ANOTHER TOWN OR VILLAGE, EVEN AFTER THEIR PUNISHMENT.

CONTROLLING A FAST-CHANGING WORLD

During the early medieval centuries there were wide variations in legal practices in different parts of western Christendom, reflecting the stronger Germanic influences in the north and a greater survival of the Roman legal system in the south. On top of such variations, there continued to be a separate system of religious or canon law for the Church which included virtually anyone who could read or write. Even as late as the 11th century some European countries did not have written laws and many still relied on memorized 'customary law'; where written laws did exist they tended to be little more than lists of punishments for specific crimes.

Although rulers 'made laws', these had to be based on what people regarded as natural justice, the customs of that people, precedence or what had gone before, and on Christian principles. The only really consistent law was the canon law which the Papacy had imposed on virtually every part of the Catholic Church and would soon attempt to impose on the secular authorities as well.

The importance of legal precedent meant that detailed records were being kept. This development led to a need for trained legal staff, ranging from qualified lawyers to humble scribes. Certain schools were recognized as producing the best lawyers. Here, students formed themselves into associations which came to be known as 'universities'. The most prestigious was at Bologna in Italy, although Paris was also important. All focused on Roman law, which included the Code of Justinian, the Romano-Byzantine Emperor from 527–565, dating from after the fall of the western Roman Empire. There was however, tension and sometimes hostility between the Church's canon lawyers and the university-trained secular lawyers.

Each country put a different emphasis on its various sources of law. In France, for example, Roman law was slightly more important than in England. Nevertheless customary law still underpinned the rights of the crown. During the 12th and early 13th centuries, however, the French legal system was overhauled using canon law as a structural pattern and Roman law as the ideal. The fact that agreements were now written down placed clear limitations on the power of the aristocracy and gave great influence to lawyers like Henry de Bracton in England (died 1268) who became the Crown's greatest allies in its struggle with the barons.

Despite these changes, archaic legal ideas survived even in the most advanced parts of 15th century Renaissance Italy, where a townsman was legally 'worth' two peasants, and an aristocratic Count was 'worth' no less than sixteen.

Hue and cry

Law enforcement became more standardized because almost everywhere it had to rely on the simplest methods of identifying and arresting criminals. In the 11th century, many barons and even ordinary knights still considered that they were free to fight their own private wars, bringing chaos to parts of southern France and Germany. Since rulers were generally too weak to stop these private wars, the Church stepped in with various Peace of God movements, which generally insisted that private wars could only be fought on particular days of the week. However, the Church still needed the help of the knightly elite to impose a Peace of God since only they had the power to stop other knights ignoring the law.

Discipline in even the best-organized medieval armies left a lot to be desired. In this manuscript painted in the mid-14th century, rioting soldiers loot a house in Paris.

Meanwhile, kings and senior barons tried to impose other regulations, specifying who could fight private wars, who could be attacked, when and where. Nevertheless, by the 12th and 13th centuries peace had been restored to most parts of western Europe, except for widespread 'official' wars between states or kings and barons.

Many members of the knightly class gave up the profession of arms in favour of more peaceful pursuits, yet their social position meant that they were still responsible for maintaining law and order in their own fiefs. There were no police, other than a few sergeants employed by various local author ities, and so the catching of criminals depended on raising a 'hue and cry'. This meant that all free men had to help in finding and arresting a suspect. In many ways this was like the 'posse' summoned by a sheriff in the days of the American Wild West.

Methods in France were reasonably typical of the way less immediate crimes were dealt with. Here, in the 12th century, someone who wanted to bring a legal case first made a 'supplication' to the appropriate authorities. An official enquiry followed, often with an appeal by the accused. Written documents had to be produced by the litigants, authenticated by the seal of an authorized person.

In southern areas where Roman law survived largely intact, local notaries validated such documents. As the use of notaries became ever more widespread, anyone who wanted to secure his rights in any matter had to pay a scribe to write the necessary papers, a notary to validate them and a lawyer to plead his case in court. This resulted in an expanding and often well-paid legal profession. The cost of going to law had always been high – and risky – so ordinary people did what they could to settle their own disputes.

Throughout the medieval period the aristocratic elite often set a very bad example and only the king was strong enough to curb them. Justice was uneven, but the imposition of law and order could be even more arbitrary. Foreigners or strangers were so feared that, in some places, travellers were not permitted to lodge outside a walled town unless their host accepted personal responsibility for their good behaviour. Watchmen at city gates were usually ordered to detain strangers, since it was common for bands of robbers to enter a town in disguise then emerge to plunder the market fair. As a result, suburbs outside a city wall tended to be lawless places where the authorities had little jurisdiction.

Trials could be a strange mixture of primitive and modern ideas. Ordinary justice was dispensed by the local lord or his steward. In

England there were courts of law at manor, 'hundred' and shire levels in ascending order, while Royal courts normally only dealt with matters affecting the king or senior barons. Originally law courts were held in the open air, and even in the 14th century local village courts could still take place in the church porch. In the early days, juries of local free men were merely witnesses to a fair trial, though were eventually asked to decide on suitable punishment.

The accused might also bring a certain number of witnesses to court, depending on the seriousness of the accusation, to support his good character. Or the accused might have to undergo an ordeal where God was expected to show his guilt or innocence. This could entail carrying a heated bar over a certain distance then having the hand bandaged for a specified time. If the hand had healed, then the person was innocent; if not, he was guilty. This was probably effective as long as those involved believed in it, in which case a guilty conscience probably showed in an accused person's behaviour.

Trial by combat

Trial by ordeal died out in England in the 13th century, but the idea of trial by combat survived much longer, particularly in disputes between members of the aristocracy.

Falling foul of the law tended to be a painful and humiliating business in the medieval period. Here, in a 15th century French manuscript illustration, prisoners are interrogated by a judge while their statements are carefully written down by his clerk.

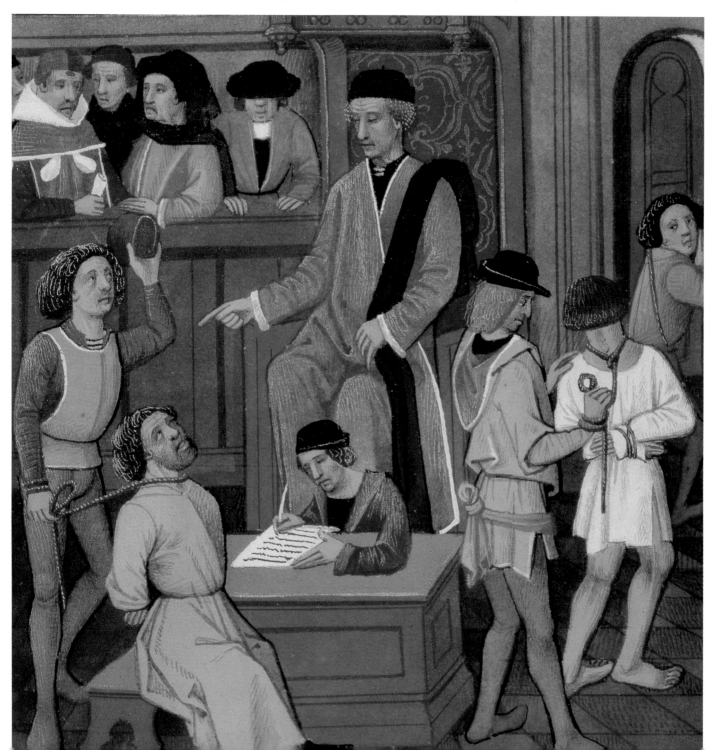

Right: Another widespread vice in medieval Europe was drunkenness. Here men dressed as middle-class merchants keep the cellarman busy, though the one on the far right has already drunk far too much. The picture comes from a late 14th century moral treatise.

Below: Parading those convicted of adultery naked through the streets of town, as illustrated in the 13th century Law Book of the French town of Agen. Public shame was one of the most powerful forms of punishment in medieval society where communities were normally so small that everyone knew their neighbours.

For ordinary people, trial by combat could involve the opposing litigants themselves or, in the case of those unable to fight, it might be between hired champions often recruited from disgraced soldiers or professional thugs. On the other hand senior church dignitaries also sometimes had 'champions' to defend their legal rights; one of the pickaxes used in trials by combat appears on the effigy of Robert Wyvil (c.1375), the Bishop of Salisbury's champion, in Salisbury Cathedral.

The weapons involved were painful, but non-lethal; one person either won outright, or the accused demonstrated his innocence by resisting until sunset. In England the system of Circuit Judges, which is still used today, was introduced. These judges were appointed by the Crown and toured the country, dealing with the more important cases in regional Assize Courts with a trial normally conducted in front of a jury.

By the end of the medieval period, a slightly different legal system had developed in France. As in England, serious crimes initially went before a local baronial lord or his representative. Firstly the plaintiff lodged a plea that the accused should be brought to justice and powerful people could insist on a higher court. If a crime involved the death penalty, it was considered 'high justice' and the accused had to

attend – whoever he was. Written testimony remained a vital part of the trial process in southern regions where Roman law survived, and written legal codes or the records of previous cases seem to have had an almost mystical power over an illiterate population. Even at village level, a priest was expected to write down all civil or legal contracts and, by the 11th century, every

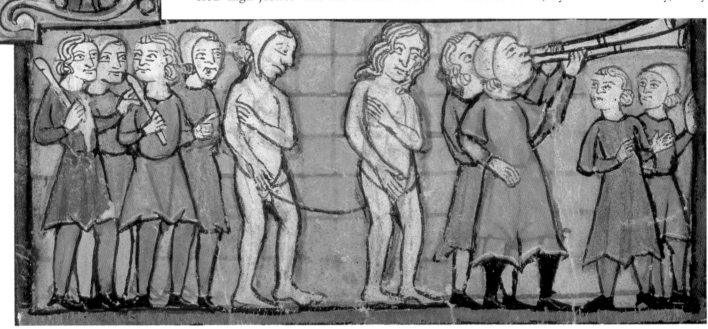

member of the aristocratic elite needed a legal expert or 'juris peritus' in his household. As has been mentioned, these men soon had enormous influence.

The distinction between civil and criminal law was not as clear as it would later become, but crimes against the rules which governed business, trade and the quality of workmanship were tried by those most directly involved. Thus a city judged citizens who broke its own laws, and market author

the opportunity of swearing to leave the country, which in England meant taking the first available boat from the nearest port – whatever its destination.

Punishment in medieval courts ranged from the barbaric to the lenient. In England, murder was punished by hanging or, in the most vicious cases, by drawing and quartering. Treason against the king remained the most serious crime, but theft of anything above the value of a shilling (roughly the

Capital punishment was imposed for a great many crimes in medieval Europe, but it was almost more important that such punishments should be done in public so that the whole community could see that justice was done. Here, in a late 13th century manuscript, King Louis of France teaches his children, apparently showing them what happened to those who broke the law.

ities or guilds tried those who broke trading regulations; the trials themselves mirroring those of the king's or Assize Courts. Meanwhile the Church also tried and punished its own people in ecclesiastical courts. Since the punishments imposed here tended to be less severe than those meted out by secular courts, anyone with the slightest claim to being a 'clerk' demanded trial by the Church rather than the state.

The Church also provided sanctuary for those pursued by secular legal authorities. Fugitives were, for example, immune from arrest for 40 days as long as they stayed inside a church building. After that the accused might be starved into submission or be given

equivalent of 12 days' work for the average workman) was also punishable by death. Lesser thefts could lead to the thief's hand being cut off. Cheating in business or selling inferior goods in the guise of better quality items led to exposure in the stocks.

Prison was used for minor offences, and with the ducking stool served to punish women who gossiped about their neighbours. The punishments imposed by guilds on their own members could be quite devastating. One case in 15th century England saw a miner, who had stolen lead from his fellow miners, having his tools and workshop burned before his eyes. He was then banned from ever working as a miner again.

BYZANTINE LAW

Byzantine law was based on Roman law as formulated and rewritten in Greek for the Emperor Justinian in the 6th century, but it was strongly influenced by Christian principles. The period from the 9th to 12th centuries also saw attempts to make existing legal codes more workable. As a result, many legal treatises were written at about this time, but it was not until the 11th century that law was taught to anyone other than the Corporation of Notaries or professional lawyers. In 1054, a third university was estab-lished in Constantinople to teach law to aspiring government officials. One of the last Byzantine legal codes, dating from the 14th century, continued to be used by the Christian Balkan population of the Ottoman Turkish Empire since the Ottoman state had separate legal systems for each of its disparate religious communities.

Law enforcement in the Byzantine Empire was relatively straightforward, though not always effective. Each city had an eparch, or prefect, who controlled trade and the quality

of goods, supervised guilds and dealt with breaches of commercial law. He was assisted by a symponos, or assessor, responsible for law and order, supported by troops from the local garrison, as well as a logothete in charge of law courts, and numerous junior assistants. Since the eparchs controlled the judiciary, they were very influential figures, but legal affairs were less clear-cut where the rural population was concerned. Here a sort of rural police force tried, with mixed success, to control banditry.

Trials and corruption

Byzantine trials also owed a great deal to Rome and included the right of appeal to other courts, with the Emperor as the final arbiter. As in western Europe, there was a clear distinction between secular and religious courts, but following the Byzantine recapture of Constantinople from the Latin Crusaders in 1260, however, the distinction became increasingly blurred and both systems were soon replaced by a single structure of regional courts.

Even so the Byzantine legal system had become so corrupt by the end of the 13th century that the Emperor Andronicus II created, in 1296, a completely new High Court; yet even this failed to solve the problem. Punishment seemed extremely cruel and included cutting off noses, tongues or limbs. However, the Byzantines, like many medieval civilizations, regarded torture and mutilation as more humane than death or destitution resulting from fines or imprisonment, probably because physical punishment only hurt the condemned offender, whereas imprisonment or financial penalties also hurt his innocent dependants.

As with most other aspects of Byzantine civilization, Byzantine law had a huge influence on its Christian neighbours. The Armenians, however, had their own legal system based on the edicts of the earliest Church Councils, while the Georgian legal system had a variety of roots, ranging from early Church Councils and the Byzantine Empire to local customary law and the influence of several passing conquerors. Rates of compensation for injury or murder were assessed in silver coins, yet in reality the lower social orders were largely at the mercy of the military and feudal elite. The biggest and clearest Byzantine legal impact was on the Slavs to the west and north, many of whom translated Byzantine legal texts for their own use.

The ruins of the 13th–14th century Despot's Palace at Mistras are on the side of a mountain, beneath the fortress but above the medieval town of Mistras which hugs the slope below. The whole complex formed the capital of this isolated southern outpost of the fragmented late medieval Byzantine Empire, and overlooked the plain of Sparta in southern Greece.

The Russian truth

The basis of Russian law was an amalgamation of tribal custom and Byzantine influence, modified by medieval Russia's unusual abhorrence of the cruel punishments found elsewhere. Its foundation was the Russkaya Pravda or 'Russian Truth', written for Yaroslav the Wise, ruler of Kiev from 1019 to 1054. One of its most notable features was the high degree of legal rights given to women as compared to Romano-Byzantine law, and its declaration that all free men had an equal 'bloodwite', or compensation value, in case of murder or injury.

As the years passed, however, this blood-price soon varied according to social status. During the later medieval centuries, Mongol power across Russia diminished, to be replaced by domination from Moscow and characterized by a steady growth in legal codes and institutions during the 15th century. This was to unify laws which had developed regional variations under the fragmented Russian principalities of the 12th to 14th centuries.

Law enforcement in the vast and sparsely populated principalities of Russia was, naturally enough, very different from that seen in the urbanized Byzantine Empire. It also seems to have included an element of mercy which was characteristic of medieval Russia as a whole. For example, discovery of a theft would be announced publicly, after which the thief would have three days in which to return the stolen goods. If the goods had already passed to a third party, he or she was similarly expected to return them and then to help identify the thief. In fact, the whole community was expected to take part in the pursuit of thieves or bandits, and failure to do so led to possible charges of complicity.

In its original or primitive form, Russian law only expected the suspect and his accuser to take part in any trial. There was as yet no mention of judges, though the confrontation took place in front of local people, who made a final decision on guilt or innocence. Later, Russian legal codes did include judges, formal trials and more detailed forms of law. Under the Novgorod Code, for example, the city's militia commander was in charge of commercial cases, probably because he and his men acted as a police force.

Elsewhere, courts could be supervised by local government officials, senior churchmen or representatives of local princes. In all cases, unruly supporters or partisans of accused and accuser were specifically banned from the courtroom, where all litigants had to kiss the Christian cross as a sign of their willingness to tell the truth. Witnesses were called, but did not testify to the facts of the case, only to the reputation of those involved. Three kinds of evidence were accepted: written, oral and by ordeal. A surviving legal code from Pskov listed several forms of ordeal, ranging from kissing the cross, which could be highly effective in such a deeply religious society, to fighting a duel.

The harsh physical punishments typical of Byzantine law were replaced by fines and/or religious penances. Even the right of blood vengeance, which was initially permitted to the family of a murdered man, was substituted by financial compensation during the 11th century.

THE LAW OF ALLAH

Ever since the mid-7th century, there had been tension at the heart of Islamic civilization between the ideal of a society built on Divine Law and the efforts of mortal men to build such a society. As a result there was little argument about what was wanted, but plenty of disagreement about how to put Muslim law into practice. The law itself was the Sharia, as written in the Koran and clarified by Hadith, or the traditional saying of the Prophet Muhammad (c.570–632). Everything attempted to build directly upon the foundation of Sharia.

Another characteristic of Islamic society was that Muslim Law did not recognize corporate bodies, but only accepted the rights of the individual, even in family law. This meant that everyone, male, female, young or old, was in the final analysis, equal

The arrival of the Seljuq Turks in the mid-11th century began a process of fundamental but contentious change as they started to separate spiritual and temporal powers. The new element which the Turks, and subsequently the Mongols, introduced was the Yasa, or Central Asian customary law, which, at first, only affected the ruling and military elites, while the bulk of the Arab or Persian population still lived under Sharia law. Like the Sharia, however, the Turco-Mongol Yasa was regarded as being above the ruler, who was expected to enforce its provisions.

The Turks also conquered a large part of the Byzantine Empire following their victory

Abu Zaid tricks the governor of a city, in comic story telling how a clever rogue fools the rich and powerful, painted by al-Wasiti in 1237.

at Manzikert in 1071. Here they adopted a tolerant approach, which tried to accommodate existing legal systems. This approach was similarly taken by the Ottoman Turks at the end of the Middle Ages as their vast empire incorporated different legal codes for each of the main religious groups.

Even where the dominant Muslim population was concerned, the Ottoman state recognized two separate legal structures: the religious Sharia and the secular Kanun. The latter arose from Sultan Mehmet II's (1451–1481) efforts to unify the secular laws of his huge realm. It also made official an earlier Seljuk idea that the Sultan was secular co-ruler, with the Caliph as 'religious ruler'. As a result, the Ottoman Sultan's secular laws covered administration, trade, land holding and taxation, while the Caliph retained authority over religious matters and moral behaviour.

Two pillars of justice

Medieval Islamic civilization had a remarkably uniform legal structure built upon two pillars: the 'qadi', or judge, with his staff of the 'judgement system', and various enforcement authorities. Whereas the 'judgement system' hardly changed over the centuries, the enforcement agencies changed according to the political climate at the time.

In most of the larger or more formally organized states there was at least one qadi for each city or region, plus a qadi for the army. Each belonged to one of four recognized schools of law and had studied in a 'madrasah', or religious college. The qadi's independence from local political pressure

was supposedly guaranteed by a regular salary from the central government. The head of the system was the Grand Qadi, who had to be a man of recognized knowledge, piety and energy. Though paid by the state,

Right: Instead of a feast in the desert or countryside, this illustration by al-Wasiti shows a party in full swing in a 'winehouse'. Upstairs men drink in comfort while downstairs a musician entertains them on an Oud, the ancestor of the lute. Over on the right a servant treads the already half fermented grapes to make nabid, a sweet and slightly alcoholic wine still made in the villages of Syria and Jordan.

he also had authority over the government's actions and could usually rely on popular support when criticizing irreligious or excessive behaviour on the part of the ruler himself. The authority of Sharia law was, in fact, so strong that it remained notably free of corruption.

Meanwhile the 'muhtasib' and his staff had a foot in both law enforcement and 'judgement'. They supervised markets, guilds, business life and improper behaviour in a public place, yet their authority was far less than that of the qadi. Whereas the muhtasib was an almost permanent feature of Islamic cities, other law enforcement agencies changed over the years. In 12th century Syria, for example, every urban quarter, tribal community and village had its own 'rais', or 'head'. They could

be powerful figures, who not only defended the interests of their own people, but also were held responsible for any serious or persistent breaches of law and order. In fact the rais could be an amalgamation of sheriff, militia commander, mayor and leader of local merchants. The Ahdath was an urban militia which was also headed by a rais who tried to maintain law and order, as well as defending the city from predatory neighbours.

Another law officer was the Shihna, originally simply a Seljuk Turkish military governor who, by the 12th century, had evolved

into a local police chief commanding the garrison and Shurta. The Shurta first appeared as an elite bodyguard, but then became a mixture of local police, firemen and troops.

Law enforcement in the Ottoman Empire

A development of the basic system of Islamic law continued under the Ottoman Empire (c.1299–1922). Although all were subject to the Sultan's law, or Kanun, each millet or religious group was also governed according to its own laws. Where Muslims were concerned, this involved the qadis who interpreted Sharia law and pronounced judgements. In practical terms, the qadi's employees investigated criminal cases, arrested and interrogated suspects, summoned witnesses and punished the guilty after the qadi had made his final judgement.

They were also helped by the local Sancak Bey, or military governor, but he was often away on campaign, so it was the local Subasi, or police chief, who played a more important role in finding and catching suspects. The Subasi also had authority to arrest suspects on his own initiative, though not to try them. Judgement had to be carried out in the presence of local witnesses to ensure fairness, while the trials themselves relied on the testimony of witnesses, both to the litigant's character and the facts of the case.

The legal profession developed early in Islamic history. At its heart were the Ulema, recognized religious scholars qualified to interpret Sharia law in practical terms. They advised the qadis, who were also recruited

Left: Other pictures in the stories by al-Hariri illustrate everyday life in perhaps gruesome detail. Here, for example, a man slaughters a camel for a feast, while below two men cook the meat over a fire and a woman carries stew to guests out of the picture. Strict Islamic dietary laws dictated that an animal's throat had to be cut before it could be eaten.

from their ranks. The science of Fiqh, or
jurisprudence, was studied at a madrasah or
religious college. Fatwas were pronounce-
ments on the basis of Sharia law, while those
qualified to serve as legal consultants were
called Faqihs or Muftis, with at least one in
every town or district. A less common institution was the Dar al-'Adl, or Palace of Justice,
staffed by Mazalim, or those knowledgeable
in law, whose task was to control abuses of
power and serve as a Supreme Court.

Punishment and compensation

Different schools of Sharia demanded different degrees of evidence before a guilty verdict
was passed; a condemned person had to be of
sound mind, or he was not considered
responsible for his actions. The punishments
accepted by Islamic Sharia law were varied
and occasionally ruthless. The concept of
compensation rather than vengeance was central to Sharia law, although the concept of 'an
eye for an eye' remained and murder was punishable by death or by a hefty fine.

Adultery was punished by stoning to
death, but could only be proved if there were
four eyewitnesses, while persistent theft
could result in the amputation of part of the

hand. Physical mutilation was, in fact, less
frequent than in the Byzantine Empire.
Fornication was punishable by 100 lashes
and banishment for a year; drunkenness in a
public place by 80 lashes and all such punishments had to be carried out in public to
show that justice was being done and to
ensure that nothing further was inflicted.

One of the most important Hadiths, or
sayings, of the Prophet Muhammad stated:
'Let there be neither injury nor vengeance for
that injury', and this, with the Koranic verses
which advocated mercy, ensured that the
maximum penalty was usually exacted only
in serious cases.

The ancient Persian tradition that a ruler
should do all in his power to win loyalty
probably accounted for a remarkable chapter
in a book of advice written by a Persian ruler
for his son in 1082. In it, Kai Ka'us Ibn
Iskandar wrote that trivial offences should
not be punished and forgiveness should be
offered wherever possible. Nevertheless the
Turks introduced other punishments based
upon Central Asian traditions, but these
applied only to political crimes by the political elite. Nevertheless they included stran-
gling, hanging or, in the worst cases of
treason, skinning alive.

LAW IN A
BUREAUCRATIC EMPIRE

Chinese law was deeply conservative and legal codes tended to repeat what went before whilst adding an increasing corpus of case law. It was built upon 'lu' or legal statutes, 'ling' or imperial ordinances, and 'li' or 'supplementary' provisions dealing with legal details. Each was an expression of the government's will, not of the people's rights.

In fact the law was not there to defend individual rights or restrain abuse of power; it was merely a system for coping with crime and dereliction of duty by government officials. Legal regulations were, however, remarkably detailed in terms of daily life, agricultural obligations and the infliction of proper punishments. In contrast to most other cultures, where equality before the law was at least theoretically recognized, Chinese law offered preferential treatment for those of higher rank.

Korean law was in several respects virtually identical to Chinese, where the National Code of 1471 has been described as more Confucian than Chinese law itself. China also provided a model for the imperial edicts of early medieval Japan. Here, however, the increasingly powerful police commissioners built up their own body of case law and, by the 11th century, they were largely ignoring the old imperial edicts. The situation changed yet again during the civil wars of the 12th century. These years saw each feudal clan develop its own 'house laws' based upon ancient Japanese patriarchal values. These 'house laws' involved the internal affairs of the clan, rather than deep legal principles. Nevertheless 'house laws' themselves evolved into the Kamakura Code, which dominated the later medieval feudal age.

Genghis Khan and the Yasa

Another legal system developed amongst the Turco-Mongol nomads of Central Asia. This was the Yasa, meaning decree, law or order, which was backed up by Yusun or tribal custom. Each 'khan' or ruler supposedly had his own Yasa which was written down by scribes and copies sent to subordinate rulers.

No complete version of Genghis Khan's famous Great Yasa survives, but recent evidence suggests that Genghis Khan did not formulate a Yasa at the start of his reign and may, in reality, never have done. The laws and precepts used by Genghis Khan could simply have been developments of existing Mongol customary law which his successor Ogedai may have then had collected and written down as Genghis Khan's Great Yasa. Genghis Khan's sayings or maxims, known as biligs, were similarly treasured.

Meanwhile the chief judges of the Mongol Empire wrote down their decisions in a 'blue book' of legal cases, which then became binding as Khan's Great Yasa and it supposedly formed the basis of the Yarghu-nama, or legal code, of the Muslim Mongol Il-Khan rulers of Iran and Iraq. The Mongol Yuan dynasty of China similarly based their laws upon the supposed Great Yasa, though in reality there were several separate codes operating in Mongol China, one for each ethnic group.

Surprisingly little is known about how laws were enforced in medieval China. The officials who ran the legal system came through the usual bureaucratic examination system, but they lacked legal training. They did, however, rely on persuasion and coercion to maintain law and order, assisted by ordinary citizens who were supposed to practise archery during the second and third months of the year and check their weapons during the ninth month.

Chinese laws covered a multitude of sins, ranging from making anti-government statements and using parts of the road reserved for members of the imperial retinue, to forging documents and taking bribes, while crime sounded disturbingly modern. It was highly organized, with criminal associations that carried out sophisticated confidence tricks and had burglary down to a fine art. The Ming dynasty, which expelled the Mongols in the 14th century, attempted to return to traditional legal systems, but they also established a highly efficient secret police system.

Early medieval Korean government apparatus consisted of six ministries, one of which was called the Board of Punishments, which dealt with laws and litigation. The law itself was administered by five Circuit Provinces and two militarized Border Regions. There was also an increased reliance on a Chinese style examination structure, emphasizing literary skills, and lower status exams dealing with subjects such as statute law.

During the earlier unified period of Japanese history a government department known as the Police Commission had evolved

126

Right: Buddhist art often portrayed heaven and hell in terms of the everyday world where the artist lived. Here a Chinese artist of the T'ang Period shows the king of hell as a judge, and the dead souls as prisoners with heavy wooden blocks fastened around their necks.

Below left: A demonic feudal lord dispenses ruthless justice with apparent relish in a 13th century Japanese painting. In reality there seems to have been a fairer system of justice in Japan around this time than there had been for many years.

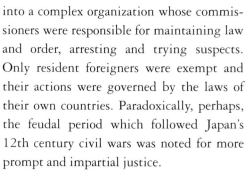

into a complex organization whose commissioners were responsible for maintaining law and order, arresting and trying suspects. Only resident foreigners were exempt and their actions were governed by the laws of their own countries. Paradoxically, perhaps, the feudal period which followed Japan's 12th century civil wars was noted for more prompt and impartial justice.

The legal system of the Mongol empire was well organized. Here the Great Khan was assisted by a Yarghuchi, or chief judge, responsible for seeing that the Yasa or legal code was obeyed. Most of his duties seem to have concerned robbery, fraud and the fair distribution amongst the dominant Mongol tribes of spoils of war, including conquered people.

Punishment according to rank

Criminal trials in China sometimes seem to have been ruthless affairs. An accused person was usually manacled, interrogated, and often flogged. The fact that a confession was essential before a case could be proved meant that torture was also commonplace. Another distinctive feature of Chinese trials was that there was invariably a guilty verdict because, if the accused was found innocent, his accuser would be punished for making a false accusation. Trials were usually carried out by a county magistrate, who was, in effect, detective, judge and jury.

On the other hand condemned criminals might escape punishment altogether, as the Emperor often announced amnesties to celebrate some auspicious occasion. The Japanese trial system owed something to the Chinese example and in the later feudal period these were normally carried out by the 'Bakufu' or military authority. Most of the procedure was written down and consequently the households of feudal leaders had to include a staff of skilled clerks as well as skilled warriors.

Punishment in China tended to be harsh. Execution could be carried out by cutting the body in half at the waist and mutilation was common. In extreme cases, the guilty person's entire family would be punished, though persons of higher rank generally suffered lesser punishments, perhaps merely losing certain privileges. The Mongols introduced the concept of 'slow death', but retained the principle of different punishments for different ranks. In Japan, the death penalty had theoretically been abolished as a concession to Buddhist feelings, though various forms of cruel mutilation remained.

PUNISHMENT THROUGH MANY LIVES

The basis of Indian law was the Hindu Dharma Sutra, or manuals on human conduct, dating from the 6th to 2nd centuries BC. These were later refined and interpreted in the *Dharma Shastras*, which were in verse form, though codification of the law continued well into the medieval period. Legal texts were written by the brahmin caste (the elite group in society) and reflected their point of view, which was primarily concerned with the 'correct way of doing things' in all aspects of life.

Meanwhile the legal systems of the Indianized states of south-east Asia were firmly based upon those of India itself. In fact, Indian 'dharma' or laws proved remarkably compatible with the existing customary law in those states and by the 11th and 12th centuries, the south-east Asian ruling elite had accepted and implemented a system based on detailed knowledge of the concepts, methods and terminology of Indian law.

It is even possible that the Khmer of Cambodia and the Cham of southern Vietnam did not have their own legal codes,

but relied on Indian legal texts. The Vietnamese of the north were, meanwhile, under the Chinese rather than the Indian legal influence.

The laws of Thailand appear to have been based on Khmer practice and surviving 14th century Thai codes divided the legal system into separate sections, dealing with such things as civil contracts and marriage laws. The first known laws from Burma date from the late 12th and early 13th centuries and show strong Sri Lankan Buddhist religious and cultural influence. Buddhism and its legal systems survived in Burma, but in the later Middle Ages in Malaya, the medieval Hindu or Buddhist states largely converted to Islam. Nevertheless earlier characteristics remained, including debt slavery for those unable to pay legal fines, which was strictly contrary to Muslim Sharia law.

Most foreign visitors described medieval India as a law-abiding civilization, but Indian sources paint a different picture. Urban crime and rural banditry were a serious problem and some groups of robbers or bandits even formed themselves into 'castes' with their own customary laws, including murder as a ritual duty. In the face of such dedicated law breaking, some Indian states had special officers, called Duhsadha-sadhanika, to pursue and arrest bandits. Those in charge of the urban forces of law often had a large staff of administrators, police, informers and even secret agents comparable to modern undercover detectives.

As all legal transactions were recorded in writing, the administration of law in India involved a large body of clerks. Beneath the king, the most important legal figure was the Pradvivaka, or chief legal advisor, who headed the system and was himself sometimes a judge. Magistrates were recruited from learned and religious people, presumably of brahmins, and could suffer extreme punishments if they were found to be corrupt or prejudiced.

Lawyers and trials

A class of professional lawyers did not, however, appear until the later medieval period. The majority of the population seem to have been barred from acting as witnesses, women and those with criminal records being excluded, along with members of lower castes in any cases brought against higher castes. Trial by ordeal was used; one example involved touching a heated ploughshare with the tongue to see if the accused developed blisters, based on the belief that a guilty conscience made a person's mouth dry by restricting the flow of saliva.

The little that is known of trials in southeast Asia indicates that a plaintiff could file a complaint before the court where a 'reciter of the *Dharma Shastra*' quoted a relevant Sanskrit legal text. There was also considerable use of torture and trial by ordeal.

Punishment in Indian law was based on ancient principles, above all the concept of blood-price, religious penance and financial fines. Imprisonment seems to have been rare. It was also widely believed that if a guilty person escaped punishment in this life, he or she would suffer in future incarnations. Capital punishments were varied and often intentionally cruel as a deterrent to others. Perhaps the most notable feature of punishment in India and the Indianized states was the more exacting punishment imposed on those of great rank as it was believed that the higher castes should lead by example. The most common form of execution remained impalement while being trampled to death by elephants and was reserved for particularly serious offences.

Opposite: The brothers Sunda and Upasunda fight over the female spirit Tilottama in an episode from the Mahabharata Hindu religious epic.

Below: The story of the Jain monk Kalaka, in a manuscript from Gujarat. Jains abhorred the killing of any creature, often sweeping the road in front themselves to avoid standing on tiny insects.

8 | WARFARE AND THE ARMY

HISTORY SHOWS THAT IN MANY PARTS OF THE WORLD, WARS WERE MORE FREQUENT DURING THE MEDIEVAL PERIOD THAN IN ANY OTHER ERA. YET MOST OF THESE WARS WERE SMALL-SCALE AFFAIRS, USUALLY INVOLVING ONLY THE RULING ELITE, A FEW PROFESSIONAL SOLDIERS AND THOSE UNFORTUNATE TO BE DIRECTLY IN THE PATH OF FIGHTING ARMIES. CASUALTIES WERE RELATIVELY LOW, WHILE SLOW SIEGES OR BRIEF RAIDS WERE MORE COMMON THAN GREAT BATTLES. MOST MEDIEVAL WARFARE WAS REALLY ONLY A BRUTAL FORM OF POLITICS, RATHER THAN THE DEVAS-TATIING CLASH OF NATIONS SEEN TODAY. THERE WERE EXCEPTIONS, SUCH AS THE MONGOLS, WHO SLAUGHTERED HUGE NUMBERS OF PEOPLE.

WAR-TORN WESTERN EUROPE

Most medieval western European armies were made up of knights, squires who would fight in an emergency, cavalry sergeants, who were professional but non-knightly soldiers, infantry sergeants, such as elite crossbowmen, and 'levies' whose standards of training varied enormously. Nevertheless the infantry remained vital, particularly in urbanized Italy and 14th century England, whose famous longbowmen won the battle of Crécy in 1346 and Poitiers in 1356.

During the 11th and 12th centuries, the knights changed from being professional cavalry soldiers to become members of a new military aristocracy. In an emergency, a leader could still 'knight' as many squires or merchants as he could afford to equip.

There was plenty of variation in medieval European armies. When the Pope proclaimed the First Crusade which captured Jerusalem in 1099, for example, he probably did not expect such huge numbers of knights and ordinary people to 'take the Cross'. One aspect of Crusading warfare was the Military Orders, whereby knights who wanted to lead a religious life but also wanted to fight, could join a particular order such as the Templars, Hospitallers or Teutonic Knights. They became the shock troops of the Crusades and were so feared that they were usually killed rather than being taken prisoner.

These Military Orders attracted large numbers of ordinary knights, who then became 'brother-knights', whilst volunteers who were not knights served as sergeants or as non-military servants. Other variations on the basic form of medieval European army were found in Scandinavia which was old-fashioned, the Iberia peninsula which was strongly influenced by Islamic warfare, Italy which was more urbanized than elsewhere,

and in Hungary where the ideal of recruiting troops from as wide a selection as possible reflected eastern ideas.

Military recruitment also changed in the later medieval period. In Italy, wealthy cities were usually run by rich merchants, who preferred to hire mercenaries rather than rely on local levies. As a result, mercenary leaders soon started recruiting their own knights, squires and infantrymen to make a ready-made army. One of the most famous was the White Company led by the English knight John Hawkwood (c.1320–1395), which fought for Florence in the 14th century.

In England and France a similar system developed, though under stricter government control and, by the 15th century, most soldiers were professionals. Archaeological excavations and descriptions of battles in medieval literature show that the most common injuries were to arms, legs and head, as the body was largely protected by armour and shield. Knights, however, tried to avoid killing each other as it was more profitable to capture a fellow knight for ransom, or to take his expensive war-horse, than it was to risk a blood-feud with his family.

New ideas in arms and armour

Arms and armour changed a great deal between the 11th and 15th centuries. Initially, mail hauberks, wooden shields and segmented iron helmets were virtually the only form of protection, with sword and spear for cavalry, axes, javelins and bows for foot soldiers. The 12th century, however, saw several new forms of equipment being adopted from the Muslims, while the Mongol invasions of the 13th century stimulated even more experimentation.

Opposite: One of two small and very damaged pieces of a late 11th century manuscript which was probably made in France or Norman southern Italy. It is probably part of a Biblical scene, showing an army blessed by God marching off to meet a shipload of Saracen or Byzantine invaders, not shown here, who are led by a dark-skinned African. The only man to have full armour is the commander on the left, which was probably quite normal at this early date.

As a result, by the start of the 14th century the mace, broad dagger, quilted soft armour, semi-rigid coat-of-plates, bascinet and brimmed 'war-hat' helmets, movable visor, separate mail coif and aventail attached to the rim of a helmet, decorative surcoat, separate armours for arms and legs, and horse-armour were in widespread use. The infantryman's longbow had also been widely used in England, Italy and parts of Scandinavia, but practically everywhere except in England simple hand-bows were now replaced by more powerful, albeit slower, crossbows. The best 15th century plate armour was made in Italy and later in Germany, with both countries exporting to Europe and beyond.

Military training included hunting, which polished a knight's riding skills, trained him to use cover, understand the lie of the land and to co-operate with other huntsmen. But, above all, training focused on the use of weapons on horseback and on fighting in a close-packed, highly disciplined cavalry formation called a 'conrois'.

Above: The longbow and the crossbow were in many ways rivals from the late 11th to 15th centuries, both illustrated in this early 14th century English manuscript. Whereas the longbow needed considerable strength and life-long practice to use effectively, a man could be trained to use the crossbow within a few months or even weeks.

Right: The Crusaders introduced some horrific ideas to Middle Eastern warfare. In this manuscript, made in Paris in 1229, they toss the heads of dead Turkish soldiers into the fortified city of Nicea in an effort to undermine the morale of the Turkish garrison.

Flanking attacks and tactical reserves were used, but not to any great degree until the later medieval period. The conrois remained the knightly cavalry's main offensive tactic, whereas the infantry largely relied on a close-packed shield-wall to resist a cavalry charge.

The cavalry conrois was the tank of medieval warfare and only the most disciplined enemy could resist if it hit its target. Seated on tall saddles with raised front and back, the knights were very difficult to topple from their horses. Even so, good infantry could fight off heavy cavalry, as the Italian Lombard League did when they defeated the German Emperor Frederick in 1176.

Disciplined urban infantry in 13th and 14th century Italy used pikes as a first line of defence, supported by crossbowmen, with cavalry ready to deliver counter-charges. This was virtually identical to the tactics of the pre-Turkish armies of the Middle East. In the 15th century, however, the Italians developed a remarkable system of battlefield co-operation between light infantry and heavy cavalry, usually operating from strongly fortified encampment. New weapons such as steel crossbows, cannon and hand-guns had an impact but in reality the technology of armour kept pace with the technology of weapons right through the 15th century.

Stone walls and wooden walls

Sieges were more important than any other aspects of medieval warfare, and the art of fortification advanced dramatically with various new types of castle appearing in the 11th century. These were very different to the Roman style of fort used throughout the early Middle Ages. During the 12th and 13th centuries, larger and more numerous towers were added to curtain walls to act as firing points for new stone-throwing trebuchets, introduced from the Middle East.

Like their Muslim foes, the Crusaders built some remarkably large and complex fortifications. Siege machines also became more powerful. Roman types of siege-

engines continued to be used and the man, or often woman, powered beam-sling mangonel was introduced from China even before the idea of putting a large counterweight on one end of the beam appeared in the Middle East. In fact, siege and counter-siege, such as the French king Philip Augustus' capture of the English-held castle of Chateau Gaillard in 1204, involved the most technologically advanced aspects of medieval warfare.

The first thing defending forces did if enemies came near was to make sure the castle had enough food, water, wine, and military supplies. Then inflammable build-

Medieval siege warfare was a mixture of hard work and quite advanced technology. In this 14th century French manuscript miners cut away at the base of an enemy's wall while the defenders try to smash their protective wooden 'shed on wheels' with rocks or burn it with flaming torches.

133

Naval warfare

There was very little real naval warfare during the early Middle Ages, though ships were vital for transporting supplies in many areas. The most powerful European maritime powers were in the Mediterranean, in particular the Italian merchant republics of Venice and Genoa. This was partly because of their bigger ships and wealth, but mostly because Italian mariners were by far the most effective in naval warfare.

Medieval naval warfare did not, however, rely on the ship-smashing rams seen in Greek and Roman times. The ram had been replaced by a beak, raised above the waterline to serve as a boarding device. Naval fights usually started by archers attempting to wound enemy oarsmen. A captain would then try to crash the beak of his ship over the enemy deck, whereupon his marines would rush across to capture the enemy vessel intact.

There were almost no galley-slaves at this time, except amongst the Crusader Military Order of Hospitallers based on the Greek island of Rhodes since 1309. Instead oarsmen were volunteers working for pay or loot. Merchant ships, often called 'round ships' because of their tubby appearance, rode high in the water and were difficult to board, but they were also so unwieldy that the galleys could shoot at the crew until they surrendered. The need to protect as well as handle these cumbersome merchant vessels meant that they often had large crews.

Another specialized form of vessel was the 'tarida', a horse-transporting galley invented by the Arabs. It was slower than a fighting galley and less efficient than a 'round ship' for carrying cargo, but was able to land men and horses right onto an enemy beach.

By the year 1483, when this Swiss manuscript was painted, arms, armour and military technology in general was remarkably sophisticated, though in many cases the ideas shown in tactical treatises seem never to have been put into practice. Here boats full of fully armoured men, some armed with hand-guns, also carry cannon as well as a degree of sturdy wooden protection.

ings near the defences would be destroyed, local wells polluted and food supplies removed. Enemies would usually be attacked before they could set up camp, but if this failed the defenders would retreat inside their walls from where they would try to destroy the attackers' siege machines. Friendly forces in the area would help by sabotaging enemy communications and stop them from gathering food or water.

Only in the most desperate situation would attackers try to take a castle by storm, normally using stone and fire-throwing machines to destroy the defenders' parapets while miners tried to make the walls themselves collapse. At first, the invention of gunpowder helped defenders rather than attackers. Only at the end of the 15th century did gunpowder artillery lead to walls becoming lower, thicker and more spread out in an effort to force artillery out of effective range. By this time the most advanced European armies had developed effective siege artillery and the devastating field artillery which defeated the English in the Hundred Years War (1337–1453).

SONS OF ROME'S LEGIONS

The Byzantine army was a highly structured organization with battalions, regiments, cavalry squadrons and infantry platoons. Even officers had ranks more like those of modern armies than those of a western European feudal force. Soldiers, like government officials, were originally paid in cash, but during the 11th century this was widely replaced by grants of land to officers and even ordinary soldiers. From the 10th century onwards, local levies increased in importance, while the famous provincial, or Theme, armies were largely replaced by great fortresses garrisoned by mercenaries.

The Byzantine Empire had traditionally recruited troops from outside territories, as well as from within, and by the 11th century, their forces included Norman cavalry, Anglo-

Saxons, Italians, Hungarians and men from eastern European countries, along with Turkish recruits.

Generally, Byzantine military commanders did not think much of the tactics of western knights when compared to the subtle stratagems used by both Byzantines and Muslims, but they had a high opinion of western fighting capabilities. The most famous western mercenaries were the Emperor's elite Varangian Guard, recruited from Vikings who arrived via Russia in the late 10th century and subsequently from Anglo-Saxons who had little chance of a military career after the Norman Conquest of England in 1066.

By the later Middle Ages, the surviving fragments of the Byzantine Empire reflected strong Turco-Islamic influence in tactics, training, organization and recruitment. In the Empire of Trebizond (1204–1461), for example, responsibility for frontier defence rested largely with the frontier barons of the high plateau, whose way of life and warfare was similar to that of the Turks, and upon the tribal peoples of the Pontus mountains, who were in many ways identical to the Georgians.

Byzantine military influence in medieval Russia was superficial. Here professional warriors served in the 'druzhinas', or military retinues, of Russian princes. They were recruited from Slav Russians, Scandinavians, Finn and Ugrian tribesmen, nomadic Turks, Persian-speaking nomads known as Alans,

Above: The helmet of Prince Yaroslav
Vsevolodovich was found under a bush,
centuries after it was lost during a skirmish
between rival Russian princes in the 13th century.

The art of medieval Italy includes some of the most advanced and some of the most primitive in Europe. On this piece of very simple stone mosaic the people of Constantinople, capital of the Byzantine Empire, surrender to a mail-clad warrior of the Fourth Crusade.

Mail continued to be used extensively, along with Islamic-style lamellar cuirasses and various forms of fabric soft armour. Some of the first illustrations of separate gauntlets in medieval European art are in late 13th century Byzantine and Crusader States' manuscripts, perhaps being the 'cheroptia' of late 13th–14th century Greek literature. According to a 13th–14th century Turkish source, some Byzantine cavalry used horse-armour which only covered the front of the animal. Though this sounds like a reversion to an early medieval style, it probably reflected the influence of Catalan mercenaries operating in the Aegean area.

A military melting pot

The idea that Russian military technology stagnated under Mongol domination is nonsense and medieval Russian troops enthusiastically copied many aspects of Mongol arms and armour. The Russians' first experience of firearms was also in the east, during their siege of Turkish Bulgar in AD1376. On the other hand, straight swords of western European form continued to be preferred in Russia well into the 14th century. The importance of axes in medieval Russia was as a result of a European infantry tradition, whereas the light cavalry mace came directly from the steppes.

More typically Russian were their helmets with broad nasals and 'half-visors' protecting the upper part of the wearer's face, while tall pointed helmets beaten from a single piece of iron but similar in shape to segmented nomad types may have been a southern Russian development. The Mongol 'khatangku dehel', the 'coat as hard as steel', evolved into the equally distinctive Russian 'tegheliay', though the Russians also used scale armour, perhaps reflecting Byzantine influence.

Byzantine defensive strategy failed against the Turks in the 11th century because these new invaders occupied the hills as well as the plains. After western Anatolia was regained in the 12th century, it was secured by a strip

and many others. In fact, medieval Russia was not only a melting pot of peoples, but also of military traditions and technologies. In fact Byzantine and Russian arms and armour were both strongly influenced by Central Asian Turkey. For example both used composite bows and were relatively slow to adopt the crossbow.

Byzantium's lack of guns until the 1390s may, however, have reflected its poverty rather than an unwillingness to use such weapons. Anthropomorphic helmet visors found in the Palace of Constantinople were comparable to those found in the graves of Kipchaq Turks and Volga Bulgars. Another form of European helmet which may have first appeared in Byzantium was the brimmed war-hat, perhaps brought from China by the Mongols in the 13th century or by their predecessors.

of depopulated no-man's-land. Meanwhile the northern coastal belt was naturally protected by forested mountains where raiders could be ambushed. In open battle, Byzantine cavalry avoided charging an enemy when the sun was in their eyes, but against Crusader forces Byzantine heavy cavalry held high ground while light cavalry harassed the enemy in the valleys.

By the 14th century Byzantine armies were quite small and this would fit Prince Theodore Paleaologus' belief that if a force was caught by surprise, it should not waste time forming divisions, but should gather into one large formation. He also maintained that the best cavalry should be in the vanguard with a division of inferior cavalry one crossbow shot behind the first.

The Russian armies

The Russian tribes had been part of a wider Central Asian world before the rise of the Kievan state in the late 9th century. Only when Russian rulers turned their back on Asia did they find it necessary to erect forts along the frontier between the forests and the steppes. In the far north Russian armies often found that winter was the easiest time to undertake long-range campaigns since they could use frozen rivers as ready-made high-

ways. In summer the only way to transport large amounts of equipment was by boat along the same rivers. Spring and autumn, however, were known as the 'seasons of roadlessness', when the landscape sank into mud. Wagons also carried supplies in the open areas of southern Russia and the steppes.

From the 11th to 13th centuries Russian forces, when facing nomad foes, placed low-grade infantry at the centre, with infantry archers shooting from behind a shield-wall and cavalry protecting their flanks. In the later 13th and 14th centuries, Russian cavalry began to copy tactics of the Mongols, whereas Russian infantry began using western crossbows in greater numbers. Nevertheless in 1380, at the battle of Kulikovo, the Grand Duke Dimitri Donskoi of Moscow still placed a river at his back and dense woods on either flank when facing a Turco-Mongol foe; as a result defeating the feared Mongol horde of Kham Mamai.

From the late 11th to 14th centuries, the Byzantine navy was in decline. During the 11th and 12th centuries, most Byzantine galleys changed from the old fashion of having oars evenly spaced to grouping them at a single level supported by an outrigger. Meanwhile the numerous rivers of Russia acted as vital arteries of communication, though river pirates were a serious problem.

In this 11th century Byzantine illustration of a naval battle, the two crews fight it out hand to hand, encouraged by military musicians. Meanwhile a swimmer from one ship is about to attack the enemy's hull, as was certainly done in many naval engagements.

THE STRUGGLE
OF CROSS AND CRESCENT

Military recruitment in the Muslim world continued to reflect earlier traditions, with a preference for mixed armies, the elite consisting of mamluks of slave origin, plus assorted tribal contingents. One development was the increased professionalism of most armies. During the late 14th century Ottoman rulers broke with tradition to create a new force, the Janissaries or 'new army'. The first recruits were drawn from the Sultan's one-fifth share of prisoners, but later Janissaries were recruited from 'enslaved' members of the Ottoman Sultan's own non-Muslim population. The Ottoman army was also characterized by its large number of Christian troops since it was Ottoman policy to leave existing military elites in place.

Traditional systems of organization similarly characterized Muslim armies. For example the Great Seljuq Sultanate of Iran and the Middle East (1037–1157) was divided into 24 military zones, each commanded by an officer who raised, trained and equipped a specified number of troops.

In Egypt, Syria and Anatolia the success of the Muslims in expelling the Crusaders in 1291 and defeating further Crusading expeditions in the 14th century reflected superior organization and logistical support. Here the army of 12th century Damascus was divided into sections: militia, part-time religious volunteers, tribal forces commissioned for a single campaign, regular troops and the rulers' elite bodyguard.

The same military structure was inherited, developed and expanded by Saladin (1169–1193), his successors of the Ayyubid dynasty (1193–1252) and even by the Mamluk rulers ((1250–1517) who had themselves been recruited as slave-soldiers. From the end of the 14th century, Ottoman military organization remained basically the same for the next three centuries, with an elite which included 'sipahi' cavalry and Janissary infantry supported by larger numbers of provincial light cavalry under their own beys, or governors, while the military organization of Muslim Andalusia had sev-

eral features in common with its Christian neighbours, remaining this way until the fall of Granada to the Spanish in 1492.

Warfare in the Muslim Middle East was constrained by ecological factors such as summer heat, winter rains and the availability of water. By the late 12th century, the Muslims realized that the only way to overcome the Crusader States was to reduce their castles and fortified cities one by one. Basically the same strategy was later used by Ottoman armies. Mobilization orders would be sent to sipahi cavalry and other provincial forces in December, the troops would muster in spring and the campaign would then normally run from August to October.

Lighter Armour but Better Discipline

In general, Muslim armies were less armoured than those of invading Christians, but were better disciplined. The primary aim of all Muslim commanders seems to have been to separate the enemy's cavalry from his infantry, but the skill of Muslim cavalry and even infantry in avoiding the fearsome Crusader cavalry charge rendered this tactic almost redundant. The formations remained traditional, with infantry forming a defensive shield-wall, supported by archers and

Above: The 12th to 14th centuries saw a renewed interest in military handbooks in the Muslim Middle East, both for commanders and for ordinary soldiers. Many of them repeated what had been written in the 8th to 10th centuries, the first great period of Islamic military studies. The Arabic manuscript shown here, however, is a mid-14th century copy of a cavalry training manual written several generations earlier for professional Mamluk soldiers in Egypt and Syria.

Opposite: The drama of the Mamluk Sultan's capture of the Crusader outpost of Tripoli in Lebanon in 1288 is certainly shown in this early 14th century manuscript. It was probably made in Italy and shows Crusaders still desperately building boats in which to escape, even as the Muslim cavalry charges down upon them.

crossbowmen, while the cavalry were divided into offensive and defensive units. The skills demanded of troops seemed to put as much emphasis on avoiding an enemy's charge as on making one themselves. The role of infantry and camel-riding mounted infantry had been of paramount importance to North African forces since the late 11th century and this resulted in very defensive tactics where a small number of horsemen made controlled charges from behind a shield-wall of spear, javelin and bow-armed foot soldiers.

Field fortifications do not feature prominently in 12th to 14th century Muslim sources, but the late 14th and 15th centuries saw a revival in their use, while the Ottomans' adoption of the 'waggenburg' made from specially prepared carts may have been copied from the Hungarians in the Balkans.

Firearms and firetroops

Composite bows dominated archery throughout the Muslim world and came in a variety of sophisticated forms, culminating in the smoothly recurved Turkish bow, the most effective cavalry weapon before the invention of firearms early in the 14th century. Firearms appeared at an early date, but were not adopted as enthusiastically as in western Europe. In 12th century Muslim armies the wearing of two mail hauberks was considered

proof against sword-blows, while the cloth-covered and padded kazaghand could also incorporate two mail shirts. The lamellar jawshan remained essentially both an Asian and Middle Eastern form of armour and could be made of iron, horn or hardened leather, while mail-and-plate armour probably first appeared in mid-14th century western Iran or eastern Anatolia.

Because of the area's climate, soft armour had always been widespread, while fireproof clothing impregnated with silicate of magnesium and powdered mica was worn by specialist fire-troops. Horse-armour had never fallen out of use in the Middle East and one of the oldest surviving examples is an iron headpiece excavated near Khartoum, dating from between the 8th and 14th centuries.

Muslim armies used various siege techniques: light troops still went ahead of the main force to blockade a castle or city, destroying surrounding orchards in an attempt to force surrender; bombardment began with the smallest engines, followed by those of increasing power to put the defenders under increasing psychological pressure. The counterweight mangonel or trebuchet was invented in the eastern Mediterranean region in the 12th century and soon came in large or small, simple or complex varieties. Fire weapons included clay and glass grenades, though the decline of fire-weapons from the later 13th century may have been as a result of their own success in driving suitably inflammable targets from the battlefield.

Despite the fact that Muslim shipwrights had led the way in building larger three-masted ships in the 11th century, some of the biggest being made on the island of Majorca, from the 11th to 15th centuries Muslim naval power in the Mediterranean was in gradual decline. By the mid-14th century even traditionally maritime Muslim North Africa could no longer challenge European domination. However, Egypt's decline as a Mediterranean power was not mirrored in the Red Sea, where the Mamluks could still challenge the newly arrived Portuguese in the early 16th century.

During the early medieval period the arms and armour of the Muslim lands and Europe still had a great deal in common. But after the arrival of the Turks in the 11th century and even more so the Mongols in the 13th century, Islamic military technology followed a very different line of development. It owed a great deal to Central Asian and Chinese influences, as shown in this picture of two horsemen in combat, probably from a copy of the *Shahnamah*, made in Tabriz, Iran, around 1480.

ARMIES OF THE KHANS

The military history of medieval Central and Northern Asia was dominated by migrations, conquest and religious conversion. The impact of ecology was also of considerable importance amongst these nomadic peoples, for example, although fighting was essential for group survival, the availability of grazing imposed a limit on the number of horses a tribe could maintain.

Armies were largely recruited from within the dominant tribal confederation and state organization reflected the military orientation of such societies. Things changed somewhat under the Mongols in the 13th and 14th centuries, with the enlistment of conquered Turks, Russians, Chinese and others. At the end of the 14th century, the great conqueror Tamerlane still claimed Mongol descent although he and his remarkable army were largely Turkish.

The fact that the Mongols were strongly influenced by the Chinese even before the rise of Genghiz Khan had a profound impact on their military organization, giving their armies a very cohesive command structure.

The horses of steppe tribes were considered 'ready for war' by autumn, which became the main campaigning season, while nomad armies tended to follow watersheds between main rivers rather than the valleys where settled populations were concentrated. Food for their enormous horse-herds was vital and the main force was usually preceded by scouts who rode ten days ahead looking for pasture.

A detailed account of the 'Battle Plan of the Khaqan' in a 13th century Indo-Muslim military treatise was probably based upon the Chinese-influenced Qara-Khitai of 12th century Central Asia and its similarity with the tactics adopted by medieval Chinese forces when facing Central Asian nomad foes is remarkable. It was, however, iron discipline which made the Mongols so formidable. They also had a habit of opening up a gap once they had surrounded an enemy, seemingly to permit escape but in reality forcing them down a corridor of murderous archery.

Archery was so important to the Turco-Mongols that bows and arrows were thought to possess magical properties, while the

Above: One of the oldest copies of Rashid al-Din's history of the world was made in Iran, between 1306 and 1314. The soldiers involved are portrayed as early 14th century Mongol warriors.

The Revenge of the Soga Brothers around 1215 became one of the classic Japanese 'revenge stories' and is the subject of this 19th century print. The Soga brother shown here is portrayed as a medieval samurai in civilian dress but armed with two swords.

Pot. Lamellar cuirasses made up of different shaped layers of slivers of bamboo were used amongst the peoples of the eastern Tibetan foothills, while bone lamellae was used in eastern Siberia and Alaska. By the late 13th century the typical Mongol khatangku dehel (coat as hard as steel) was often lined with metal scales and may have been the inspiration behind 13th–14th century western European coat-of-plates and brigandines. Recent archaeological studies suggest that horse-armour was more widely used by Mongol armies than once thought, and was usually of hardened leather, though sometimes of iron.

The strategy of minimal damage

China served as a primary source of military influence for peoples near and far. Nevertheless Chinese culture remained deeply pacifist. China's Sung dynasty (960–1279) is often regarded as being particularly unmilitary, although it had enormous armies including militias selected from registers of local families.

The Sung seemed particularly concerned to prevent rebellions and no army could be mobilized unless its commander had two halves of a marked tally in his hands, one of which he always kept and the second of which was kept in the Imperial capital. Palace troops rotated between the capital and the provinces as this was thought to toughen the men, but it proved very expensive and was abandoned in favour of raising the status of frontier troops. Another Chinese concept was the military–agricultural colony.

The Koreans were similarly unwarlike. The Koryo rulers of Korea (935–1392) even abolished the early medieval 'bone rank' aristocratic system and replaced it with a bureaucratic military administration. Korean influence may, however, have been behind some aspects of Japanese military organization, although later medieval Japan was dominated by warrior clans, leading to an almost unique form of military government.

paucity of references to spears in Central Asia presumably reflects the low status of this weapon. The first waves of Mongol conquerors also had specialist Chinese fire-troops in their ranks.

Mongols introduced a more rounded headpiece of Chinese origin to western Asia and Europe, sometimes with peaks at the front, which eventually evolved into a 17th–18th century western European helmet popularly known in England as the Cromwellian

Given the deep-seated dislike of Chinese civilization for any sort of warfare, it is not surprising to find defence always taking precedence over offence. It was even acceptable to assassinate members of the enemy leadership in order to avoid a more widespread or prolonged war. Nevertheless, although the Sung tried to avoid any conflict, many famous military treatises were compiled during their reign.

Some traditional Chinese battle formations, as presented in these sources, were a mixture of the practical and the semi-magical; a typically Chinese element being the 'golden bridge' or gap so that an enemy would not fight to the bitter end – almost the direct opposite to the 13th century Mongols' use of a comparable gap to force the enemy into a 'killing zone'. Other imaginative Chinese tactics were to use dummy soldiers to make their numbers appear greater, drag brushwood behind their troops to raise sufficient dust as though from a larger army and plant poisoned spikes in drinking places.

The importance of hand-held crossbows can hardly be overestimated in Chinese warfare and by the 11th century this was the strongest weapon in China's armoury. The manufacture of helmets and sword-blades similarly demonstrated China's advanced metallurgy techniques, while scale-lined armour was constantly being refined and improved. Lacquered leather lamella was also typical in some parts of China and Japan, which was done for decorative and weatherproofing reasons.

In siege warfare Chinese armies used wooden palisades or thorny obstacles to defend their positions. Offensive devices included the extendable 'cloud ladder', the wheeled 'heaven bridge' or movable siege-tower, and the 'goose carriage' which incorporated an extendable platform. Stone-throwing mangonels were placed inside the walls rather than on top, being directed by forward 'artillery observers'. During the early medieval period, many Chinese ships also had

stone-throwing artillery, while marines were armed with crossbows. By the 14th century, gunpowder cannon were also used in naval or riverine warfare. In 1222, troops of the Sung dynasty even attempted to relieve a siege with a squadron of man-powered paddlewheelers. In fact, rivers played a major role during internal Chinese conflicts and there were several instances of full-scale naval battles being fought on lakes or rivers.

Japanese armour was perhaps the most decorative of the Middle Ages. This armour includes a Do or lamellar cuirass, laced with silk, and is in a late 14th century style, though it was almost certainly made much later.

WAR AND THE KSHATRIYA CASTE

India had distinctive military traditions based upon Hindu religious principles. Competition for land between peasants and aboriginal forest tribes led to both being warlike, despite warfare being theoretically confined to the kshatriya warrior caste. In Burma the elite ahmudan 'guards' of the 12th to 14th centuries were recruited from an established aristocracy while in what is now Indonesia, society was also organized along Hindu caste lines. The little that is known about military organization here is summed up in a surviving Manual of Court Organization which describes the functions of senior courtiers, including the prime minister responsible for internal security and military affairs.

The Arthashastra text on good government written in the early Middle Ages indicates that an Indian army consisted of a hereditary elite, plus mercenaries, short-term contingents from 'guilds', allies and aboriginal auxiliaries, while the apparent inexorability with which Muslim forces pressed southwards loosened the military caste system still further. According to the Atharvaveda, an army was commanded by the 'sena pati' and traditionally consisted of four arms: infantry, cavalry, chariots and elephants, though in some areas a naval fleet was also added.

Following the collapse of the Gupta state around AD 510, Hindu armies reverted to ponderous tactics, positional warfare and a reliance on fortifications. Infantry predominated, though elephants replaced chariots as the 'heavy shock' element in medieval Hindu armies. In fact Hindu Indian armies were clearly less mobile than their northern foes, with apparently outmoded strategy, an inferior cavalry arm and considerable reliance on the impact of elephants. Remarkably, some enemy horses were even trained to walk on their hind legs so that their riders could reach and attack men riding high above them on these elephants.

Infantry archers was so important that the most complete Indian military manual was called the Dhanurveda or 'science of archery'. The simple bow survived throughout southern and south-eastern Asia, whereas composite bows were not suited to the humid climate unless waterproofed with lacquer. The straight sword remained in favour long after the Middle Ages and probably evolved into the straight 'sundang' of south-east Asia in later centuries. The most extraordinary sword was, however, a reverse-curved weapon widely shown throughout Hindu art at least until the 13th century.

Ritualized violence

The use of exotic weapons may, in fact, have indicated the ritualized character of violence in Hindu civilization. In southern India special throwing sticks were used by aboriginal peoples, but unlike the Australian boomerang, they were not intended to return to the thrower. An even more unusual Indian weapon was the sharpened throwing disc. Light types were thrown horizontally like a quoit, while heavier types were dropped vertically upon attackers.

The most distinctive form of late medieval Indian armour was the coat of a thousand nails, which had appeared by the 15th century, combining Sino-Mongol scale-lined and Indian fabric covered or padded defences. India also had a strong tradition in soft-armour and may have been the source of various forms of quilted armour seen in the Middle East and Europe.

Siege warfare was extremely primitive in south-eastern Asia, but was highly developed in India. Scaling ladders were the normal means of direct assault and were secured to mud-brick walls with iron pegs. Indian armies also used elephants with protective iron plates on their heads as live battering rams against gates. Indian references to the use of fire and smoke to defend fortresses sometimes sound so devastating that they recall the weapons used by gods and heroes in

Hindu religious epics rather than the reality of the limitations of medieval warfare.

Meanwhile the Indian Ocean was peaceful compared to the Mediterranean, although Malaya did become a major centre of piracy in the 13th to 15th centuries. Evidence from 13th century Indo-China indicates that the crews of very large war canoes largely fought with archery while river warfare also played a major role in Burma. In India the only big rivers were in the north, but here the open terrain lent itself to wide-ranging campaigns on land with little reason to fight on water.

Opposite: The late 12th or early 13th century carvings on the Buddhist temple of Bantei Serai in Angkor shows warlike scenes as well as everyday life and religious events.

Below: Indian cavalry were regarded as ineffective by their Muslim foes during the earlier medieval period, but by the end of the Middle Ages they could compete on equal terms.

9 RELIGION AND BELIEF

THE MIDDLE AGES WERE A VERY RELIGIOUS PERIOD AND MOST PEOPLE IDENTIFIED THEMSELVES FIRST BY THEIR FAITH. RELIGION ALSO LAY AT THE ROOT OF THE MOST RUTHLESSS WARS AND DEEPEST MISUNDERSTANDINGS. SOME CIVILISATIONS WERE, HOWEVER, MORE TOLERANT THAN OTHERS; CHINA AND THE MUSLIM WORLD, FOR EXAMPLE, PROCLAIMED TOLERATION IN THEORY, IF NOT ALWAYS IN PRACTICE, WHEREAS CHRISTIAN EUROPE RARELY EVEN PRETENDED TO ENTERTAIN OTHER FAITHS.

'TWIXT HEAVEN AND HELL

Christianity of the Latin or Catholic form was the dominant religion in medieval western Europe, though it was not the only one. In some outlying areas paganism survived, while pagan 'folk beliefs' remained deeply entrenched in most parts of Europe amongst the poorer rural communities. Several places also had a sizeable Jewish population.

In some parts of southern Italy Greek Orthodox Christianity was the dominant form, while Muslims not only existed, but also ruled over large parts of the Iberian peninsula almost to the end of the 15th century. Another Muslim community existed in Sicily, but was transported en masse in the 13th century to the Italian city of Lucera, where it survived for several decades.

Religion of whatever denomination was central to the everyday lives of medieval people. The Church also played the leading role in education, helping the needy and tending the sick. Most men and women believed that some sort of penance would wash away sins and save their souls from Hell. Although expensive, one of the most important forms of penance was to make a pilgrimage to one of many Christian holy sites, particularly Rome or the Holy Land.

However, even the poor could visit the tomb of a local saint as every country in Christendom had its own pilgrimage centres, and as a result, pilgrim routes criss-crossed Europe. Nevertheless, this was a hazardous undertaking; the main dangers were disease, shipwreck or attack by robbers, yet there were monasteries and sometimes special hostels run by friars, which provided accommodation along the main routes.

Conditions became easier in the late Middle Ages, when knights, merchants, prosperous peasants and an increasing number of strong-minded women went on pilgrimage just for enjoyment. They had evolved into something more like the modern tourist than the highly devout pilgrim of earlier centuries.

Like tourists, pilgrims brought back souvenirs; most seem to have been lead 'badges' which usually portrayed something associated with the saint whose tomb had been visited, the most famous of these being the scallop shell of St. James, whose tomb was believed to be at Santiago de Compostella in Spain.

Conversion at sword-point

The spread of Christianity into the fringes of Europe was rarely peaceful, continuing since the early Middle Ages to be preached at the point of a sword. The most violent 'evangelizing' was seen in the Spanish and Portuguese campaigns of the *reconquista* against Muslims, and in the Baltic's Northern Crusades against both pagans and Russian Orthodox Christians. In neighbouring Scandinavia and the Viking communities of the Scottish islands, Christianity co-existed with Norse paganism, but was then forcibly imposed by the ruling elite.

Some of the first Scandinavian settlers in far-off Greenland seem to have been Christian and, by the mid-11th century, their colonies formed part of the north German diocese of Bremen. Meanwhile, Christianity spread amongst the pagan Finns and Lapps of the far north. Northern European paganism was, in fact, shamanistic and consisted of many different local beliefs. It was characterized by drums used to make contact with the spirit world, animal sacrifices associated with unusually shaped rocks or trees, and a belief that the bear was a sacred animal.

Opposite: The poet Lygate and the pigrims leaving Canterbury after the completion of their pilgrimage to the tomb of Thomas Becket, as shown in a 15th century manuscript. The road might only be a stony track but the pilgrims look well dressed and fed, while the fine buildings in the background suggest a prosperous world.

Peter the Hermit leading an advance force of the First Crusade in a late 13th or early 14th century manuscript. Peter's followers would soon be virtually wiped out by the Seljuk Turks as soon as they reached Asia, since they only included a small number of professional soldiers.

The Church was the only truly international organization in medieval Europe. Nevertheless, ecclesiastical boundaries were almost always the same as political boundaries, except where major wars had changed the latter. The whole of western Christendom was divided into archdioceses headed by archbishops, dioceses under bishops and parishes with their local priests. Priests were often also supported by deacons and other men of 'minor orders'.

As the authority of the Catholic Church spread, so new dioceses and parishes were established. At the same time monasteries sprang up as centres of prayer and, concurrently, taming the surrounding land. The new puritanical Cistercian order of monks, founded in France in 1098, took a particularly prominent role in this pioneering agriculture, helped by 'lay brothers' who tended the fields or pastured the sheep owned by the order, often living in a grange attached to the monastery or in nearby farms.

The wealth which flowed into the monasteries as a result of such activities also encouraged monastic orders to invest capital in other sorts of economic activity, but this in turn contributed to the cynicism and corruption which afflicted many monasteries by the end of the Middle Ages. During the 13th century, a new sort of religious order appeared. These were the two orders of Friars established by St. Francis (1181–1226) and St. Dominic (1170–1221). Instead of remaining in monasteries to work and pray as did the monks, friars lived in the outside world. They preached the gospel and helped ordinary people in more immediate ways. However, they too became rich from the gifts of believers and were soon being sharply criticzsed for their corruption.

The alliance forged between the Church and the knightly elite in the 11th and 12th centuries was always a difficult one. A knight's role in society was basically a violent one, although his sword was expected to be used only against evil-doers and enemies of the Church.

Meanwhile, the Church tried to strengthen its psychological hold over the knights by playing a bigger role in the ceremonies where men were raised to the status of knights and such ceremonies thus became as impressive as possible. Swords, which had once merely been blessed to ward off the 'Evil Eye', now became sharpened versions of the Christian Cross.

Splendour and dissent

From the 13th to 15th centuries the Church changed in several significant ways. The majority of people remained firm believers and took great pride in their own local church building. Increasing wealth also enabled them to spend more on beautifying even ordinary village churches with carvings, wall paintings, stained-glass windows, crosses and altars. In many cases, old structures were pulled down and replaced by a completely new church in the current style.

As a result there are more village and town churches dating from this than in any other period in European history. Increasing corruption, however, meant that the practice of one priest having responsibility for more than one parish (and their revenues) became widespread. The higher ranks of the Church, including archbishops, cardinals and popes, were often political and ambitious men, despite being very learned, but such problems were more apparent in some places than in

Right: A 14th century illustration of Fransiscan friars. By this date, friars were no longer the simple poor men, preaching to ordinary people as St. Francis of Assisi had intended. They had become rich and often corrupt, though many were still, of course, dedicated to God.

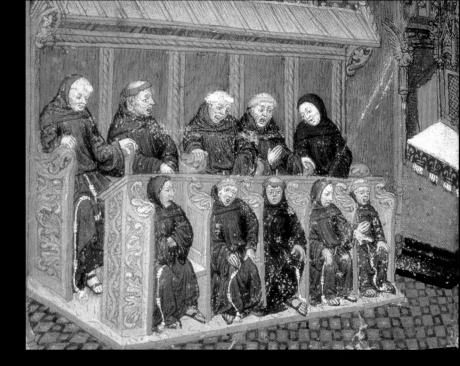

Below: Heretics begging for forgiveness as they are burned at the stake in front of the French king, illustrated with horrifying reality by Jean Fouquet in the second half of the 15th century.

others, and the fact that so many bishops were Prince-Bishops or local rulers meant that they could not avoid getting involved in the tangled, violent politics of central Europe.

Protests against the Church

The problems of the Church in the 13th century prompted Francis of Assisi to set up his order of friars; for a while it seemed as if this movement would be declared heretical, as the corruption of the official Church structure stimulated religious heresies. In the 11th century there had been the Patarini of Milan, in the 12th century the Petrobrusians and Henricians of France, and the Waldensians and Humiliati of France and Italy.

These were as least Christian, but the Cathars or Albigensians of 12th and 13th century France, Italy and Germany adopted a 'dualist' faith which believed that the world was a battleground between equally powerful forces of light and dark, good and evil. It was rooted in the Manichaean faith of early medieval Persia and had spread to Europe via the Byzantine Empire and the Balkans.

The 14th century saw bands of unauthorized 'poor preachers' touring the countryside, denouncing the sins of the aristocracy and the Church. Educated people wrote savage satires about the religious leaders of their day and religious questions were taken so seriously that rival supporters would brawl in the streets.

Men such as the late 15th century preacher Savanarola had fanatical followers who demanded reform in the Church and repentance from everyone else. Savanarola went so far as to welcome the French invasion of Italy on the grounds that the French king was the 'Scourge of God', foretold in the Bible. He also condemned much Renaissance art as pagan and was deeply anti-

Semitic – one way or another it was hardly surprising that Savanarola ended with few friends and was burned at the stake as a heretic in 1498. These were, in fact, the first stirrings of the Reformation which would be taken up in 16th century Germany.

Anti-Semitism was deeply engrained in medieval Christian society, unlike in the neighbouring Muslim world, where it was virtually unknown. As the Christian merchant class grew, and the guild system took control of most trade, Jews were excluded from virtually all professions other than money-lending which was theoretically prohibited for Christians. This role in society, however, merely deepened the fear and ignorance of Jews that was felt throughout Europe.

Nevertheless Jewish communities flourished in several areas, protected by local rulers and a Church which found them useful. The most important centres of Jewish life were France, England, Germany and Italy, though there were older Jewish populations in Spain and southern Italy. Most such communities were, however, driven out so that by the end of the 15th century the main Jewish centres were in northern Italy and some German cities. Newer communities grew in Poland, Lithuania and under the tolerant rule of the Ottoman Turkish Sultans.

Right: A Jewish Rabbi celebrating Passover, in a Hebrew Jewish prayerbook made in the 14th century. Jewish art, and above all manuscript illustrations, were almost always made in the same style as that of the country where the artist lived. So a Jewish painting from France would look French while a Jewish manuscript from Syria would look Islamic. Apart from small differences, the same would also be true of the costume worn by the people in the illustrations.

THE MOST CHRISTIAN EMPIRE

Religion played an even more central role in the Byzantine Empire. The schism between the Orthodox and Catholic, Greek and Latin, Churches dated from 1054, but the feelings of difference had been growing for centuries. The Fourth Crusade of 1204, when a western army conquered Constantinople, naturally made Orthodox Christians even more antagonistic towards Catholics. Many efforts at reconciliation were attempted in following years, but all failed, the last one being made in 1453 – the year the Byzantine capital of Constantinople fell to the Ottoman Turks.

Orthodox Christians had a deep belief in the power of faith and ordinary people considered that miracles, great or small, were an almost everyday occurrence. They also had a very literal view of the Bible, but what distinguished them most of all was their faith in icons or religious images. Back in the early medieval period, during the iconoclastic or 'icon breaking' controversy, the Byzantine Empire had been the stronghold of the icon-

oclasts who felt that faith in religious images was misplaced. Meanwhile the strongholds of the iconophiles, or those who approved of holy images, was in what would become the Catholic west. By the 11th century, however, iconoclasm was a thing of the past and icons played a major role in the religious life of people, from the Byzantine Emperor to the humblest Russian peasant. As a result Orthodox Christians were regarded as little more than idol-worshippers by many of their Muslim neighbours.

Monasteries also played a fundamental role in medieval lives, though Orthodox monasticism remained closer to the ascetic ideals of the first Christian monks than did Catholic monasticism. Byzantine monks were almost entirely concerned with prayer, religious study and the making of icons. It was also quite normal for members of the ruling elites to enter monasteries when they retired from public service. Even the warrior Emperor John Cantacuzenus VI became the monk Ioasaph after his abdication in 1354; much the same happened in Russia.

Pilgrimage was at least as popular amongst eastern Christians as it was in the Catholic west, while the Holy Land itself was not far away. Nevertheless, embarking on a pilgrimage was still hard and dangerous, although the Byzantine authorities provided some inns. It is interesting to note that on Sundays and religious feast days inns were only allowed to serve wine from eight in the morning to eight at night.

Religion was similarly central to the sense of identity of eastern Christian states such as Armenia and Georgia. At various times the Armenians had to fight off Byzantine, Turkish, Crusader and Mongol onslaughts, before they finally fell to the Mamluks. It is perhaps why the Armenian Church had a

Above: Much less is known about Greek Orthodox convents than is known about monasteries although a large number existed in the Middle Ages.

An icon of the Virgin and Child in the Glykophilousa or 'sweetly embracing' style. It is a 14th century Byzantine miniature mosaic in which the tiny tesserae are fastened to a panel of wood. These were always rare and highly prized.

Asiatic Khanate into a Christian realm whose rulers modelled themselves on the greater 'Tsar', Caesar or Emperor in Constantinople. The decision to accept spiritual leadership from the Orthodox Patriarch in Constantinople rather than the Latin Pope in Rome divided Europe into east and west up until modern times.

A monastic republic

The Byzantine Church was a strictly hierarchical organization headed by the Patriarch of Constantinople, who had a close religious and political relationship with the Emperor. This enabled the Byzantine Empire to use the Orthodox Church to influence other Orthodox states and, as a result, the position of the Patriarch of Constantinople was a highly political one.

In complete contrast, Orthodox monasteries were spiritual retreats, often in extremely inaccessible places, such as Mount Athos on the easternmost finger of the Khalkidiki peninsula in northern Greece. The other-worldly character of many Orthodox monasteries did not, however, stop them growing rich from donations of money and land.

Nor were their leaders reluctant to interfere in the outside world when they felt that political morals were slipping. Much less is known about Byzantine nunneries and they were most often mentioned as places of virtual exile for ladies who, for reasons of age, political circumstances or indiscreet behaviour, abandoned the outside world.

As the Byzantine Empire crumbled away, some groups of monasteries became virtually autonomous, the most famous being Mount Athos, which was handed over from Emperor to Patriarch in 1312. It preserved its separate status even after the Balkans were conquered by the Ottoman Turks. Because they owned huge estates, many Orthodox monasteries had a large staff of servants and agricultural labourers. Many monasteries also employed their own garrison troops, as it was common

deep distrust of practically all neighbours, though it eventually came to a compromise with the Catholic Church which basically left the Armenians to their own devices. From the 11th to 13th centuries, Georgia steadily grew into a major regional power most notably under the warrior Queen Tamara (1184–1213), of which one characteristic was the frequency with which its bishops led troops into battle.

Meanwhile the conversion of the vast medieval Russian state to Orthodox rather than Latin Catholic Christianity in the late 10th century had a profound impact on the Russians' neighbours to east and west. The Russian state now changed from a settled

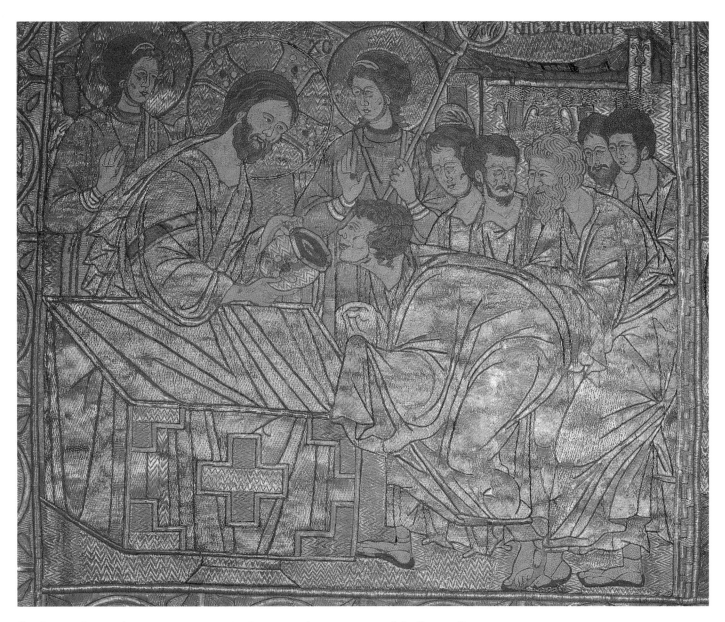

for the monks to take up arms in a crisis. In fact some parts of eastern Europe were dominated by a monastic economy comparable to that seen in Buddhist Tibet.

Despite the frequently appalling oppression which Byzantine peasantry endured at the hands of their own aristocracy, there were few revolts because of the people's unswerving loyalty to the Church, particularly in the face of Muslim encroachment. When loyalty did die, it was associated with non-Greeks, with complete changes in religion or extreme heresies. For example, the Paulician heresy, which had flourished amongst the Armenians of early medieval eastern Anatolia, spread to the Balkans, where it led to the emergence of the Bogomil movement. This flourished particularly amongst Bosnian Slavs and Albanians, precisely those communities where Islam later won its greatest number of converts following the Ottoman Turkish conquest in 1463.

There was very little religious dissent in medieval Russia where the Orthodox Church tolerated ancient shamanist beliefs amongst the uneducated peasantry. These contributed to the promiscuity, excessive drinking and the popularity of wandering minstrels called 'skomoriki' amongst the Russians. The skomoriki were believed to have been descended from shamanist medicine men of pre-Christian times.

The richness of some Byzantine textiles amazed western Europeans during the early medieval period, and even in later centuries their standard of workmanship remained extremely high. This, the Last Supper, shown on the gold and silver embroidered silk Epitaphios of Thessaloniki, is one of the greatest examples of Byzantine textile art and was used in the service of the Eucharist.

DAR AL-ISLAM – HOUSE OF PEACE

Muslims believe in One God, whom they call by the Arabic name Allah, but who is regarded as the same God worshipped by Jews and Christians. Many Muslims would say that all religions, even the most primitive, worship Allah though in ways which have become corrupted because of thousands of years of human interference. For this reason Muslim toleration, though often more theoretical than real, could extend to any group which acknowledged the existence of a Supreme Creator.

Muslims also regard Muhammad as the Seal of the Prophets, in other words the last in the line of prophets going back to Adam himself and including Old Testament Jewish prophets, Jesus Christ, several pre-Islamic Arabian prophets not recognized by Jews or Christians, and, in the eyes of some Muslim thinkers, the founders of all the world's earlier religions. Muhammad is seen as the last Prophet – no later claimants being accepted. The other basic aspects of the Muslim faith are prayer, fasting, giving alms to the poor and, where possible, making the Haj, or pilgrimage, to Mecca.

Within less than a century of the Prophet Muhammad's death in 632, the Muslim community split into two factions: the Sunni, sometimes called orthodox, and the minority Shia. Apart from tiny differences in doctrine and ritual, any disagreement between the two concerned religious authority.

While the Sunni accepted the idea of an elected Caliphate, the Shia considered that spiritual leadership most remain with the direct descendants of the Prophet Muhammad, who were considered to have inherited the personal sanctity required by the Imam or spiritual guide. In practice, the elected Caliphate of the Sunni was chosen only from the Abbasid family, and then sometimes only on the basis of which of them had actually seized power.

Meanwhile the Shia fragmented several times because of disagreements about which of the Prophet's descendants should inherit the Imamate. Some minor but locally powerful groups sometimes would leave the Muslim community altogether, but this was rare, as Muslim toleration usually enabled the Umma, or 'community', to embrace even such groups as the Bektashi dervishes, who drank wine, left their womenfolk unveiled and included non-Muslims.

Mosques and religious beliefs

For ordinary medieval Muslims, however, religion continued to dominate everyday life, with obligatory daily prayers, congregational prayers each Friday, fasting during the Ramadan and saving up for the pilgrimage to Mecca – the wish of all pious Muslims.

The mosque, meanwhile, was not considered sacred like a Christian church or a Hindu temple, but was merely a place of communal prayer which needed to be respected and kept clean. Some mosques did, however, take on the character of shrines for other reasons, usually because they included the tombs of important religious figures. Other mosques served as religious colleges, or as centres where sufi brotherhoods would gather to celebrate in their own somewhat unorthodox manner – celebrations which could include religious music and dance.

Many parts of the medieval Muslim world held unorthodox beliefs, which could include beliefs in jinnis and demons, even amongst the ruling classes. Jinnis were thought to be creatures created from fire, just as mankind was created from clay, and, like humans, they included male and female, good and bad, Muslims and non-believers. There was a similarly widespread belief in magic, talismans, and prediction of the future.

Islam was not structured in the same way as Christianity. Even the Abbasid Sunni Caliphs of Baghdad (750–1258) had lost most of their temporal power by the 11th century, but survived, as little more than puppets, long after the medieval period. The Shia Fatimid Caliphate of Cairo (909–1171) was overthrown in the 12th century and the rival Caliphs of the western parts of North Africa did not survive much longer.

Basically, the Islamic religious establishment consisted of the Sharia legal system and junior imams who led prayers in local mosques. They were not, however, priests, as no such people existed in Islam, but they were men with sufficient religious education to be accepted by their local communities as religious leaders – beyond that, the imam had virtually no official spiritual authority.

Because religion was central to Islamic society, rulers took a close interest in the religious leanings of the legal establishment, teachers and local imams. Thus the Seljuk sultans of the 11th and 12th centuries, who were Sunni Muslims, sponsored a revival in Sunni theological colleges and preachers to act as potent political and spiritual weapons against the rival Shia Fatimid Caliphate in Cairo.

The Seljuk sultans of Anatolia (1077–1300) followed the same policy to stem the spread of Shia ideas and to encourage Islam amongst subjects who were still largely Armenian or Greek Christians. Yet Seljuk Anatolia was the birthplace of the Mevlevi or 'whirling dervishes' founded by the mystic and poet Jalal al-Din Rumi (1207–1273). They managed to remain within the Sunni establishment while still providing an outlet for those who needed a more emotional religious experience.

Another characteristic of later medieval Turkish Anatolia was the large degree of Christian influence upon Islam at the village

One of the few more serious pictures in al-Wasiti's illustration of Abu Zaid's adventures shows a funeral in a cemetery As the body is placed in its grave the women tear off their veils and even show their long dark hair as a sign of grief, while the men sob more soberly into their white sleeves.

Strictly speaking, religious subjects should never be shown in Islamic art. However, there are many illustrations of religious activity, many of them satirical. Here the comical hero Abu Zaid pretends to be a religious scholar and preaches from the pulpit. The picture was painted by al-Wasiti in Baghdad around 1237.

or tribal level, resulting in some highly unorthodox practices. On the other hand, these made conversion from Orthodox Christianity to Islam much easier.

A spread of religious mysticism was, in fact, one of the most notable features of later medieval Muslim society in many countries. It not only flourished in the towns, but also involved wandering dervishes, extreme ascetics, disaffected tribal groups and down-trodden peasants. Shia doctrines had by now largely been driven underground and, in their more extreme Ismaili versions, served as a sort of revolutionary undercurrent.

Even the powerful Ottoman Sultans only really joined the orthodox Sunni Muslims in the 15th century and, even then, the Ottoman Empire remained home to a large number of varied dervish sects. One of the most unusual was that of the Bektashis, whose doctrines and practices included many Buddhist concepts dating back to the time before the Turks converted to Islam. Not only did the Bektashi welcome Christians and Jews into the lower ranks of their brotherhood, but they also developed a close relationship with the Janissaries, the Ottoman Sultan's elite infantry troops.

The artist al-Wasiti was very good at showing crowds in very small spaces. Here soldiers from the Caliph of Baghdad's army announce the end of the fasting month of Ramadan, which meant that people could celebrate with feasting. The soldiers are led by trumpeters and a drummer riding a mule.

THE CONFUCIAN WORLD

In Europe there was frequent friction between Church and state, while in the Muslim world these were theoretically one and the same. In China religion and government were again closely linked, but for different reasons. Here religion was a means of social control, and the beliefs at the heart of Confucianism based upon the teachings of Confucius in the 6th century BC were not so much a religion, as a view of mankind's place in the universe.

Chinese philosophers constantly strove to achieve an ideal society based on deeply held conservative values and a view of history seen as a series of cycles rather than a continuing progression. Strict Confucian scholars considered that virtue brought a reward and argued in favour of moral principles. Yet a fatalist view that wealth or success resulted from irrational external 'powers' remained deeply entrenched in Chinese civilization, engendering a widespread interest in predicting the future and summoning help from spirits or dead ancestors.

State-sponsored worship

Since the Chinese state openly used religion as a form of social control, the government supported local shrines and ensured that local authorities maintained them in good condition. Similarly the local authorities ensured that religious sacrifices were made and festivals observed to preserve good crops and clement weather. Mount T'ai in eastern China was believed to be the most important shrine where new Emperors were supposed to give an account of their actions.

Meanwhile the spirit of the soil was thought capable of both good and evil and needed to be restrained with suitable rituals.

Most Chinese also believed that two main forces were at work in the universe: Yin which was dark, cold and female, and Yang which was bright, warm and male. All mankind could hope for was the maintenance of a balance between the two.

The individual soul, however, was the concern of ascetics and hermits rather than of ordinary people, but the Confucian emphasis on family obligation meant that the Chinese paid enormous attention to family graves and shrines. At the New Year's Day festival, for example, offerings were made to dead ancestors by the entire family in order of seniority. In the villages, agricultural produce would similarly be shown to the ancestors' graves at special ceremonies which were almost like spiritual 'company reports'.

Confucianism may have been the state religion of China, but several other faiths were tolerated. Taoism, for example, dated from the later part of the Han period (206BC–AD 220) and offered a 'path ' whereby a person hoped to achieve immortality, though by the later Middle Ages, the Taoists had developed themselves into a structured political and social force with a recognized hierarchy.

Buddhism reached China from India during the later part of Han period (206BC–AD 220) and soon proved popular with soldiers because it weakened the link between individual and family spirits, meaning that it did not really matter whether or not a person was buried at home or in a distant place. The essence of Buddhism is to release the human soul from a cycle of reincarnations through meditation, good works and self-discipline, ultimately leading to nirvana, or total enlightenment.

But Buddhism soon divided into two main schools: the Hinayana school concentrated on

Tibet, Central Asia, China, Korea and Japan. Meanwhile the Chinese also developed a system of spiritual exercises called Ch'an, which was known in Japan as Zen, a mixture of Buddhist and Taoist philosophies.

Buddhism and its rivals

Buddhism also took root in Korea and, despite the fact that Confucianism was encouraged by the ruling elite, Buddhism became the dominant religion. Nevertheless a revised form of neo-Confucianism became the state creed in the late 14th century, particularly under the first few rulers of the Yi or Li dynasty (1392–1910), while at the same time an indigenous shamanism survived.

Buddhism similarly spread to Japan, where the native faith of Shinto responded to the challenge and became more formalized, surviving alongside Buddhism. In fact Buddhism did not really spread amongst the population until the 12th century, leading to a liberalization of doctrine and an emphasis on a single deity, Amida, as the saviour of souls. Another characteristic of the fragmented feudal age which then followed was the way in which the samurai military elite adopted Zen meditation to serve as a bridge between the new 'popular' forms of Buddhism and the orthodox religious structures.

Buddhism had been introduced to Tibet by the ruling elite in the 7th century, but then virtually disappeared with the collapse of the early medieval Tibetan empire in the 9th century. It slowly revived in the 10th century and thereafter dominated the life of the Tibetan people. Here 'enlightened ones' were believed to have willingly delayed their own final enlightenment for the sake of others, a living example being the Dalai Lama.

The 11th to 15th centuries also saw a flowering of monastic culture in Tibet; the main monastic orders included the ancient Nyingmapas, the Sakyapas who developed in the 11th century, the Kargyupas who appeared in the 12th century, and the Gelugpas who were founded in 1409.

The Bodhisattva Fugen shown on an 11th century painted silk. Japanese Buddhist art of this period was a mixture of Chinese, Central Asian and northern Indian elements, plus native Japanese styles.

monastic discipline and had little interest in the god or gods, while the Mahayana school put greater emphasis on the goal of immediate enlightenment through meditation and the intercession of saints of Bodhisattvas. Hinayana flourished in southern and southeastern Asia, while Mahayana took root in

The gigantic bronze statue of Amida Butsu, the Great Buddha, at Kotuku-in was made for the samurai leader Yoritomo in 1252. It is one of the most astonishing examples of religious art from the Kamakura period.

The Buddhist civilization of Central Asia had much in common with Tibet. Here Mahayana Buddhism survived alongside earlier shamanist beliefs while the latter dominated the northernmost tribes of the Siberian forest and Arctic fringe. Nestorian Christianity also had many adherents amongst the Turco-Mongol peoples of Central Asia in the 13th century and Islam was also beginning to spread.

Mongol shamanism had no fixed dogma and the universe was believed to contain an infinite number of spirits, including ancestral ghosts. These accounted for all aspects of nature and geography while Tengri, the god of the sky, watched over everything as a supreme spirit. Tengri also had a special relationship with rulers on earth, but did not have much impact on the everyday life of ordinary people, to whom Nachigai, the earth goddess, was of more immediate significance. As a variation on a widespread form of ancestor worship Genghis Khan's (c.1162–1227) battle standard became a very important totem as the Great Khan's spirit was believed to live in it.

In fact Mongol shamanism involved a great many idols, including small 'ongghon' made by women out of felt or silk. Meat and drink would be offered to the ongghons whose mouths would be smeared before meals or other important occasions.

The Temple of the Silver Pavilion at Ginkaku-ji is a typical example of how the Japanese tried to set their religious buildings in harmony with surrounding nature. It was built in 1482. The garden was as important as the building, and was designed by Soami.

HINDU SOUTHERN ASIA

Although the concept of a supreme deity underlies Hinduism, in practical terms the Hindus worshipped many gods. They also had more tirtha, or pilgrimage sites, than any other major religion, particularly in the Himalayan mountains, along the Ganges river and on Cape Comorin at the southern tip of India. Many of these sites also attracted the Buddhists and Jains. Since only higher Hindu castes studied the Vedas or religious texts, ordinary people tended to focus on the physical evidence of Divine presence.

The most important pilgrimage centres, which included free kitchens providing food for visitors and also served as study centres for religious students. The great temples of southern India had huge staffs to maintain them – one in the Chola capital also included four hundred sacred prostitutes who dedicated their bodies to the service of the gods. Seasonal religious fairs were also popular with wandering ascetics, who used them to discuss the religious problems of the day.

Hinduism and Buddhism both spread south-east, although the only area to adopt the Mahayana Buddhism was northern Vietnam, while a form of Hinduism dominated southern Vietnam, Java and several neighbouring islands including Bali. Meanwhile Hinayana Buddhism spread across Cam-

bodia, Thailand and Burma. Both Buddhism and Hinduism blended with existing south-east Asian cults; amongst the Khmer, for example, ordinary people had for centuries looked upon their tribal chiefs as embodiments of the god or spirit of the soil and a rice-burning ritual may have developed from a harvest festival or sacrifice.

On the other hand, Hinayana Buddhism seems to have become the religion of the bulk of the population in medieval Burma far more quickly than in other parts of south-east Asia and for many centuries it remained the cult of a ruling elite.

Following a period of Buddhist domination, a Hindu revival started in the early Middle Ages in southern India. Rulers spent huge amounts of money on temples and sacred art to emphasize their own role as links between men and gods; in fact the depiction of gods and kings sometimes seem to have been interchangeable and temple art was also used to record military victories. The temples themselves consisted of many buildings within a complex which developed into a small town in its own right. The temples owned large tracts of land and employed thousands of agricultural workers, buying up those who fell into debt slavery.

Whereas Buddhism declined steeply on the Indian mainland, it remained the dominant religion in Sri Lanka where monasteries were often incorporated into royal centres because rulers wanted, where possible, to control the religious hierarchy.

In south-east Asia, meanwhile, the religious affiliation of an area seems to have depended almost entirely on the leanings of the local ruling dynasty, who would, in turn, use religion to extend influence over more distant islands. Here vast stone structures called candi symbolized the power of the gods, while Buddhist stupas tended to be situated a short distance from the town; both temples and stupas were maintained by local villagers in return for tax exemptions. Temple complexes covered an even bigger area in Indo-China, where the 12th century

temples at Angkor in Cambodia cover an area almost 25 by 10 km and remain the largest single religious complex made by man.

The greatest religious change that took place in south-east Asia during the later medieval period was the arrival of Islam. It first took hold in northern Sumatra, then the Malayan coast, then Java and the Sulu islands during the 14th century and the Moluccas by the late 15th century. The spread of Islam was, however, carried out by merchants and wandering dervishes rather than by conquering armies, while Hinduism, Buddhism and local animist beliefs survived in several areas.

Above: The four-armed Hindu god Siva Nataraja, as portrayed in a late 11th century bronze statue from the Chola kingdom in southern India.

Opposite: Many medieval Indian Hindu temples were practically covered with statues, both inside and out. In some cases they were highly erotic, as on these 11th century carvings at Khajuraho in Madhya Pradesh, central India.

10 STATE AND EMPIRE

One of the most extraordinary features of medieval history was the way in which some parts of the world were covered by vast empires which remained loyal to distant rulers, while in other areas, political authority was fragmented into many tiny, constatntly changing states. Then there were even bigger, but far more short-lived, empires carved out by nomadic peoples from Central Asia, of whom the Mongols were the most famous.

RIVAL KINGS, EMPERORS AND POPES

By the start of the 11th century, the Christian states of western Europe were very different to what they had been in the 9th century. Central authority was weaker, the local autonomy of barons greater and the new class of knights was, in many cases, virtually beyond government control. For most of the states of the European heartland, the next few centuries would see huge efforts by central authorities to reimpose control. France, England and some Scandinavian countries succeeded; the collective Empire of Germany, Austria, Switzerland, Italy and its large neighbouring provinces did not. The Papacy, as leader of the Latin Church, also tried to impose its own hegemony, but largely failed.

On the frontiers of Europe there were other priorities; in what are now Spain and Portugal, several small states pressed south against Muslim Andalusia whilst in central Europe, Poland, Bohemia and Hungary survived German expansion by adopting German political systems. In the north, the Scandinavian kingdoms remained a poor and ignored corner of Christendom. The Celtic north-western fringes remained even more 'backward', despite being so close to England which, by copying French models, had become one of the most 'advanced' states following the Norman Conquest of 1066. In fact, efforts by the Anglicized kings of southern Scotland to impose their rule on the highlands were never really successful.

In many parts of western Europe an early medieval tradition of free men being able to bring complaints directly before their king continued throughout the 11th and 12th centuries, while senior barons were considered almost equal in rank to the king and therefore had to be consulted on all major issues. Furthermore, in most parts of Europe,

towns grew in wealth and influence, and all these factors contributed to the development of early forms of parliament.

Parliamentary debates

The English experience was in some ways typical. The Magna Carta of 1215, King John's charter encompassing the basic rights of political and personal liberty, was a result of his need for ready cash to defend his French territories from attack by the French king. When the Church joined the barons in resisting King John's financial demands, he had to recognize aristocratic rights.

The first parliaments were elected by those with power, with representatives being selected from the same classes. As the burden of taxation spread down the social order, so parliamentary representation followed. In England, representation was eventually achieved at shire or county level, closer to ordinary people. In most countries, representatives from different social classes either met separately or formed distinct groups, such as in the three 'arms' of the Aragonese Cortes. In England, the Church and baronial representatives evolved into the House of Lords, while those of town and county became the House of Commons.

The 14th century also saw the emergence of political members like Peter de la Mare, the first 'speaker' of the Commons, in 1376, whose legal, political and financial experience made the House of Commons increasingly effective. As yet, however, there was no freedom of speech within England's parliament, and any member who criticized the monarch too much could find himself in trouble. England was then less democratic than several other places in Europe.

Opposite: The very cold climate of Greenland and its very small population meant that many relics of two small Scandinavian settlements survived to astonish modern archaeologists. This is part of the ruins of Brattahlid, the so-called 'eastern' or more accurately the south settlement founded by Erik the Red in the late 10th century.

The most dramatic political developments were in Italy. Here states like Milan became 'tyrannies' governed by a military dynasty, while others, such as Venice, were republics with power firmly concentrated in the hands of an oligarchy of elite families. In more fluid republics such as Florence, power was constantly shifted between wealthy families like the Medicis, who usually preferred to 'pull strings' behind the scenes rather than lead from the front. Yet they steadily rose to dominate this city state from 1434 to 1737.

Loyalty to family was paramount in medieval Italy and, as a result, any government tended to be characterized by feuding between powerful families, murderous vendettas, assassination and brawling in the

The triumphs and disasters of the Crusades remained popular subjects of literature, particularly amongst the knightly class, long after the Muslims had retaken the Holy Land. In this early 14th century illustration the Christians are shown as fully armoured knights of the time when the manuscript was painted, whereas the Muslims are inaccurately shown as turbaned savages.

streets. The situation in medieval Germany developed in a slightly different way and by the end of the 15th century the wealthiest regions could be described as socially and politically fragmented.

Power to the people

At local level political power was also changing in fundamental ways. The old Carolingian militia of the 9th–10th centuries had become the new knights by the end of the 11th century, serving as a link between the king and ordinary people. The latter would also look to the knights for advice, as well as protection, in a political system which worked remarkably well – as long as the knightly elite clung to the old ideals of public service.

By the 14th century, however, tensions resulted in peasants' revolts in many parts of Europe, the most famous of which were the Great Revolt of 1381 in England and the Jacquerie of 1358 in France. Yet the term 'peasant revolt' can be misleading since it was not always those at the very bottom of the hierarchy who rose up against oppression, but rather those who had gained some prosperity and now considered that they should have some say.

Once again the situation was different on the outer fringes of western Christendom. In Scotland, for example, survivals from the earlier medieval period included the Earldom of Moray which was descended from a Pictish kingdom. Elsewhere in the highlands and islands, local Toisichs dominated the power structure, owing a distant allegiance to a High King who eventually became the King of Scotland himself. Free members of society consisted of extended families; taxes were paid in kind rather than in cash. From the 12th century onwards the old tribal structure began to evolve into the Scottish clan system of later years. In fact the remoter regions of Scotland were probably the only part of Europe where tribalism increased rather than declined during the Middle Ages.

For entirely different reasons, local political structures in medieval Italy also developed along distinctive lines. Here the flourishing cities felt a need to dominate their 'contado', or rural area immediately outside their walls, for political, economic and military reasons, as well as to ensure constant and reliable food supplies .

Several ideologies competed in medieval Europe. From the 11th to 13th centuries, the Catholic Papacy unsuccessfully claimed temporal as well as spiritual domination. This clashed with the 'imperial' ideology of

what had become a German–Italian Empire, based on the Emperor Otto III's efforts at the start of the 11th century to continue Charlemagne's work. Like Charlemagne, Otto III wanted to rebuild the Roman Empire in a Christian form, with himself and his successors as leaders of all the kings of Europe, equal to the Byzantine Emperor in Constantinople and partners of the Pope.

'Brotherhood of arms'

Meanwhile the Church also encouraged a sense of Christian 'brotherhood of arms' amongst the knightly elites of western Christendom, particularly in relation to the military elites of neighbouring non-Christian lands. At this time the knightly class was regarded as Christendom's main defence in a frightening and hostile world. The uniquely western European system of heraldry developed during the 12th and 13th centuries as a way of distinguishing this military elite.

More importantly, perhaps, it also served to identify individuals and groups within the knightly class, since extended family relationships often spread beyond national boundaries. Furthermore heraldry could proclaim political allegiance as well as identity. In fact western heraldry eventually developed into a pictorial language with strict rules where designs were handed down from generation to generation.

There were even cases where men made pictorial jokes about their own names. Some rich merchant families who had risen from humble origins to knightly status took pride in this fact by including motifs representing business or farming on their coats-of-arms. Heraldic ruler were not, however, as universal or rigid as is sometimes thought.

Meanwhile western Christendom was on the offensive against practically all its neighbours. The most dramatic campaigns were those of the 12th and 13th century Crusades, though these were also the least successful. Such failures puzzled churchmen who were convinced that God was on their side, while the knights were equally certain they were the best fighting men in the world. Though

Left: People paying their taxes to the town's official representative, as shown in a 13th century law book. Careful accounts were kept; much of the money going to maintain law and order or to repair the town's defensive wall.

Below: A view of the port of Hamburg, in a 15th century manuscript. As one of the Hanseatic League of trading cities, Hamburg became extremely rich. The man on the left of the picture is probably a customs officer.

Di commence li liures du graunt Caam qui parole de la graunt Ermenie de perse et destartars et dynde. Et des graunz merueille qui p le monde sont,

The Polo brothers leaving Venice at the start of their epic voyage to the east, in a late 14th century version of the travels of Marco Polo. Marco Polo's detailed account of his travels through Asia, his service under the Great Khan Kubilai, and his return via the Indian Ocean, was not really believed when he got home. On the other hand, the merchants of Venice and Genoa had a far better idea of the world beyond Europe than did most other people in western Christendom.

these events are seen as very important in western history, they are generally viewed by the Greek Orthodox and Muslim worlds as damaging barbarian invasions.

Far to the north, the Baltic Crusades were more successful. Here knights, sergeants and warlike priests forced Christianity upon the pagan natives. Campaigns known as the 'reconquista' pushed the Christian frontier southwards, eventually overrunning Andalusia and even proposing to attack North Africa in 1354. One interesting outcome of these aggressive campaigns was the creation of states ruled by the Military Orders, the largest being that of the Teutonic Knights, who ruled most of what is now northern Poland, Latvia and Estonia by the 13th century.

Europe's expansion across the north Atlantic also suffered a little-known setback at the end of the medieval period. Two colonies in Greenland which were based around deep fjords in the late 10th century became part of Norway's overseas territories in 1261 and a royal commissioner, or 'umbodsmadr', took up residence. Trade improved and there is evidence that there were unofficial links with western Scotland. But the climate gradually changed, there was political turmoil in Scandinavia and clashes with the native Inuit Eskimos grew worse.

The last official sailing to Greenland was in 1410 and the settlers were probably finally absorbed into Inuit Eskimo society around 1500.

BYZANTIUM'S COLLAPSING EMPIRE

The Byzantine Empire was the surviving eastern part of the old Roman Empire. Indeed, people still called themselves 'Romans' right down to the fall of Constantinople in 1453. It had existed alongside the Muslim world since the 7th century, often at war but more commonly at peace. Then in the 11th century another threat appeared – the newly converted Muslim Turks, who overran the eastern provinces until partially driven back at the start of the 12th century.

The Byzantine Empire began to collapse and fragment under pressure from both Muslim Turks and Latin Catholic western Europeans, finally falling to the Ottoman Turks in the mid-15th century. Meanwhile other Orthodox and eastern Christian states survived and in some cases even flourished, including Cilician Armenia, and Georgia, which reached its greatest splendour in the 13th and 14th centuries.

Taxation and the poor

Within the Byzantine Empire and its fragmented successor states, autocratic rule was the ideal and taxation was normally very high because of the need to maintain a large military structure. The traditional pomp of the Byzantine court also cost a great deal, as did Byzantium's elaborate but failing bureaucracy. The Byzantine economy had traditionally been a cash economy, in which the state owned a great deal of rural land, urban property, mines and quarries.

Most government revenues came from customs levies on imports and exports, inheritance, consumer goods and agriculture, where the rural village was the basic taxation unit. Here a man's neighbours had joint tax responsibility if an individual was unable to pay his dues. After the introduction of a quasi-feudal system, those who held pronoias, or fiefs, still had the right to raise some local taxes. Meanwhile the imperial government found it increasingly necessary to buy the loyalty of political and military followers, either with pronoia or with cash salaries in the old Romano-Byzantine manner. This became even more noticeable under the fragmented Byzantine statelets of the 13th to 15th centuries. Yet the rulers of these much reduced 'empires' and despotates still tried to govern their little states in much the same manner as their mighty predecessors.

In the neighbouring Christian kingdoms, Georgian government had originally been modelled on Byzantium, though with a strong Persian influence. The result was very complex with a sophisticated hierarchy which reached great splendour under King David the Builder (1089–1125). A monarch ruled by Divine Right and central government was undertaken by five 'viziers', or ministers, while the provinces were ruled by 'eristavis', or dukes.

Emperor Michael I proclaims Leo V as co-Emperor in 813. They are shown being lifted up on a shield, which had been the Byzantine army's way of recognizing and accepting their ruler.

Other members of the aristocracy were given elaborate court titles such as Master of the Royal Stables and Chief Wine Steward. During the 12th and 13th centuries, Georgia came under strong Crusader influence and as a result developed many features in common with western European feudalism. The status of the minor aristocracy rose, while the burden of taxation fell on the peasantry where the old class of free peasants declined steeply.

The land of rival princes

The government of medieval Russia was supposedly modelled on that of Byzantium, but circumstances were so different that new structures were bound to appear. The old unified Russian state based upon the city of Kiev had been founded by Scandinavian merchants who probably took over the administration of what had been a part of the Judeo-Turkish Khazar Khanate. During the 11th century, the rulers of Kiev imposed their authority across a vast area of small, scattered settlements, this remarkable state reaching the peak of its power in the 12th century.

The Russian Principalities, including the northern 'republic' of Novgorod, then fell under Mongol domination. Even before the Mongol conquest, however, the centre of gravity of the Russian states was already moving from Kiev to central Russia. By the end of the 15th century, Russian power was based around Moscow.

The way medieval Russia was governed was also distinctive. There were several leading, but rival, families or clans, who claimed descent from Rurik, the founder of the Kievan state. They acted as governors of the increasingly fragmented Russian principalities, tending to move from state to state, ruling one or more principalities at any given time. Yet this system of rule by competing families led to feuding and eventually to fragmentation as the Mongols invaded.

Below the princely elite came the boyars, an aristocratic class which had emerged from a mixture of older tribal, landholding and

military elites. Unlike the aristocracy of western Europe, the boyars were legally free to offer their allegiance to whichever prince they wished and to retain their lands, even if they entered the service of a rival ruler in some distant part of Russia.

Medieval Russian society was, in fact, more fluid than that of medieval western Europe and even the free peasantry was, at first, free to move around the country. Such peasant farmers could pass their farms on to their sons, but were obliged to hand agricultural land over their local boyar if they had no son. However the boyars were free to pass on their lands to a son or a daughter. A great many peasant families had, in fact, fled northward from the southern steppes and neighbouring lands even before the Mongol invasions and this clearly benefited the cities of the central Russian principalities.

The subsequent centuries of Mongol domination effectively insulated Muscovy, as the lands around Moscow in east-central Russia were called, from western interference, which, in turn, enabled Moscow to take gradual control of its neighbouring principalities.

The later medieval period also saw a steady centralization of power by the ruling princes, particularly the ruler of Moscow, at the expense of the boyar aristocracy and of Veche town councils. Initially, this meant little change for the rural peasantry, but by the time Ivan III, known as Ivan the Terrible, came to the throne in the second part of the 15th century he ruled more like a Mongol Khan than a European prince.

Above: An 11th century mosaic showing Mary and the Child Jesus between the Byzantine Emperor Romanos and the Empress Irene. The Empress has red hair, since she was of Russian origin, and offers the Virgin a manuscript while Romanos offers money. Their heavily jewelled robes were characteristic of an imperial court where ceremony played an extremely important role.

Opposite: A map-like 'aerial view' of Constantinople, capital of the fast shrinking Byzantine Empire in 1422. In reality the famous defensive walls enclosed several village-like areas of houses separated by vegetable gardens, orchards and waste ground. The city only filled up after it had been taken by the Ottoman Turks. On the other side of the Golden Horn is the separate suburb of Galata, inhabited by European and other foreign merchant communities.

A THEORETICAL THEOCRACY

Within Islamic territories, rulers were theoretically autocrats who governed within strictly defined laws. This gave enormous power to any religious establishment which decided whether any policy was legal under Sharia law. The Ulema or recognized religious scholars and the civilian bureaucracy together formed the 'men of the pen' while the military formed the 'men of the sword'.

In theory, as the focus of popular discontent, an unjust government could be overthrown by the Ulema, while extortionate government was believed to fail because its actions made the people unwilling to work

and thus undermined its own financial foundation. In fact the link between wealth, power and legitimacy was more openly recognized in Islam than in any other medieval civilization. On the other hand, violence was always just under the surface and remained the normal way of settling internal and external disputes.

By the 8th century, the 'men of the pen' were a distinct and often highly educated class present in almost all medieval Islamic states. As such, they had parallels in the Byzantine Empire but not in western Europe. By the 11th century, the old Greek, Aramaic and Persian administrative elites had been largely Arabized, though not Islamized as Christians still played a major role in Iraq, Syria, Egypt and Andalusia. Together with their Muslim colleagues they were known as the katibs, or scribes, and were headed by the vizir, or 'prime minister'. At first they received regular monthly salaries, but in later years, as the cash economy deteriorated, senior bureaucrats were given iqta fiefs comparable to those offered to military officers.

In reality, of course, between the 11th and 15th centuries there were considerable variations on this basic system. In the Fatimid Caliphate of Egypt (909–1171), for example, the Caliph himself had had little power since the rule of the probably insane Hakim at the start of the 11th century. Instead power rested in the hands of viziers, who in turn owed their position to one or more sections of the army. For its final century of existence the Fatimid Caliphate was, in effect, a military dictatorship. Nevertheless the government still had to supervise agriculture, irrigation and trade, as well as defending Egypt from no fewer than five Crusader invasions between 1118 and 1169.

The Turkish variations

While the Fatimids claimed to govern in a traditional manner, the Seljuk Turks and their successors in the eastern and central Islamic lands openly introduced new administrative features. They were military states where the efficiency of the army remained paramount. Under the Seljuks (1037–1157), themselves, rule usually passed from father to eldest son, while younger brothers governed the provinces. The ruler was himself assisted by a Vizier, as well as the newer figure of the Pervane, or Lord Chancellor, and was advised by a divan, or council. They in turn were supposedly supported by 24 secretaries, half of whom dealt with financial affairs whilst the others dealt with military matters.

Almost everything was written down, with paper imported from China used for the most important documents. Government paperwork was done in Persian, religious law in Arabic, while Turkish was only used in everyday life. This sophisticated administrative structure included a secret police to root out corruption amongst officials and would itself form the basis of subsequent Turkish states including the Ottoman Empire.

Friction between the Persian and Arabic 'men of the sword' and the less educated Turkish 'men of the sword' was characteristic of many states, though each recognized the importance of the other. The need to defend the state was obvious, but the soldiers similarly knew that trade and manufacture gave the taxation base which provided their salaries. These elites also loved titles and display – the Master of Ceremonies being one of the most important officials at all Turkish courts, although the Turks' traditional concern for pure water meant that the Master of Water was almost as significant. Next in seniority came the ruler's personal doctor, who was frequently Jewish or Christian.

The Ayyubid government (1169–1250) in Egypt and Syria continued to use the Fatimid administration while at the same time adding several Seljuk ideas. The Ayyubid system was

in turn utilized by the Mamluk Sultans to the end of the medieval period. There were continuous efforts to keep the 'men of the pen' separate from the 'men of the sword' and, despite a gradual decline in the status of the bureaucratic elite, Syrian and Egyptian katibs, or scribes, contributed as much to the survival of the Mamluk state as did the army. It is also worth noting that many katibs were recruited from the descendants of Mamluk soldiers, since only first-generation slave-troops were considered worthy of elite military status.

The Ottoman state was supposedly modelled on that of the Mamluks, but in reality differed in many ways. In its early days, the Ottoman administration was largely tribal and relied on Turco-Mongol yasa laws rather than the Muslim sharia. However, as it attracted refugees fleeing from Mongol oppression as well as defectors and converts from a crumbling Byzantium, the Ottoman state absorbed both Persian and Byzantine civil administrative concepts.

The Byzantine impact became even more pronounced in the later 14th–15th centuries after the Ottomans had crossed the Dardanelles in 1348 and went on to conquer the Balkans. In fact the Ottomans now cre-

Opposite: Muslims are usually portrayed very inaccurately in medieval European manuscripts, except in those from Spain and Portugal. Here the Moors or Andalusians were the Christians' immediate neighbours. They also often used virtually the same arms and armour, though their civilian costume was very different. Both civil and military costume is shown in this late 13th century picture of the Muwahid governor of Seville holding a council of war.

Below: On this page from the adventures of Abu Zaid illustrated by al-Wasiti, the governor of Maragha in north-western Iran discusses problems of local administration with his officials. Medieval Islamic civilization was, in fact, highly bureaucratic and the katibs or scribes were an influential group.

ated the first European Islamic state since Muslim Andalusia had declined far to the west. By the end of the 15th century the Ottoman Empire had developed into a new Muslim Byzantium which gave considerably more freedom to its peasantry, was more open to new ideas and was considerably more favourable to commerce than the old Byzantium had been.

During this period the administration of western Islamic regions in North Africa and Andalusia remained far more traditional, though by no means unchanging. Most states were now monarchies, though some claimed to be Caliphates. Cities and palaces reflected the glory of their rulers, often employing huge numbers of servants and functionaries.

Much of the countryside, however, was still dominated by local clans which had been given land by a government in return for loyal military service. In other cases they merely received official recognition for land they already held in return for not causing further trouble. Here the peasantry was protected by provincial elites in exchange for taxes in a simple form of feudal relationship.

The only surviving picture of the great Saracen hero of the Crusades, Saladin, is this simple little Fatimid-style picture. Salah al-Din, or Saladin, was of Kurdish origin, brought up and educated in a sophisticated Arab aristocratic environment, while his army was largely Turkish. Here he is portrayed as a turbaned Arab prince seated cross-legged on a carved wooden dais.

Right: The World Empire carved out by Genghiz Khan in the 13th century astonished subsequent generations. Here, the Mongol warriors are shown in 14th century arms and armour.

PLATE A

PORTRAIT OF SALADIN (?)

FATIMID SCHOOL

About A.D. 1180

THE BUREAUCRATIC IDEAL

By the 11th century there had been a considerable increase in China's population and the old early medieval military elite had ceded power to a new bureaucratic class. The main source of government authority came from information detailed in registers of land holding and inhabitants based on frequent censuses, which were essential for tax gathering. The most important element of this was the collection of one thirtieth of all produce, bringing in massive revenues. The tax-gatherers were themselves frequently checked by senior authorities as a system to stop corruption and fraud.

From the 10th century onwards Chinese forms of administration were adopted in neighbouring Korea, where the bureaucracy was given Chinese-style ranks while officials were paid salaries, given land grants or allocations of rice according to circumstances. By the 10th century, the two main southern islands of Japan were divided into 62 provinces and the Japanese imperial administration was again based on a Chinese model.

Yet this attempt to adopt the complex Chinese system did not prove suitable in economically backward Japan and as a result many individuals had impressive titles without real function. In fact form and ceremony became more important than effective administration. By 1185, the centralized government had collapsed and the Japanese imperial court was bypassed rather than destroyed, while what was left of central government fell into the hands of a military headquarters known as the Shogunate. Most government was, however, localized and more efficient than in earlier years.

Amongst the Turkish peoples of Central Asia government was much simpler, leadership passing to the eldest surviving brother or to the strongest brother or son. The Mongols largely copied this system and tribal leaders often came together in a great council to decide upon their overall ruler. Genghis Khan was himself elected in this way in 1206, though he went on to impose a greater degree of loyalty to the concept of a Mongol 'people' than had ever been seen before.

Beneath him there were some 95 governors responsible for enforcing law, gathering taxes and imposing military conscription in a state which was organized like a vast army. Further north amongst the more primitive peoples of the Siberian forests, meanwhile, the old system of tribal princes supported by mounted warrior elites remained in place until modern times.

Local government in medieval China was closely tied to the census system and the entire population was divided into officials and non-officials. The rigidity of this structure served as a form of social control and every family was categorized according to wealth, profession and traditional status. To modern eyes, Chinese administration often

Tamerlane holding court at Balkh in what is now northern Afghanistan, as illustrated in a Persian versified epic made in 1538. The tall pointed red caps worn beneath the white turbans were not worn in Timur's day and in fact, until the Safavids seized power in Iran at the end of the 15th century, they were often regarded as the mark of Kizil Bash 'Red Head' subversives and revolutionaries.

since taxation was assessed on the basis of land. These Sho estates were not, however, owned outright. Instead various people had different rights to use land, impose dues or labour on those who lived there, or to take a proportion of the crops. As a result no individual actually owned the land but might have had rights in several different places; rights which could be changed or transferred as rewards for service.

Clans and mandates from heaven

Land-holding was of relatively minor importance amongst the peoples of Central Asia, where control of people and herds was much more significant. Here the basis of Mongol society was the clan, claiming descent from a common ancestor. A group of kindred clans was called a 'bone', and marriage within the clan was forbidden, each clan being controlled by its dominant family.

The clans were also grouped into a tribe, which itself formed part of a 'people', Freemen of the lower class could win the title 'tarkhan' for valour in battle and thus enter the minor aristocracy. Above them the nobility were called 'noyat', or 'noyan' if they were of princely rank, while at the top of the social order were the Khan and his immediate family.

seems oppressive, taxes high and conscription harsh. Imperial edicts ranged from amnesties for criminals, rewards or bribes for a whole community or gifts to local leaders. They also covered minor matters of personal behaviour. Corvée labour could be demanded of virtually the entire Chinese population and might take up to one month a year for ordinary peasant families.

In Korea, taxes also came in several forms and included corvée labour, though the continued deep-rooted concept of hereditary status excused the land-holding elite from more onerous tasks. As central Imperial authority crumbled in Japan, local administration revolved around the Sho or estates given by the aristocratic landowners to loyal supporters. This also had the benefit of reducing the burden on great landowners

The ideology of the Chinese state was rooted in the belief that the ruler had a mandate from heaven and could only be removed if he failed in his duty. Several periods in Chinese history had seen considerable changes, although deeply rooted Confucian values continued to provide an unbroken thread. Although a conservative dynasty, the Sung undertook several attempts at political reform. Most were more theoretical than real, though the great Chinese reformer Wang An-Shih's 'Ten Thousand Word Memorial', written in 1058, had a profound impact. It was primarily concerned with keeping lower ranking administrators loyal and honest.

In Tibet, the earliest kings were believed to have come from heaven and to have returned there at the end of their reigns.

More earthly rulers began with the semi-mythical Grigum Tsanpo who is said to have accidentally cut his rope to heaven and thus been unable to return. Tibet then entered upon a period of expansion in the 7th–8th centuries, characterized by clashes with the Chinese but generally good relations with the Muslims.

The Mongols could hardly have been more different. They may not, however, actually have wanted to conquer damp and relatively backward Europe, their primary interest being the conquest of China. On the other hand the Mongols rapidly adopted the administrative systems of those they conquered. The Mongol Yuan dynasty (1257–1370) of China, for example, ruled in a largely Chinese manner, while the Mongol Il-Khan dynasty of Iran and Iraq (1256–1349) ruled much as their Arab, Persian and Turkish predecessors had done.

Even within the Central Asian steppes, most of the Mongol successor states were administered along traditional Turkish lines, usually being divided into three provinces or frontier marches. In Russia the princes were largely left alone as long as they recognized Mongol supremacy and paid taxes.

This picture of the Mongol 'World Conqueror' Genghis Khan in his tent was made in Herat, in Afghanistan, for Shah Rukh around 1435. The figures are dressed in the style of the Timurid rather than Mongol Empire, but the six white horse-tail banners on the right were a mark of senior rank shared by Turks and Mongols alike.

STATE, CASTE AND TRIBE

In medieval India statecraft was regarded as a science known as Arthashastra, which included administration, economics, agriculture and even the arts. Books on kingship advised a ruler how to avoid the 'six enemies' of lust, avarice, pride, anger, drunkenness, insolence, and the 'four temptations' of hunting, gambling, drinking and womanizing. Traditionally anyone who had a grievance went on hunger strike before the palace gates until such time as his wrongs were redressed.

Kingship itself carried with it a halo of divinity, with the king's main function being to punish wrongdoers, to attack his enemies and to encourage agriculture. Such traditions underpinned the Chola state which had brought stability to southern India in the

11th century. The Cholas, however, lacked the closely-knit bureaucracy of China and power remained largely in the hands of the aristocratic dynasties because the Cholas were frequently at war with rebellious vassals. Local government was centred on the villages, the largest of which had assemblies with authority to tax citizens. Similarly the provincial towns had nagaram councils which were, in many respects, more like dominant merchant guilds.

In south-east Asia, many states tried to model themselves upon the Hindu concept of a concentric universe, with the ruler and his territory at the centre surrounded by vassals. However, many rulers were more like glorified village headmen, being merely first amongst equals in relation to neighbouring leaders. Such kingdoms rarely had fixed boundaries but seem to have merged from direct rule to vassal to non-vassal areas.

Their rulers were assisted by professional civil servants, drawn from a quasi-bureaucratic nobility of families of priests who administered the central regions, while the ruler himself served as a link between his people and the heavens. In Indonesia the priestly caste were intermediaries between rulers and gods via the offices of a statue or idol in what might have been a survival of the cult of worshipping ancient ancestors. Rulers also donated large areas of land to temples or monasteries to ensure their own and their subjects' spiritual well-being.

Most south-east Asia kingdoms were centred upon rivers, even in Indonesia, although some of its coastal states never acquired much inland territory. The most detailed information comes from the Javanese kingdom of Majapahit, which never had a fully centralized administration; outlying regions were

administered by Rakryan governors drawn from the premier family who ruled in the same way as the king did in central regions. Senior aristocracy, priests and military commanders were often given land in newly acquired territories which they were expected to develop and colonize and these often evolved into vassals or autonomous regions. The ruler also rewarded individuals and villages with land, thus introducing the concept of private ownership to an area where land had previously been held communally.

In the Buddhist Khmer state in Cambodia, the rulers were always selected from the priestly caste, although their power depended on the main aristocratic families. The king himself was an almost godlike figure who only left his capital on the back of an elephant with gilded tusks, surrounded by cavalrymen, priests, bands and palace maidens. All onlookers touched their foreheads to the ground as he passed. Senior religious posts were reserved for long-established priestly families, usually inherited through the female line. Vast expenditure on temple buildings and court ceremonials may actually have contributed to the decline of Hindu and Buddhist south-east Asian states in the 13th century, although some of them were also under military assault from the Mongols. Only eastern Java continued to flourish.

Based on a Chinese model, the administration of the medieval Vietnamese state differed from that of its south-east Asian neighbours, while further to the east, some of the Philippine islands may have been under the tenuous suzerain of the Majapahit maritime empire based in Java during the 14th and 15th centuries. The Chinese also claimed to have imposed some form of suzerain during the Ming period (1368–1644). After several clashes with the Mongols, Burma was left largely to its own devices, but even the Burmese kingdom suffered a slow decline towards the end of the Middle Ages.

Above: Medieval India was a land of powerful fortresses such as Jaisalmer in Rajasthan. It was an important centre of Hindu resistance to Muslim conquest but eventually fell to the invaders. This fortress is made of stone but in some parts of India most fortifications were of mud bricks or of earth and timber.

Opposite: Amongst the little-known 14th–15th century paintings from Nam Giang, northern Vietnam, is this illustration of 'Foreign Countries'. It illustrates a procession of representatives from various countries, each dressed in their distinctive costume.

11 WORLDS APART

THE CIVILISATIONS OF THE MEDIEVAL PERIOD WERE NOT SO IGNORANT OF EACH OTHER AS IS SOMETIMES THOUGHT. EUROPEAN SCANDANAVIAN COLONISTS LIVED IN GREENLAND AND TRADED WITH THE INUIT ESKIMOS, WHILE THERE WAS A STRONG CONNECTION BETWEEN ALASKA AND EASTERN SIBERIA. EVEN THE AMERICAS AND AUSTRALIA WERE TENTATIVELY LINKED TO NEIGHBOURING CONTINENTS. AUSTRALIA SEEMS TO HAVE BEEN VISITED BY INDONESIAN FISHERMEN AND MERCHANTS.

A VERY VARIED WORLD

The medieval period has sometimes been described as the 'World of Divided Regions', which suggests that different parts of the inhabited globe were more isolated than those of earlier or later centuries. This is incorrect, though some cultures did remain more or less separate from their neighbours.

Ethiopia was the most advanced civilization in sub-Saharan Africa. It had been Christian since the 4th century and this was central to its sense of identity in relation to both Muslims to the north and pagans to the south. All men, including priests, had to marry unless they were to become monks, and marriage itself came in several forms. Girls were married from the age of 12 and were expected to resist their husbands on their wedding night; they in turn were helped by their best men to overcome such resistance. Although men were permitted to take concubines, the wife must first agree.

Medieval Abyssinia was similarly characterized by numerous religious fraternities, which met once a month in a member's hut, with separate fraternities for women. In reality, these fraternities seem to have been more social than religious.

Much is known about the cultures of medieval America. By AD 1000, Inuit Eskimo encampments included well-insulated sunken houses which served several families. Whale hunting formed a major part of the Inuit culture, for which they used dog-sleds as well as kayak canoes. It appears that some North American cultures of the east and centre seem to have been matrilineal, with a chief presiding over four social classes. The elite were often placed in timber coffins in mortuaries on top of mounds and left until only the bones remained when there would be a second elaborate burial ceremony.

The cultures of south-western USA were influenced by the sophisticated civilizations of Central America. By the 12th century, most were based in agricultural river valleys where the Pueblos lived in fortified villages, often huddled against the sides of canyons. Central and South American civilizations were noted for displays and huge ceremonial structures while religion clearly played a major role in these often warlike cultures. Even a game played with a large ball in a stone court was probably religious.

In the Pacific islands, the Polynesians built their houses of wood, but, owing to the lack of timber, the inhabitants of Easter Island built theirs of stone. Polynesian tools reflected the choice of materials available to them and included fish-hooks and coconut graters made of sea-shells. Their diet consisted of fish, pork, chicken and dog, while the presence of sweet potatoes in their diet confirms a link with South America.

The aboriginal people of Australia did not follow an unchanging 'stone age' way of life, but like all societies responded to changing conditions; for example stone technology actually declined from the 1st to 19th centuries. Frequent droughts meant that huge areas were often temporarily evacuated, although people took advantage of the conditions to burn the land in order to stimulate the growth of edible roots. Members of tribes assumed a family relationship and families were generally polygamous, self-sufficient units with a strict division of labour according to sex.

Opposite: The famous bronze statues and heads made by the Benin people of west Africa first appeared in the late medieval period, though some of the best come from the 16th century. This example is a portrait of Idia, who was credited with using magical powers to help Benin defeat its Igala enemies.

Below: This manuscript from pre-Columbian Mexico shows a marriage ceremony between a man and woman of noble birth. Their names are shown by signs above their heads while the woman's married status is shown by her plaited headdress. The little footprints leading up the page between the figures point to their future children.

FORGOTTEN ABYSSINIA

The Madonna and Child on a 15th century wall painting in the rock-cut church of Abune Yemata in Ethiopia. Ethiopian art showed its origins in the Coptic art of Egypt and that of various other Christian sects in the Middle East.

Cultural links between medieval Ethiopia and the Copts of Egypt were strong and it was only the collapse of the Christian kingdom of Nubia at the end of the Middle Ages that cut Ethiopia off from the rest of Christendom. During the medieval period the Dabtaras, or 'learned men', played a major role in Ethiopian culture as manuscript copiers, teachers, scribes, musicians, choristers and liturgical dancers. The Ethiopians also wrote biographies of saints, royal chronicles, religious poetry, battle songs and verses in praise of leaders.

Much was translated from Greek and Arabic, including the earlier Arabic Kebra Nagast or 'Glory of the Kings', which became Ethiopia's national epic and told their history from the time of Menelik, supposedly the son of the Queen of Sheba and King Solomon, and who was believed to have been the ancestor of Ethiopia's rulers.

Ethiopian church music was largely sung in a pentatonic scale like early Coptic and Armenian music and their wandering minstrels were renowned for singing outrageous satires about current leaders. Ethiopian art was also closely related to that of Middle Eastern Christian art, Biblical illustrations being stylized, traditional and very colourful.

Down the eastern coast of Africa a new Swahili civilization developed from a blending of Bantu African and Arab–Islamic cultures, but Muslim culture did not spread far inland. In west Africa, however, Islam spread south of the Sahara where, by the 14th century, Mali and Timbuktu became new centres of learning. The forest states between the grasslands and the coast refined their arts of metalwork and ceramics to a high degree, culminating in the famous Benin bronzes of the 15th century. Several cultures developed in the southern half of Africa during the medieval period, but little of their art survives since most of it was fashioned from perishable materials. Nevertheless more recent art from south Africa includes rock drawings similar to the ancient rock art of the Sahara.

A civilization of cities

The natural resources of land and sea along the north-western Pacific coast of North America enabled rich cultures to develop, but again most artefacts were constructed of perishable wood. In the dry south-west of the USA., the Pueblo cultures were strongly influenced by those of Mexico and Central America, copper-working techniques arriving from the same direction.

The Maya of Central America created a civilization based on cities built around ceremonial architectural complexes. The greatest period of Maya civilization ended in the 10th century, but they continued to produce stone and wood carving, wall painting, stucco and ceramics of great sophistication. The Maya were also the only literate civilization in pre-Columbian America. By the late medieval period in Mexico, the warlike Aztecs were in control, whose art owed a great deal to their predecessors like the Maya.

The Aztecs also employed subject tribes to make leatherwork, ceramics, mosaics and golden jewellery. Meanwhile the Incas and the other civilizations of the Andean mountain regions of South America appear to have shown less artistic originality than the peoples of Central America. In recent years the artefacts of an unknown and remarkable medieval civilization have been discovered in the Amazonian basin, including ceramic containers shaped like human figures.

The Polynesians retained a considerable cultural homogeny, probably because their spread across the Pacific Ocean was relatively recent. Yet after AD 1000, for reasons which remain unclear, the Polynesians largely abandoned the making of pottery, while metallurgy spread no further than New Guinea. The main divergence from Polynesian cul-

ture was in New Zealand, where the Maoris adapted to a larger landmass and more temperate climate. Another variation was found far away on Easter Island, which was not only cool, but also extremely isolated. Here a series of huge statues remain one of the enigmas of art history – their production came to an abrupt halt around 1600, probably because the inhabitants ran out of timber and suffered a shortage of food.

This medieval ceramic figurine from Columbia shows a man playing a form of pan-pipes. Relatively little is known about the medieval cultures of Columbia but they clearly had some features in common with the Maya of Central America as well as the Inca in the Andes Mountains further south.

CHURCHES FROM THE VIRGIN ROCK

The Church of St George at Lalibela in Ethiopia is one of the most famous of the churches cut from the rock itself in the 13th or 14th centuries. The internal and external style reflects the architecture of Coptic Egypt, ancient Yemen and even of India.

The rock-cut churches of Lalibela, Ethiopia's new capital in the 12th century, are still one of the marvels of world architecture. Though cut from the ground in great pits, the free-standing rock churches were planned and decorated in styles which recall aspects of Coptic Egyptian architecture. However, Abyssinian architecture really developed from that of the Yemen, with most important buildings using the ancient Arabian mixture of timber and stone set in mortar made from mud.

Another original form of architecture developed along the east African coast where mosques and palaces were made from brilliant white coral, whereas the massive dry stone enclosures of Great Zimbabwe further inland were quite different and date from the 10th to 15th centuries. Most of them were built around granite boulders topped with ritual monoliths.

The architecture of pre-Columbian America ranged from the temporary structures of nomadic peoples to the tall mud-brick fortified villages of the Anasazi Pueblo culture. Many of the elaborate stone temples of the various Central American peoples stood within sprawling cities. Only a few decades before the arrival of Spanish invaders the Incas built their remarkable new capital of Cuzco consisting of an inner city of stone palaces for the nobility, bureaucrats and learned elite, surrounded by a grid-pattern of streets laid out in the form of a great cat. At the centre was a Holy Place which the Incas regarded as the centre of the world.

Not surprisingly the architecture of the Pacific island peoples was on a much smaller scale. Nevertheless, the Polynesians built characteristic paved platforms and court-yards as part of their temples, known as 'marae' in most places, as 'heiau' in the Hawaiian archipelago and as 'ahu' on Easter Island. It was here that the Easter Islanders erected their astonishing stone head statues.

The Maoris of New Zealand, meanwhile, added their own distinctive contribution in the form of Pa fortresses defended by ditches and palisades. Elsewhere in Polynesian culture there appear to have been no fortifications whatsoever.

FARMERS AND HUNTER-GATHERERS

One characteristic of the Americas, Pacific islands and Australasia during the medieval period was their huge variety of rural life. In medieval Ethiopia, for example, the rural population was scattered across the countryside in isolated farmsteads rather than being grouped into villages. To avoid seasonal floods, most habitations were on high ground, either on the lip of one of the gorges which dissected the plateau or on a ledge within the gorge, while the plateau was largely left to semi-nomadic pastoral peoples.

Feasting and fasting

Everywhere religious feast and fast days marked the seasons and people fasted before noon on Wednesdays and Fridays. The Ethiopian New Year's Day was early in September, marking the end of the rainy season when the land was carpeted with flowers. This was followed by the feast of Masqal, which was an occasion for general merry-making, with warriors singing boastful songs and when a form of inter-community hockey was played. Another game called guks involved pairs of horsemen pursuing each other at a gallop, the leader holding his shield at arm's length while the pursuer tried to hit the shield with a blunted javelin.

In the pre-Islamic states of west Africa, grasslands people grew sorghum, wheat, vegetables and cotton, raised camels, cattle, sheep, goats and horses. Further south cattle raising predominated, with families migrating between high and low grazing areas according to the season. In East Africa, most agriculture was confined to the coast where bananas, coconuts and sugar cane had been introduced from south-east Asia. Before the expansion of the iron-working Bantu from the north, large parts of southern Africa were inhabited by Hottentots and bushmen while the many inhospitable regions still remained uninhabited.

Several edible plants such as potatoes, maize and chilli peppers were still confined to the New World during the medieval period. In the far north, the medieval Inuit were essentially whale hunters. The people of the northern Pacific coasts also hunted whale, sea lions and otter, but also gathered shellfish and fished for salmon. From the 9th century, the bow and arrow replaced the javelin and spear within the cultures of eastern and central North America, which ranged from nomadic forest tribes to agricul-

A silver model of a maize plant. Many pre-Columbian American cultures relied on the cultivation of maize as their basic source of food, and the plant was so important that it also had sacred associations. In addition maize was used to make a form of beer called 'chicha', which was drunk in huge quantities during religious festivals. This particular object comes from the Inca civilization of South America and dates from the late 15th or early 16th centuries.

tural villages. In the south-west, intensive hunter-gathering also survived alongside agriculture where irrigation permitted the growing of maize, squash, cotton and perhaps tobacco.

Agriculture underpinned the great civilizations of Central and South America. Amongst the Incas, two thirds of all agricultural produce was taken in tax. Until recently the Amazon basin was thought to have been inhabited by peoples relying on hunting, gathering and crude slash-and-burn agriculture. Now, however, evidence of intensive agriculture has been found in several areas – a recently excavated village near the mouth of the Amazon, which flourished from the 5th to 12th centuries, consisted of a large oval earthwork enclosing houses where men and women lived separately, with a ceremonial platform at one end of the community. The women did most of the agricultural work.

The rapid Polynesian colonization of the Pacific islands during the Middle Ages brought new edible plants, walled fields, terraces and irrigation to some islands. In New Zealand, the previously untouched flora and fauna rendered farming almost unnecessary, but, as various species were hunted to extinction, by the 12th century the Maoris of North Island had become dependent on agriculture. Meanwhile the South Island provides a rare example of an agricultural people actually abandoning cultivation in favour of a return to hunter-gathering during the medieval period.

The Australian aborigines were similarly a nomadic hunter-gathering society, where larger groups fragmented in lean times, but came together in good ones. Evidence from the south-east of the continent suggests that here there were annual gatherings of extended families to exploit seasonal bounty.

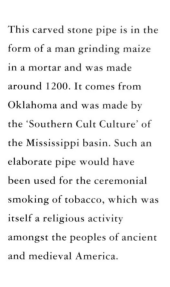

This carved stone pipe is in the form of a man grinding maize in a mortar and was made around 1200. It comes from Oklahoma and was made by the 'Southern Cult Culture' of the Mississippi basin. Such an elaborate pipe would have been used for the ceremonial smoking of tobacco, which was itself a religious activity amongst the peoples of ancient and medieval America.

LINKING LOST WORLDS

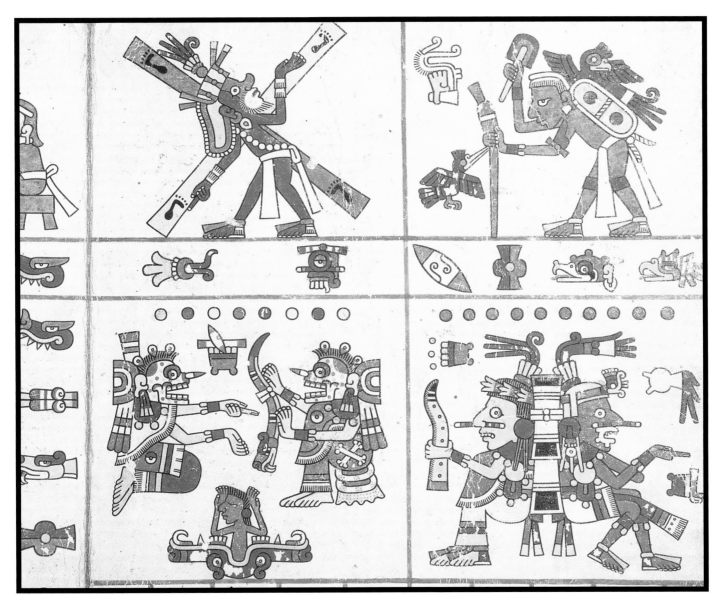

Medieval Ethiopia was not urbanized, yet small towns existed and trade flourished. Imports ranged from foreign luxuries to vital bars of salt from neighbouring deserts. East Africa had complex trading links, though the major urban centres were on the coast which exported mangrove wood and served as transit areas for iron and ivory from the interior.

Trade between east Africa, the Middle East, India and Indonesia had existed for hundreds of years but, with the Muslim conquest of India and the beginnings of Islamic conversion in south-east Asia, it expanded. Despite cultural differences, the coast and interior of east Africa were economically interdependent, with the most densely populated inland areas being close to sources of iron and gold which was then exported as far as India. In return, the ruling elites of the interior imported Islamic and even Chinese luxuries.

West Africa also experienced a major development in trade with north Africa and

Not many manuscripts survive from pre-Columbian Central America, but this one in Mixtec style comes from Mexico. It is made of deerskin and shows, in the top register, Yacatechuhtli or 'Lord Nose', the patron god of merchants. On his back he carries the symbol of a crossroads marked with merchants' footprints.

185

The so-called 'cliff palace' at Mese Verde in Colorado, USA. It is one of the most magnificent of cliff dwellings and was built by the 'Basketmaker' culture and the Pueblo Indian civilization which followed. This location was one of the main centres of civilization in this part of America in the 11th and 12th centuries, including over two hundred rooms and twenty-three circular ceremonial chambers.

for ordinary people, had mud-plaster walls and thatched roofs. Some of the Pueblo cultures of the south-western USA also had close trading links with Mexico. Here the great cities of the Maya functioned as administrative centres, with sprawling suburbs around them and populations of up to 5,000 people.

In South America, several other civilizations developed extensive trade and had large urban centres – for example, Chan Chan, the capital of the Chima state, was sited right on the Pacific coast. To control their expanding empire, the Incas constructed new towns, including Machu Picchu high in the Andes, which was surrounded by terraces dotted with small thatched houses. Inca towns were also centres of manufacture while the Inca communications system enabled caravans of llamas and human porters to carry food to the main cities.

Navigational talents

By the year AD 1000, the Polynesians inhabited a vast expanse of ocean dotted with islands, covering less than one per cent of the total area. This dispersal was deliberate, performed in open canoes which carried men, women, livestock and seeds for planting. In fact the medieval Polynesians were the greatest navigators in history. Given the flourishing maritime heritage of south-east Asia, it is not surprising to find that Indonesians visited Australia long before Europeans arrived. Timor is less than 500 miles away and during the early modern period sailors from the Celebes came to collect the sea cucumbers in what is now Arnhem Land.

One possible source suggests that a close trading link existed between Java and northern Australia until the 12th century and there is strong evidence that Chinese explorers reached northern Australia by the 15th century. The main evidence of trade or exchange before the arrival of European colonizers lies with ceremonial items, particularly ornamental sea-shells found within the Australian landmass.

Egypt during the medieval period, exporting slaves, gold, ivory and animal pelts in return for horses, luxury items and salt from central Saharan oases. As a result Islamic weights and measures were used throughout west Africa until the arrival of the European slave-traders. Meanwhile local trade within the savannah grassland and forest regions was largely in iron ore, dried fish and cereals. The forests also produced iron, ivory, ebony wood and wood for fuel in metalworking.

This complex situation encouraged the emergence of urbanized states, of which Ghana was the most important in the pre-Islamic period. Its capital was divided between the royal palace and a quarter reserved for foreign merchants separated by the houses of local inhabitants. Flourishing trans-Saharan trade similarly stimulated urbanization within the forest zone, where the remarkable civilization of Benin flourished from the 14th to 19th centuries, relying on the export of slaves for its prosperity.

By the 8th century, small towns existed in the Mississippi basin of North America where the houses of a ruling elite were grouped around an open space within a wooden stockade. Larger longhouses, perhaps

TECHNOLOGY WITHOUT SCIENCE

So little is known about the scientific or medical knowledge of medieval Africa, the Americas, Polynesia and Australasia that it is often assumed that the peoples of these areas had no science and that their medical knowledge was barely worth considering. Yet increasing appreciation of what is now called 'alternative medicine' gives a new slant on what were once regarded as primitive medicinal superstitions.

In medieval Ethiopia, for example, the 'dabtaras', or scribes, were often experts in herbal medicines and similar tribal experts were found in all African cultures. Their traditional cures were still used when European missionaries burst upon the scene in the 19th and early 20th centuries, precisely the time when western science was at its most arrogant in relation to the 'pre-scientific' lore of native peoples.

In some respects, earlier European travellers provide a less prejudiced view of traditional knowledge. The 18th century Mandingoes of west Africa, for example, were described as paying great attention to the phases of the moon which marked the seasons and had a direct effect upon daily life, but supposedly had little interest in the stars. Though they made great use of amulets to cure diseases, they also inhaled herbal vapours to cure fevers and treated dysentery with the powdered bark of a certain tree. Far to the south the bushmen of the Kalahari desert used the jaws of giant flesh-eating ants as stitches to close a wound; the body of the ant was then cut off, leaving its huge jaws clamped around the wound.

The Maya of Central America used remarkably advanced stone technology but are most famous for their astonishing astronomical observations. These had a numerical system based upon the number 20, rather than on ten as in almost every other part of the world, and for reasons which are still unclear, the resulting calendar calculations used 3 August 3114 BC as their base date. Such calculations enabled Mayan priests to make extremely accurate predictions of dates which were believed to be suitable for certain ritual activities or ceremonial events; these dates were regarded as being under the protection of a particular god.

The 'quipu' was a series of knotted strings which served as a form of code or record keeping system. By using such objects the bureaucrats of the Inca Empire in South America kept records of the number of llamas needed as baggage animals or the volume of agricultural produce from a particular province.

CHRISTIAN HIGHLANDS TO PAGAN ISLANDS

One of the remarkable Maui statues on Easter Island in the far south-eastern quarter of the Pacific. They are unique, and were all made within a relatively short period. Then quite suddenly work on them stopped, probably because the islanders ran out of both timber and food.

The Ethiopian Church was an offshoot of the Coptic Egyptian Church, its single Abuna, or bishop, being selected by the Patriarch of Alexandria. Each rural church served some 1,000 inhabitants, while monasteries were similar to the first monastic retreats in early Christian Egypt, being loosely knit groups of individuals. Hermits lived entirely on their own, eating wild roots and herbs. Ethiopian law was administered in the open air where

accused and accuser both handed over sums of money to be forfeited if either lost his case. Then came a ritualized question and answer session, with the judge sitting between the litigants. Punishments could include flogging, imprisonment or fines and a debtor could be roped to his lender until he had paid off his debt. In the pre-Islamic sub-Saharan states, kings had a semi-divine status; their funerals were often accompanied by human sacrifice. Ancestor worship played a major role in the religion of these areas, as it did throughout much of southern Africa.

Gods and human hearts

The religious practices of pre-Columbian America seem to have included the most bloodthirsty rituals in religious history. Human sacrifice was enormously important amongst the Maya and Aztecs, who believed that the end of the world could be delayed by feeding the gods with human hearts; 20,000 captives were slaughtered during one four-day festival. The religious beliefs of South America are less well known, though a creator god had been worshipped by some Andean civilizations since the 11th century. The Inca king was regarded as a descendant of the sun, while ordinary peasants worshipped an array of spirits and sacred stones.

On the Pacific islands, carved statues probably symbolized various gods while ritual activities took place on the paved areas which characterized Polynesian culture. The aboriginal peoples of Australia had a distinctive view of time, stating that ancestral beings created the world's natural resources in an ancient Dream Time; these were protected from over-exploitation by a complex system of taboos and dietary restrictions.

LOST EMPIRES

The administrative systems of some sub-Saharan states were partly an indigenous development and partly influenced by the civilizations of Egypt, the Sudan and Nubia while, with the spread of Islamic culture, their armies became increasingly similar to those of north Africa. Within the forest belt to the south, states rose in response to alterations in trade patterns between sub-Saharan Africa and the Muslim world. Here, however, there was minimal Islamic administrative or military influence. In east Africa, Great Zimbabwe was the biggest of several regional capitals, each 65–70 km apart.

Archaeological evidence shows that there was a major decline in population, probably as a result of epidemics, in central and eastern North America in the 15th century before the arrival of the Europeans introduced new diseases. The Pueblo culture also declined, perhaps as a result of crop-failures and attack by the ancestors of the Apache and Navajo nomads. Toltec rule had collapsed in Mexico around 1170, followed by anarchy in which city states competed for dominance. The last to triumph were the Aztecs, who carved out an empire ruled by priest-kings.

Before the 11th century, two empires developed in the Andes mountains of South America; their civilization was taken over by the Incas in the 14th century, which then grew into the largest of all the pre-Columbian states under a ruler who had absolute authority in religious, political and military affairs. Perhaps the most remarkable thing about the Inca state was the fact that its complex bureaucracy had no system of writing but instead kept records on lengths of knotted string. Following the arrival of European diseases, the states of the Amazon basin collapsed so totally that even their ex-

istence was dismissed as a baseless Eldorado legend. Only now has there been a rediscovery of the truth that chiefdoms dominated tens of thousands of square kilometres.

By the start of the 11th century, Polynesian expansion was completed, but states do not appear to have developed until the 13th century. In the 14th century the 'classical' Maori era began in New Zealand's North Island with massive fortified earthworks and extensive agricultural systems. There were, however, neither states nor extensive chiefdoms in aboriginal Australian society. Here the basic tribal unit may have been around 500 people who claimed religiously sanctioned hunting rights over certain territory, the boundaries of which were marked out by natural features.

Several different artists worked on the illustrated Skylitzes Chronicle, probably in 13th century Sicily. This one clearly had a much greater knowledge of Islamic and African costume, perhaps suggesting that he had once worked in these areas. In this picture he shows an ambassador from the Bulgarian King Simeon being received by the ruler of Tunisia, Ziyadat-Allah III.

Ahdath Urban militia in some Muslim cities.

Ahmudan Elite guard unit of Burmese rulers.

Ahu Paved area probably used for religious purposes on Easter Island.

Albigensians Dualist heretics in southern France.

Alchemy Belief that basic materials can be changed into different basic materials.

Althing Local political assembly in Scandinavian territory.

Ars Nova New form of music in 12th–13th century Europe.

Arthashastra Science of government in Hindu India.

Assize Court Local legal court in England.

Astrolabe Device similar to a sextant for measuring the altitude of stars.

Aventail Flexible neck and throat protection attached to the rim of a helmet.

Ayurveda Indian medical sciences.

Aznauris Georgian minor aristocracy.

Bakufu Japanese military government.

Bascinet Helmet which protected the sides and back of the head.

Beak Extended prow of a warship designed to ride over the side on an enemy vessel.

Bektashi Member of a mystical Muslim brotherhood.

Bent Entrance Fortified gate which forced attackers to expose their unshielded sides.

Bey Ottoman local and military leader.

Bilig Sayings attributed to a respected Mongol ruler.

Bloodwite Compensation paid in case of murder or physical injury.

Bodhisattva Buddhist saint or semi-divine personage.

Bogomils Members of a Dualist faith or heresy in the medieval Balkans.

Boyar Member of the aristocratic elite in Russia and some Balkan countries.

Brahmin Priestly caste in Hindu society.

Brigandine Fabric or leather body armoured lined with small scales.

Caliph Spiritual and originally temporal ruler of the Muslim world.

Canon Law Christian religious law.

Caravel Small Portugese and Spanish merchant ship.

Caste Rigid form of social class division in which individuals are nor supposed to change their rank.

Ch'an Chinese Buddhist spiritual exercise.

Chanson de Geste Heroic tale or song.

Chatris Kiosk on top of a fortified gate in India.

Christendom region of the world in which Christianity dominated

Cistern Underground water-storage tank.

Clerk Any person in priestly or minor orders.

Cloisonee Coloured enamelled decoration on metalwork.

Coat of a Thousand Nails Indian protective coat lined with scales.

Coat-of-arms Heraldic device or pattern identifying one family, state. city, etc.

Coat-of-plates Body armour of scale-lined cloth or leather.

Coif Protective hood made of mail.

Common Land Land attached to a village and used for grazing by all members of that community.

Composite Bow Powerful bow usually made of glued strips of wood, horn and sinew.

Concubine Unmarried sexual partner.

Condottieri Leader of mercenary soldiers in Italy.

Conrois Very closely packed cavalry formation.

Cortes Parliament in one of the Iberian Christian states.

Corvée Forced labour demanded by the state.

Courtly Love System of behaviour between men and women of the knightly aristocracy based upon mutual admiration and sexual restraint.

Crossbow Bow attached to a wooden stock provided with a locking mechanism and trigger.

Crusade War conducted on behalf of Christianity or the Papacy.

Customary Law Law based upon accepted traditional rules.

Dabtara Member of the Ethiopian 'learned men'.

Dar al-Imara Office of the governor in an Islamic city.

Darbazi Form of Georgian house with a pyramid roof.

Dervish Islamic mystical religious fraternity.

Despotate Fragmented Byzantine state or province.

Dharma Sutra Hindu manuals on correct conduct.

Divan Advisory council in an Islamic state.

Druzhina Military retinue of a Russian prince.

Drystone Building technique using stone without mortar.

Dualism Religious belief that the powers of Good and Evil were roughly equal in power.

Duhsadha-sadhanika Police official in Hindu India.

Eparch Governor of a Byzantine city.

Eristavi Georgian duke.

Faqih Muslim legal expert.

Fatwa Judgement based on Islamic Sharia law.

Feudalism Theoretical structuring of society on the basis of mutual obligation.

Fief Portion of land allocated to a knight to maintain himself and his household.

Fiqh Science of Muslim law.

Friar Member of a Christian preaching rather than monastic order.

Gaeoinggars Wealthy elite in Scandinavian Orkney Island society.

Ger Mongol nomad tent.

Godar Local Scandinavian chieftain.

Gonikeia Form of Byzantine peasant farm.

Gothic Name originally given as an insult to the art of the pre-Renaissance period in western Europe.

Grandeur Style of life expected of the aristocratic elite.

Greek Fire Petroleum based fire weapon.

Guild Association of those engaged in a particular trade or craft.

Guks Ethiopian cavalry game or exercise.

Hadith Sayings of the Prophet Muhammad.

Hamam Public baths in Islamic towns and cities.

Harem Private section of a house reserved for women and their immediate family.

Hauberk Armour in the form of a mail shirt.

Heiau Paved area probably used for religious purposes in Hawaii.

Heraldry Recognized language of signs, images and colours used to identify aristocratic families, states, cities, etc.

High Justice Accusation and trial which could result in the death penalty.

Hinayana One of the two main forms of Buddhism.

Horse-archery Cavalry tactics using the bow on horseback.

Household The family unit plus servants and dependants.

Hue and Cry Obligation of all members of a community to pursue a criminal.

Humanism Belief that human beings are at the centre of Creation.

Hundred Local territorial division in England.

Icon Religious painting in the Orthodox Christian Chuch.

Iconoclasm Fundamental disapproval of religious illustration.

Imam Muslim spiritual leader or guide.

Iqta Piece of land allocated to a member of the Islamic military or administrative elite.

Irgen Mongol tribe.

Janissary Elite infantry soldier in the Ottoman army.

Jawshan Lamellar body armour used in Muslim armies.

Jihad Individual struggle against evil in Muslim society, or a war in defence of Islam.

Jinni Supernatual being created from fire in Islamic mythology.

Kakawin Indonesian poetry based on Indian themes.

Kamal Form of sextant used as a navigational aid by Muslim sailors.

Kanun Secular law in the Ottoman Sultanate.

Katib Scribe or member of the bureaucratic elite in Islamic states.

Kavya Indian epic stories.

Kazaghand Cloth-covered mail armour of the Muslim world.

Keep Tall central main tower in a castle.

Khan Turkish or Mongol ruler; also a hostel for merchants or travellers in Muslim countries.

Khatangku Dehel Form of Mongol armour.

Kremlin Fortified citadel in Russian towns.

Kshatriya Warrior or aristocratic caste in Hindu society.

Kuriltai Gathering of senior Mongol leaders.

Lamellar armour Armour made from small rigid pieces, usually of metal or hardened leather, laced together with thongs.

Lay brothers Members of a monastic community who have not taken monastic vows.

Li Chinese supplementary legal rules.

Ling Chinese imperial decrees.

Livery Form of uniform worn by members of a particular household.

Locatores Those charged with establishing settlements in new territory.

Logmadr Leader of one of the Scandinavian colonies in Greenland.

Logothete Official in charge of Byzantine law courts.

Longbow Large bow made from a single piece of wood.

Longhouse Single story domestic building eventually including several rooms.

Lu Chinese legal statutes.

Madrasah Teaching mosque or school.

Mahayana One of the two main forms of Buddhism.

Mail-and-plate Form of armour incorporating mail and metalic plates.

Mail Armour made of interlocking metal rings.

Mamluk Elite Muslim soldier of slave origin.

Mangonel Beam-sling stone throwing device used in siege warfare.

Manichaeanism Dualist religion of Persian origin.

Manor Area of land under the authority of a local knight or squire.

Marae Paved area probably used for religious purposes in Polynesia.

Master Craftsman Person who has achieved sufficient skill to be recognized as a Master by his guild.

Military Order Monastic order dedicated to fighting for the Christian faith.

Militia Part-time military force enlisted from local inhabitants.

Millet Religious community within the Ottoman state.

Minor Orders Rank in the Christian religious heirarchy below that of a priest.

Minstrel Professional singer or songwriter.

Money Fief Source of revenue allocated to a knight instead of a piece of land.

Motte and Bailey Form of castle incorporating a fortified mound and pallisaded enclosure.

Mou Small piece of land used to measure agricultual land in China.

Mufti Islamic legal expert.

Muhtasib Official in charge of maintain public services and legal trading in an Islamic city.

Nagaram Town council in Hindu India.

Nirvana Total enlightenment in Buddhist belief.

Nomadism Pastoral way of life in which families moved randomly in search of animal grazing.

Notary Person with authority to draw up or confirm legal documents.

Noyan Mongol aristocracy.

Obok Mongol clan claiming descent from a common ancestor.

Ongghon Small Mongol idol.

Pa Maori fortress in New Zealand.

Pagoda Tower-like Chinese religious building.

Pastoralism Rural way of life dependant on animal herds.

Patriarch Senior member of the Church heirarchy, one grade beneath the Pope.

Peace of God Church-led movement attempting to limit private wars between members of the aristocracy.

Penance Personal sacrifice for a religious reason.

Pervane Chancellor in a Persian or Turkish state.

Plate armour Armour made of large pieces of metal shaped to fit parts of the body.

Po Mutual support organization amongst Korean merchants and artisans.

Pradvivaka Chief legal advisor in a Hindu state.

Priyayi Villages of superior status in pre-Islamic south-east Asia.

Qadi Judge in Islamic society.

Rais Leader of a small community within Muslim society.

Rakryan Governor of an outlying part of an Indonesian state.

Ramani Dusun Village leader in Indonesia.

Renaissance Supposed 'rebirth' of Classical Latin and Greek learning in the later medieval period.

Rishi Spiritually enlightened religious authority.

Round Ship European merchant vessel with very broad beam.

Samurai Japanese warrior elite.

Sancak Bey Ottoman military governor.

Schiltron Scottish infantry formation.

Schism Separation of the Eastern (Orthodox) and Western (Catholic) Churches.

Sena pati Commander of a Hindu Indian army.

Serf Low status peasant who was not permitted to change his family's place of residence without permission from his feudal lord.

Sergeant European professional soldier of non-knightly status.

Shamanism Religious belief based upon propitiation or consulation of spirits.

Sharecropping Form of land tenure in which farmers gave an agreed proportion of crops to the landowner.

Sharia Islamic religiously based law.

Sheriff Official responsible for maintaining law and order in a specific area.

Shia One of the two main religious divisions in Islam.

Shield-wall Defensive infantry formation in which shields form an uninterruped front.

Shihna Seljuk Turkish military governor.

Sho Estates given by the Japanese aristocracy to loyal supporters.

Shogunate Military headquarters which effectively governed later medieval Japan.

Shurta Local police force in some Muslim states.

Siege Tower Siege machine in the form of a wooden tower, often moveable.

Sipahi Ottoman cavalry supported by timar fiefs.

Skomoriki Russian minstrel.

Slash and Burn Simple form of agriculture where natural vegetation was burned off and the land used for a few seasons.

Soft armour Protection made from flexible absorbant material

Squire Social rank beneath that of a knight; originally a man aspiring to become a knight or a knight's senior servant.

Stocks Device in which those convicted of minor offences can be restrained and subjected to mockery.

Strip Field System of agriculture in which large open fields were divided into numerous narrow strips.

Stupa Buddhist religious building originally consisting or a domed structure.

Subasi Local police chief in the Ottoman state.

Sufi Muslim mystic.

Sultan Muslim secular ruler acknowledging the superior authority of the Caliph.

Sumptuary Law Law governing the clothing worn by particular social, religious or political groups.

Sundang Straight sword used in parts of south-east Asia.

Sunni One of the two main religious divisions in Islam.

Surcoat Cloth garment worn over armour.

Symponos Officer responsible for law and order in a Byzantine city.

Tabby Primitive form of earth-based concrete.

Tarida Specialized form of horse-transporting galley.

Tarkhan Title given to the bravest Mongol or Turkish warriors.

Tegheliay Form of Russian body armour.

Theme Byzantine provincial army and the military province itself.

Tirtha Hindu pilgrimage site.

Tithe Proportion of agricultural or other produce handed over as a form of tax.

Toisich Local leader in the Scottish Highlands and Islands.

Torre Fortified urban tower in medieval Italy.

Tourament Mock battles or individual combat, usually with blunt weapons.

Transhumance Pastoral way of life in which families followed the same migratory routes each year.

Trebuchet Counterweight beam-sling stone throwing device used in siege warfare.

Trencher Thick slide of bread used as a form of plate.

Trial by Combat Means of settling legal disputes by combat.

Trial by Ordeal Method of deciding guilt or innocence by subjecting the accused to a physical ordeal.

Troubadour Minstrel in medieval France.

Truce of God State-led movement attempting to limit private wars between members of the aristocracy.

Tsar Supreme Russian ruler.

Ulema Muslim religious scholars.

Ulu One of the Mongol peoples as a whole.

Umbodsmadr Representative of the Norwegian king in the Greenland settlements.

Umma Worldwide Muslim community as a whole.

Uruk Dominant family in a Mongol clan.

Ushkúynik Russian river pirates.

Varangian Guard Byzantine military unit recruited from Scandinavians and Anglo-Saxons.

Vazir Georgian government minister.

Veche Russian town council.

Vedas Hindu religious texts.

Vizir Government minister in an Islamic state.

Waggenburg Temporary field fortification made of waggons.

Wako Japanese pirates.

Waqf Islamic charitable organization and its property.

War-Hat Form of helmet with a broad brim.

Wattle and Daub Form of building technique using wood and clay.

Yakata Lightly fortified residence of a Japanese samurai family.

Yangmin Free but non-aristocratic social class in Korea.

Yarghuchi Mongol chief judge.

Yasa Turkish and Mongol customary law.

Yasun Association of related Mongol clans.

Yin and Yang Two forces governing the universe in traditional Chinese belief.

Za Mutual support organization amongst Japanese merchants and artisans.

Zakupi Russian family which had fallen into debt bondage.

Zen Japanese Buddhist spiritual exercise.

INDEX

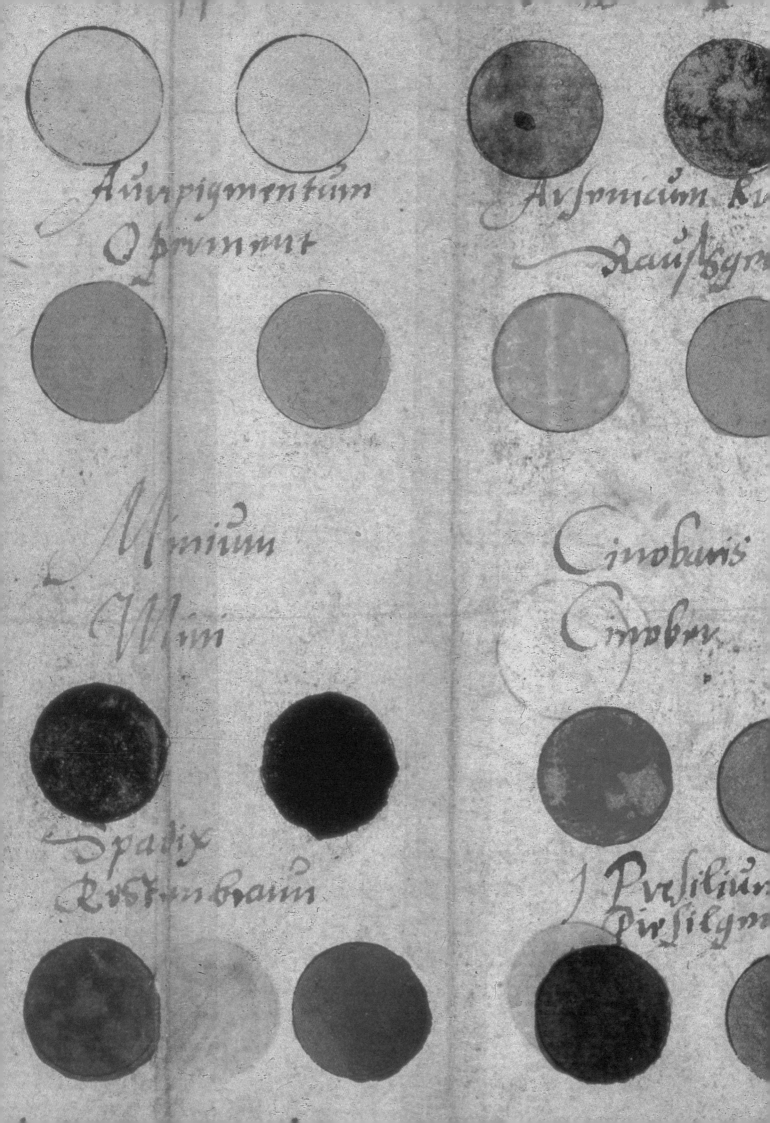

Auripigmentum
Opriment

Arsenicum r[...]
Rauschgel[b]

Minium
Mlin

Cinobaris
Cinober

Spadix
Rostenbraun

Persicum
Pirsicum